The Politics of Sports Development

las
You m...
~ried if it it.

This important new text traces the evolution of sports development in the UK in the context of broader shifts in sport and social policy. It explores the emergence of sports development from the early years of public policy for sport in the 1960s to the present day. This analysis is set against a background of policy initiatives, such as 'Sport For All', 'Action Sport', CCT and the National Lottery, and includes an examination of the contemporary political emphasis on sport's contribution to the social and cultural well-being of the nation.

Incorporating original material from major case studies of four local authorities and the national governing bodies of hockey, rowing, rugby union and tennis, the book examines the reality of 'doing sports development' within a changing social and political policy climate. By showing how sports development policy is made, remade and translated into practice, this book will be essential reading for any student of sport or leisure policy, and all practising sports development officers.

Barrie Houlihan is Professor of Sport Policy, Institute of Sport and Leisure Policy, Loughborough University. **Anita White** is Visiting Professor, Loughborough University and Independent Consultant on Sport Policy and Sports Development.

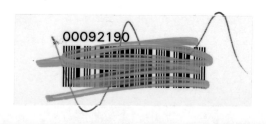

The Politics of Sports Development

Development of sport or development through sport?

Barrie Houlihan and Anita White

Routledge
Taylor & Francis Group

LONDON AND NEW YORK

First published 2002
by Routledge
11 New Fetter Lane, London EC4P 4EE

Simultaneously published in the USA and Canada
by Routledge
29 West 35th Street, New York, NY 10001

Reprinted 2003, 2004

Routledge is an imprint of the Taylor & Francis Group

© 2002 Barrie Houlihan and Anita White

Typeset in Times by Taylor & Francis Books Ltd

Printed and bound in Great Britain by
T J International Ltd, Padstow, Cornwall

British Library Cataloguing in Publication Data
A catalogue record for this book is available from the British Library

Library of Congress Cataloging in Publication Data
A catalog record has been requested for this title

ISBN 0–415–27748–5 (hbk)
ISBN 0–415–27749–3 (pbk)

Contents

Illustrations

Figures

Tables

Preface

This book has four main aims. The first is that it should provide a broad definition of what constitutes sports development both as an activity and as a set of policy objectives. As will soon become clear, such an aim is by no means easy to fulfil as the boundaries between sports development and other closely related activities such as coaching, community development, youth work and physical education teaching are blurred. Many teachers, coaches and youth workers who would not acknowledge the title of sports development officer, and some who would reject outright any association with the activity, nonetheless contribute to the achievement of sports development objectives. Correspondingly, there are many who possess the title of sports development officer who find that they are involved in activities that could easily be described as youth work or community capacity building. As with so many areas of public policy, the longed-for period of policy stability during which focus and practices can be clarified and established does not arrive. Governments change, new policy priorities are identified and inevitably the ever-adaptable, or at least the ever-pliable and compliant, service of sports development is drawn into a further round of re-evaluation of objectives and priorities.

The second aim is therefore to trace the evolution of sports development as it passed through periods of intense political scrutiny and enthusiasm and equally intense periods of neglect and disdain. As a relatively new activity, both within local authorities and national governing bodies of sport, it has for long periods been treated with a degree of scepticism as to its value to broader organisational objectives. However, a sceptical attitude towards sports development at least assumes an awareness of the existence of the activity. In many local authorities sports development has existed on the very margins of the political and administrative field of vision. In contrast, sports development could be seen as central to governing bodies of sport, but the traditions and conservative culture of many of these voluntary organisations have not always provided a positive environment for the promotion of social policy objectives.

The third aim is to examine a selection of organisational settings within which sports development takes place. As is made clear in the text no attempt has been made to select a strictly representative sample. Our concern has been to select four local authorities and four sports where sports development has been provided with the opportunity to demonstrate the contribution that the service can make to organisational goals and the different ways in which sports development policy has been made and delivered. Our intention has been to identify examples of service innovation and good practice and also to illustrate and analyse the problems and challenges that sports development professionals face and their response. The cases not only provide examples of service development and innovation, but they also help to identify issues generic to the sector which help to set an agenda for sports development officers as an occupational group.

The final aim of the book is to take stock of the sports development service as it enjoys a sustained period of political and financial support. The stocktaking is concerned not only with providing an assessment of what sports development has achieved over its brief history but also to examine the capacity of the service to survive a change in its fortunes. As is argued in the book, sport development and sport policy generally is particularly susceptible to changes in its environment such that relatively minor changes appear to generate a disproportionate impact on practice. Incoming ministers for sport, of which there have been far too many in recent years, have a capacity to translate their particular enthusiasms into policy priorities in a way that is inconceivable in other government departments.

As these aims imply, the book is not written for those who are coming to the study of sport policy for the first time. We have assumed that the readers have some understanding of the contours of the debates about broad social policy and the role of local government and also have an awareness of the evolution of sport policy in Britain since the mid-1960s. The text is aimed at those who want to examine in more detail a sector of sport policy, albeit a fairly broad sector. We should also make clear that the book takes England as its focus. While much of the history of sports development in England is common to other parts of the United Kingdom there have always been some variations between the home countries which are likely to become more pronounced since the recent granting of greater devolved power to Wales and Scotland.

The first four chapters locate sports development in the broader context of evolving social policy. The intention is to capture the shifting pattern and priorities of sport policy and show how these were influenced by deeper changes in social policy. Each of the first four chapters takes as its organising framework a conceptualisation of the policy process that emphasises the layered nature of policy change where surface activity and turbulence might disguise the power of deeply embedded values and beliefs that many sports organisations embody and which have the capacity to absorb short-term challenges so as to moderate shifts in policy inertia. The analytical framework not only helps to identify sources of long-term policy stability, but also acknowledges that policy is not static and that effective policy analysis must provide an explanation of change as well as stability. In the framework we have adopted the dynamic element in the policy process comes largely, though not exclusively, from the interplay of structural interest groups which compete for resources and other less tangible sources of policy advantage.

The early chapters provide the context for the more detailed examination of contemporary sports development policy and activity within four local authorities and four governing bodies of sport. The case studies are indicative of trends and emerging patterns of policy influence illustrative of current sports development practice and do not claim to be typical. The final chapter provides an analysis of the contemporary context of sports development, summarises the extent and depth of change in sports development policy over the last thirty-five years or so, and considers some of the potential challenges facing sports development officers in the coming years.

The authors, Barrie Houlihan and Anita White, bring different experiences and perspectives to the analysis of sports development policy and practice. Barrie Houlihan has, over the last ten years, written extensively on a broad range of aspects of sport policy and has also been involved in the provision of policy advice to a number of international, national, regional and local sports organisations. Anita White, a former international sportswoman with a doctorate in the sociology of sport, first became involved as an activist in the Women and Sport movement in the 1980s, and then worked for the Sports Council as Head of Sports Development and later Sport England as Director of Development between 1990 and 2000. By collaborating in writing this book the authors bring together a unique combination of outsider and insider insights, objective analysis and lived experience to the subject. Both authors share an enthusiasm for, and a belief in, the potential of sports development to contribute to individual and social development, and also great respect for the sports development professionals who work in the field.

Acknowledgements

Any investigation of contemporary policy results in the accumulation of debts to those who have given their time to talk to researchers and dig through their files for documents. Without exception those we have approached for interviews or specific pieces of information have been generous with their time and enthusiastic about our project. We would therefore like to record our sincere thanks to the following: Tim Bryan, Brendan Carey, Valerie Charlton, Simon Dickie, Roger Draper, Tony Featherstone, Caron Feast, Fiona Fortune, Tim Garfield, Simon Hall, Mike Hamilton, Chris Hespe, Carol Isherwood, Roland Jack, Rosie Mayglothling, Julian Pagliaro, Lynn Parker, Jan Perridge, David Shaw, Bryan Smith, Sue Sutton, the staff at the Sport England Information Centre in London and the staff of the Pilkington Library at Loughborough University.

Barrie Houlihan would also like to express his particular thanks to Neil King who, as his research assistant for a year, made an invaluable contribution to the early stages of the project. Anita White would like to express her particular thanks to Derek Casey and sports development colleagues at Sport England and other organisations with whom she worked during the 1990s. A final word of thanks to our colleagues in the Department of Physical Education, Sports Sciences and Recreation Management, particularly Mike Collins, Ian Henry and Tess Kay, for many stimulating conversations about sport policy, sports development and social policy, and also to Suzanne Whyman for her excellent administrative support.

Abbreviations

ASC	Advisory Sports Council
BAe	British Aerospace
BASES	British Association of Sport and Exercise Sciences
BOA	British Olympic Association
BUSA	British Universities Sports Association
CCPR	Central Council of Physical Recreation
CCRPT	Central Council of Recreative and Physical Training
CCT	Compulsory Competitive Tendering
CLOA	Chief Leisure Officers Association
DCMS	Department of Culture, Media and Sport
DES	Department of Education and Science
DETR	Department for the Environment, Transport and the Regions
DfEE	Department for Education and Employment
DfES	Department for Education and Skills
DNH	Department of National Heritage
DoE	Department of the Environment
ECB	English Cricket Board
ESC	English Sports Council
FSA	Foundation for Sport and the Arts
ILAM	Institute of Leisure and Amenity Management
ISRM	Institute of Sport and Recreation Management
ITI	Indoor Tennis Initiative
LA	Local Authority
LEA	Local Education Authority
NCF	National Coaching Foundation
NCPE	National Curriculum for Physical Education
NGB	National Governing Body (of sport)
NJRP	National Junior Rowing Programme
NJSP	National Junior Sports Programme
NOF	New Opportunities Fund
PAI	Priority Areas Initiative
PAT	Programme Action Team

PE	Physical Education
PEA UK	Physical Education Association of the United Kingdom
PEPS	Physical Education for Primary Schools
RDM	Regional Development Manager
SAZ	Sports Action Zone
SC	Sports Council
SCSI	School Community Sport Initiative
SDC	Sports Development Council
SDO	Sports Development Officer
SDU	Sports Development Unit
SE	Sport England
SRB	Single Regeneration Budget
SSC	Specialist Sports College
UKSI	United Kingdom Sports Institute
YDO	Youth Development Officer
YST	Youth Sport Trust

1 The origins of sports development

The 1960s to the mid-1970s

Introduction: defining sports development

Some policy areas are easier than others to plot and delimit. While all policy areas have blurred edges which indicate the current limit of government intervention or where they overlap with related areas, most have a recognisable core of objectives and practices that define the service in the eyes of users, the public and politicians. Education, for example, a policy area which overlaps with sports development, can be defined by reference to a body of legislation and regulation and also by reference to the associated pattern of expenditure and programmes of activity. Types of schools, teaching methods and the allocation of time to subjects in the curriculum provide a distinctive mix of outputs which also help to define the service. Furthermore, a service can be characterised by the intended and actual outcomes of policy programmes which, for education, would include changes in literacy levels, truancy rates and GCE A level points scores. In summary, for each major policy area a reasonably sharp profile can be drawn in terms of objectives, practices, outputs and outcomes. Moreover, in established services the profile is given additional sharpness through longevity, for while all services will reflect shifts in objectives and practices over time the extent of change is, in many cases, relatively minor and the pace of change often modest, and even in those areas which experience policy turbulence there are often long periods of relative stability.

However, there are many policy areas, or sub-areas within established services, which lack the sharpness of definition found in the core aspects of the major services. The indistinctness of a policy area and consequent problems of defining current policy may be the result of a variety of factors or combination of factors such as its recent identification by government as a legitimate focus of public policy, instability in policy objectives, variability in its salience to government, or the fact that its sphere of activity impinges on the interests of more politically significant services. To an extent sports development is subject to all these factors. First, it is a sub-area primarily, but not exclusively, within the broader area of sport policy which itself has only been acknowledged as a legitimate and regular focus for government expenditure and policy for just over thirty-five years. Second, it has suffered from a marked degree of instability in objectives which, given its short history, has made it difficult to establish the continuity of practice that often provides a foundation of a public profile. Third, sports development is normally at the margin of the government's field of vision. Only rarely over the last twenty years has sports development been a salient issue for central government. The urban riots in the early 1980s and the brief period of office of John Major, an enthusiast for sport, brought sport and sports development closer to the centre of the political stage, but then only temporarily. The New Labour government had priorities other than sport, but by the end of its first term had produced a comprehensive and prescriptive 'Government Plan for Sport'. Finally, and most importantly, sports development is located in a sector of government activity that is crowded with services that are both relatively resource rich and politically weighty. Rather than conceptualising the policy area of sports development as constituting a discrete set of objectives and practices securely located within a bounded territory on the map of government activity, it is more accurate to conceptualise it as occupying policy space in the interstices of other services such as education, health, foreign policy, social services and sport itself, where its objectives and practices are frequently affected by exogenous developments.

Nevertheless, for an activity that is a recognised element of the work of the majority of local authorities and all governing bodies of sport, sports development is surprisingly difficult to define. Going back to the origins of the use of the term, one finds it dates back to the early days of the Sports Council, which was established as an advisory body in 1965. Indeed the title 'Sports Development Council' was originally proposed for this body and its remit included development of training and coaching, and priorities in sports development as well as facilities, research and planning (Coghlan 1990). It is unclear whether it is best defined as a concept, a government policy, or simply by the work being done by the growing ranks of workers in sports development, or indeed by some combination of the three. Examining the work of those whose job title is that of sports development officer and building a definition around their activity and practice, it is clear that the title of sports development officer is by no means universally adopted by those who are clearly involved in similar work. In a survey carried out in the early 1990s Collins found that fewer than half of those who considered their work as involving at least 50 per cent sports development were called sports development officers (Collins 1995). Other titles used included Soccer Development Officer, Women's Sport DO, Recreation Officer, Community DO and Leisure DO. In addition, not all those with the designation 'sports development officer' spent more than half their time involved in sports development. An alternative approach is to seek to identify the core elements of sports development from a review of current activity and accept that such a definition may cover a wide range of administrators, public officials and organisations, not all of whom will necessarily view sports development as their primary responsibility.

One view common among those involved in sports development is that it can be summed up as 'getting more people to play more sport'. This succinct statement of objectives has been elaborated by Collins who characterises sports development as 'a process whereby effective opportunities, processes, systems and structures are set up to enable and encourage people in all or particular groups and areas to take part in sport and recreation or to improve their performance to whatever level they desire' (1995: 21). A slightly different definition is provided by the Sports Council (North West):

> Sports development is a process by which interest and desire to take part may be created in those who are currently indifferent to the message of sport; or by which those not now taking part, but well disposed, may be provided with appropriate opportunities to do so; or by which those currently taking part may be enabled to do so with meaningful frequency and greater satisfaction, thus enabling participants at all level to achieve their full potential.
>
> (1991: 3)

This definition is more interventionist in tone and reflected the Council's perception of sports development as proactive, interventionist and promo-tional concerned to target groups or areas 'suffering social, economic and recreational disadvantage' (*ibid.*). Of particular importance is the acknowl-edgement by the Council that while sports development may be justified by a variety of social, recreational and health motives, it is a valid end in itself. However, perhaps the clearest, most commonly used and most succinct defi-nition of sports development is that found in the Sports Council policy document published in 1993:

> Sports development is about ensuring the pathways and structures are in place to enable people to *learn* basic movement skills, *participate* in sports of their choice, develop their competence and *performance*, and reach levels of *excellence*.
>
> (Sports Council 1993a, emphasis added)

The important point here is the recognition that pathways and structures have to be in place for people to progress, with the implication that it was the job of the sports organisations and sports development professionals to put these structures in place and enable and encourage individual progression.

Between them these three definitions capture not only the breadth of sports development but also the areas of ambiguity. In terms of scope, sports development refers to those not currently involved in sport as well as those already active, and also refers to the general or mass participant and the aspiring international athlete. Sports development has been conceptualised as an activity preoccupied with the service inputs (facility provision) and the creation of opportunities, but it has also been conceptualised as an activity whose proper focus is on service outcomes and the maximisation of benefit. In addition, at different times the emphasis in sports development has varied between reactive and proactive strategies and between participation objectives and performance objectives. Perhaps most significant in policy terms has been the tension between *development through sport* (with the emphasis on social objectives and sport as a tool for human development) and *development of sport* (where sport was valued for its own sake).

The extent of variation between definitions of sports development can be frustrating but is not so different from the problems faced in defining other areas of government activity, especially in the fields of social welfare. While most policy areas are characterised by long periods of relative stability, none remains static and a definition of sports development will reflect the past and current mix of objectives, practice, principal agents of implementation and sources of resources which, in turn, have been affected by the broader factors such as the political salience of sport and sports development and also by policy movement in contiguous areas. In order to appreciate the current blend of objectives and practices that define sports development it is important to understand the context within which the service emerged and the salient features of the current policy environment. Explanations of policy development based on rational models of decision-making have long since given way to analyses which acknowledge the extent to which political interests and ideology undermine rationality. An awareness of the factors that shape the way in which the political system responds to public issues, and indeed the way in which private troubles or concerns do or do not become public issues, is essential if the contemporary character of sports development is to be understood.

Explaining policy change

It is useful to distinguish between factors in terms of the level at which they operate within the political system. A sensitivity to the extent to which beliefs and values are differentially embedded is important in understanding the way policy, even in new service areas such as sports development, is not simply the product of the interplay of organisational and institutional power at the surface of the political process. A number of theorists have sought to explain the differential responsiveness of democratic political systems to public issues often focusing on the capacity of political systems to ignore certain social problems. Many theorists have taken as their starting point Schattschneider's argument that there were biases built into the political process that protected the interests of those with the capacity to set the rules of the political game (Schattschneider 1960). Bachrach and Baratz (1962, 1963), for example, examined the extent to which powerful interests could effectively exclude issues from the political agenda. Exclusion may be so deeply entrenched that it is taken for granted and becomes a routine response such that 'demands for change in the existing allocation of benefits and privileges in the community can be suffocated before they are even voiced' (Bachrach and Baratz 1970: 7; for a British example, see Saunders 1975). Lukes significantly extended the analysis of the theorists of non-decisions by arguing that under some circumstances the exclusion of particular interests is so deeply ingrained through socialisation and manipulation of the media that exclusionary action is an automatic and unconscious response (1974). Thus the shaping of wants and beliefs helps to reinforce and augment the power of the powerful while further diminishing the power of those on the margins of, or in a position of opposition to, the political process. The operationalisation of beliefs which differentially favour one group over another appear spontaneous because they are taken for granted. Lindblom reached a similar conclusion in his study of the relationship between business and the state where he conceded that it is possible that business can 'achieve an indoctrination of citizens so that citizens' volitions serve not their own interests but the interests of businessmen' (1977: 176) and where civil servants will unconsciously assess policy proposals in terms of their impact on business.

To understand the evolution of sports development and its current position it is important to appreciate the environment in which it emerged and continues to operate (see Table 1.1). At a fundamental level it is necessary to identify the deep-seated policy predispositions that Lukes, Lindblom and others have referred to, but it is also important to acknowledge that while the ideological context of policy will be significant so too will be factors such as the structure of the machinery of government and the pattern of interest group activity. Benson suggested that it was possible to analyse policy in terms of the metaphor of levels where each level is partially autonomous but embedded in a deeper level which sets limits on the degree of autonomy (1982; see also 1975 and 1979). At the shallowest level there is the pattern of administrative arrangements for a service which refers to the organisational location of a function, the extent of division of labour between units and the form of control exercised over subordinate units. Within the sport policy area the preferred form of service delivery is through local government (either directly or as clients and contractors), independent governing bodies, physical education, sports-related organisations such as Sports Coach UK (formerly the National Coaching Foundation) and government agencies (the various Sports Councils). Institutional/administrative arrangements might be located at the shallowest level but they do become embedded over time (Granovetter 1985) and are linked structurally to the deeper layers of the social formation and, as Goodin and Klingemann (1996: 18) observe, are 'nested within an ever-ascending hierarchy of yet more fundamental, yet more authoritative rules and regimes, and practices and procedures'.

Closely related to the pattern of administrative arrangements, and also nested within deeper structures of society, is the pattern of inter-organisational resource dependencies which is concerned with questions of the distribution among organisations of resources such as expertise, finance, facilities, potential athletes, authority and administrative capacity. An example of resource dependence in the area of sports development would be when schools link

Table 1.1 Levels of policy analysis, 1960 to the mid-1970s

Variables	*Variables applied to sport: 1960 to mid-1970s*
Shallow: more vulnerable to change	
Administrative arrangements	'Arm's-length' Sports Council; service delivery by local authorities and sports clubs.
Pattern of inter-organisational resources dependencies	SC dependent on CCPR (and ex-CCPR staff) for expertise and on grant aid from central government for finance. LAs dependent on SC grant aid to pump-prime facility development projects.
More stable: change over the medium term	
Interaction between structural interest groups:	In general interest groups were, at best, emergent during this period.
demand groups (consumers of service outputs);	Demand groups of negligible importance.
provider groups (facility/club managers, sports development officers, PE teachers, youth workers and leisure services managers);	No unified voice. Multiplicity of professional bodies but some discussion of the need to rationalise professional representation in sport and leisure management, but little, if any, recognition of sports development officers as a distinctive service group.
direct support groups (e.g. national governing bodies, CCPR and schools);	Direct support groups better organised and almost all wary of the new Sports Council, especially the NGBs who were content to receive grant aid but suspicious of Council direction on policy.
indirect support groups (related local authority services such as land use planning, community development and non-Sports Council sources of funding)	Sports services, particularly sports development, were peripheral to their main responsibilities.

Variables	Variables applied to sport: 1960 to mid-1970s
Dominant core policy paradigm	Keynesian and post-war welfare consensus; activist state; service planning; professionalisation.
Deep: entrenched	
Embedded structural values fundamental to the social formation	Patriarchal attitudes to participation in sport. Strong gender order in PE and sport. Deference. Class-based pattern of participation reflected, for example, in the persistence of the distinction between amateur and professional participation. Voluntarism preferred to state intervention.

Source: Adapted from Benson (1982) and Sabatier (1999)

with local sports clubs, with the former providing access to its pupils (potential club recruits) and the latter providing coaching expertise. Similarly, the British Sports Council has on many occasions provided pump-priming funding for local authority facility development projects where the latter provide revenue funding and administrative resources. A third element at the surface level is the dominant policy paradigm which is the set of values and assumptions that influence policy choice and administrative practice across a range of services and would include confidence in service planning, professional discretion, orientation towards selective or universal benefits, confidence in local government, preference for privatisation and the use of quangos. At the service level there will also often be a discernible dominant paradigm. In health care, for example, the dominant paradigm is characterised by reactive (as opposed to preventative) medicine, doctor dominance, scientific knowledge and individualised treatment. However, with regard to sport, it will be argued that while at one time in the late 1980s and early 1990s a dominant paradigm did emerge around a model of the sports development continuum, its dominance was at best partial. While the sports development continuum provided a rationale for sports development activities which was widely accepted among those directly involved, it was less successful in providing a robust context for policy-making that was acknowledged by those with the power to shape policy, such as civil servants and ministers for sport, but who had less direct involvement in service management and delivery. Consequently, the sport policy area might better be described as reflecting the tension between a number of competing paradigms.

At a deeper level Benson identified the interaction between structural interest groups, and the rules of structure formation. The administrative arrangements and policy paradigms can only be understood in relation to an underlying power structure. Power is articulated and reflected in administrative practice and policy commitments within the policy sector. Adapting Benson's classification there are four types of structural interest group that are relevant to the study of sports development within a British context, namely, demand groups (consumers of policy outputs), provider groups (the deliverers of services, e.g. leisure services managers, PE teachers, coaches, youth workers, SDOs and, more recently, sports clubs), direct support groups (those groups upon which organisations depend for systems support, such as national governing bodies of sport, local authorities and schools), indirect support groups (related local authority services, including land use planning, community development, and non-Sports Council sources of funding such as Lottery boards other than sport and the Foundation for Sports and the Arts).[1] It is this level that gives the policy process its dynamic quality. It is here that the distribution of costs and benefits by governments and the impact of exogenous factors such as economic recession, inflation or economic growth have a direct impact and where individual and collective interests (whether class, spatial community, age, gender, etc.) experience and interpret policy outcomes and consequently generate demands and supports within the policy area. What prevents this neo-pluralist model of the policy process drifting towards pluralist utopianism is an acknowledgement of the significance of what Benson refers to as the rules of structure formation which set the limits to policy action both by defining activities that are unacceptable and those that are. Benson's notion of 'deep structure' corresponds broadly to the ideas of Lukes and Lindblom and relates to the biases inherent in the fabric of the political process. The pattern of interaction between the prevailing rules of structure formation and the interplay of structural interests, only some of which are internal to the policy area, has considerable influence on policy. However, the concept of deep structure requires some elaboration and will be used in this study to refer to the pattern of values reflected in the construction of identity such as gender, ethnicity and class, as well as the relative weighting given to values such as freedom, equality, trust and private property. In addition, values which reflect assumptions about the relationship between the individual and the community and the pattern of resultant rights and duties would also be important elements of the deep structure of a political system. Deep structural values may be distinguished from policy or problem–issue specific values in terms of their longevity, their resistance to change and their level of abstraction.

It is acknowledged that this model is not without its problems – for example, in the identification of discrete levels of analysis, the articulation of the pattern of influence between levels, and the relative autonomy that each levels enjoys. However, it is argued that the model is nonetheless valuable in that it alerts the policy analyst to the need to take account of the importance of the context within which policy operates if policy development is to be understood and to look beyond the surface phenomena of day-to-day politics. It also provides a useful framework for investigating the problem of explaining policy change.

Sports development and the welfare state

It is hardly surprising that the evolution of the welfare state from the early 1950s to the present day should have strongly influenced the parallel evolution of sports development. However, shifts in sports development policy do not simply mirror the broader trends in welfare policy, partly because those broader trends were themselves an amalgam of sub-trends affecting specific welfare services and partly because of factors peculiar to the evolution of sport policy and in policy areas adjacent to sport. Table 1.2 presents an overview of the broad trends in welfare policy since the mid-1950s (for a fuller discussion see Deakin 1994; Wilding 1997; Field 1996; Hill 1993). Those aspects of change that are of particular importance to sports development over the first two periods are: the shift from universalism to greater selectivity or targeting of services; the introduction of compulsory competitive tendering as an increasingly important element of the context of sports development; and the greater emphasis on enabling rather than direct provision by local authorities.

Identifying the consequences for sports development of the election of the Labour government in 1997 and its re-election in 2001 is more difficult. In the early years of most governments it is difficult to see beyond the election rhetoric and post-election optimism to identify the likely degree of change for particular services. It should be borne in mind that it was ten years before the governments of Margaret Thatcher made their mark on welfare policy.

Table 1.2   Changes in welfare policy, 1950 to 2000

	1950 to mid-1970s	*Mid-1970s to mid-1990s*	*From the mid-1990s*
Prominent values	Equality of access and (to a lesser extent) of benefit; social/collective responsibility	Individual choice and responsibility	Individual choice and responsibility
Role of the state	Interventionist and service providing	Limited and service enabling/co-ordinating	Emphasis on service enabling/co-ordinating, but increasingly interventionist and directive
Perceptions of the individual	Social citizenship	Political citizenship	Political/economic citizenship
Agents of service delivery	Strong and extensive professionalised bureaucracy at central and local government level	Agencies operating in a quasi-market; blurring of the division between public and private/voluntary provision	Agencies operating in a quasi-market; mixed market in service provision
Preferred policy instruments	Universal benefits	Minimal level of benefit; means testing; private insurance, market and quasi-market solutions	Targeted benefits; means testing; partnerships and 'action zones'
Illustrative sports development policy	Sport For All	Facility development and later CCT	Talent identification programmes for youth; Sports Action Zones; World Class Performance and UKSI for selected sports and athletes

'New Labour' promised during its 1997 election campaign to undertake a fundamental overhaul of the welfare state. That the initial enthusiasm had been replaced by greater caution was indicated by the dropping from the Cabinet in 1998 of Frank Field, the minister leading the review. However, the actions of the Labour government in its first few years allow a tentative identification of areas of continuity and change from the previous government. For Powell and Hewitt, who identify areas of policy change, continuity and retreat, it is the high level of continuity that is the dominant theme (1998). Continuity exists in the acceptance of the purchaser–provider split in the National Health Service, the similarity between the Conservative government's 'workfare' scheme and the 'welfare to work' proposals of Labour, and in the general acceptance of the mixed economy of welfare. The restoration of the priority given to housing homeless people is one of the few retreats from Conservative policy and is balanced by the extension of Conservative policy regarding the payment of higher education fees. A fuller examination of current sport policy and the impact of the Labour governments of Tony Blair will be given in chapter 4.

1950 to the mid-1970s

Consensus: the golden age of welfare policy

The Labour government's involvement with sport during the mid-1960s was located within a set of well-established welfare policies and practices reflected in the post-war consensus characterised by the term 'Butskellism' which referred to the assumed, but often exaggerated, common ground between the Conservative and Labour Parties in the late 1950s and 1960s. The Conservative Party of the time was dominated by the 'One Nation Group' whose most prominent spokesperson, Iain Macleod, defended the support for welfare services of the Churchill government of the early 1950s, while eschewing the 'crass egalitarianism' of the Labour Party (Conservative Political Centre 1958, quoted in Deakin 1994: 44). Despite the somewhat half-hearted embrace of the goal of greater equality, the thirteen years of Conservative government up to their election defeat in 1964 was a period of welfare policy consolidation. Taking the twenty-five-year period as a whole, it is possible to argue that there is strong evidence of policy continuity built around an acceptance of a role for an interventionist state, a commitment to public funding for welfare services, a willingness to confine discussion on policy direction to the margins of party political debate, and an assumption that the technical nature of many issues of implementation properly resulted in a central role for the welfare professions (Deakin 1994; Powell and Hewitt 1998). Despite some disagreements about the depth of the consensus, there is a generally agreed view that the consensus held until the mid-1970s. Yet, as Deakin notes, 'within five brief years from 1974, this apparently solid edifice of common assumptions had been riddled through and through by a fusillade of criticisms from every point of the political compass' (1994: 54). The eventual collapse of the post-war settlement in the late 1980s was hastened, but certainly not determined, by the Conservative election victory in 1979.

While the consensus was both significant and substantial, it subsumed a series of tensions, many concerned with policy implementation, that sharpened as the operation of the welfare state came under increasing criticism. Four overlapping tensions are of particular importance to the early years of sports development. The first concerned the values that were used to justify and contextualise welfare policy. For supporters of the welfare state within the Labour Party, the dominant value was that of 'equality' with an emphasis not just on the provision of equality of opportunity through free access to high quality services such as education, housing and health care, but also on the prioritisation of a notion of equality which implied a concern with the quality of outcomes or benefits. Many, especially in the Conservative Party, gave priority to the liberty of the individual over equality and were deeply suspicious that many welfare policies, and the introduction of comprehensive education in particular, would lead to inferior uniformity. Insofar as the more libertarian politicians were able to support welfare policies, it was only to the extent that welfare services provided an opportunity for self-improvement which the individual was free to take or refuse. Where the balance between values gives priority to equality, it can be reflected in sports development by the greater emphasis placed on targeting of under-participating groups as opposed to the establishment of generally available facilities and opportunities. An emphasis on the pursuit of equality can also encourage sports development practice that directs investment towards the employment of sports leaders rather than the provision of facilities, as it is the former that can best ensure that participants can gain greater benefit from participation.

The second tension related to the proper role of the voluntary sector. Although parts of the welfare state, personal social services and the health sector in particular had always worked closely with, and depended heavily on, the voluntary sector, there had occasionally been tension between a perception of the voluntary sector as a specialist partner in a common endeavour, on the one hand, and as a sector perpetuating the perception of welfare as charity and often offering untrained as opposed to professional support, on the other. Within sport, the voluntary sector, represented by the governing bodies of sport and the large number of voluntary clubs, had long been the foundation of sports organisation in the UK, but had not remained immune from the consequences of this tension. While in some sports there was a rapid establishment of a complementary relationship between the public and voluntary sectors, this was not the case for all sports. Sports development activity in swimming had long rested upon a close and generally successful relationship between the voluntary club that provided coaching and competition and the local authority that provided the facility. By contrast, the growth in opportunities to play badminton at public leisure centres on a casual basis was seen, by the governing body, as undermining the role of the club.

Third, there was the differing perceptions of professions. The prevailing view in the 1950s and 1960s was that the professional brought neutrality, diagnostic expertise and technical sophistication to bear on a problem. By the mid-1970s this benign view of professionals was being challenged by a contrary perception that characterised the professional as self-serving, ineffective and ideological. While this tension did not surface till the late 1980s, the dominant role of professions in local government service provision became the model that sport, and later sports development and coaching, sought to emulate.

The final tension concerned the significance of the concept of community in welfare service provision. The late 1950s and 1960s was a period of optimism about the capacity of government to intervene and improve the quality of life. As already mentioned, the preferred vehicle for the improvement of welfare was a professionalised public service, particularly at local government level, whose members would use their expertise to assess needs and then make the necessary arrangements for them to be met. Although professionalised service delivery was the dominant mode, there emerged, during the 1960s, a complementary or, to some, an alternative form of welfare practice based on the development of self-help skills from among members of local disadvantaged communities – what, in today's terminology, would be referred to as empowerment.

Milson defined community development as 'a process – usually in neighbourhoods – where attempts are made to mobilize the total resources of the community for the protection, support and enrichment of individuals and groups being part of the whole' (1974: 26). The concept of community development appealed to both the left and the right in politics. For the former, community development offered the prospect of a counterweight to a centralised (and predominantly Conservative-government-led) civil service too closely allied to business interests and too accepting of business values. For the right, community development focused more on the return of power to the community to enable it to exercise effective control over local government and entrenched professional interests. According to Butcher (1994), the reaction to the bureau-professional model of service delivery that typified the period from the early 1950s to the mid-1970s, included the following policy and organisational characteristics: a preference for devolved/decentralised decision-making; emphasis on equity rather than equality and a more flexible and varied conception of need; greater citizen involvement in decision-making; and a stress on organisational values rather than structures. In terms of service delivery, the community-practice model stressed the role of the community in articulating need and the role of the professional as a facilitator of community articulation rather than the external analyst of need; the professional is 'on tap' rather than 'on top', and the work of the professional is with people in their communities rather than people in an individualised context. Butcher sums up the community development 'way of working' as follows:

> The professional worker seeks to forge a 'partnership' between agency and community whereby she/he can offer help in identification of needs, and formulation of plans. The worker then seeks to assist the community or, more accurately, its representative organisations, to gain access to the agencies' [*sic*] in a way that is most effective in meeting its identified needs and demands.
>
> (Butcher 1994: 16)

Among those on the political left it is by this process that the community moves from the role of passive recipient of services determined by professional definitions of need to that of a collectivity of citizens actively negotiating for resources to meet self-defined needs. Where the left and right diverge is over the role of the state. In contrast to the left, which views the state as a source of resources for the community, the right is more inclined to encourage the community to be the source of its own resources. Despite some disillusionment with the community action–development approach among the left in the late 1960s, the attraction of community development revived in the late 1970s as the left, most notably in Sheffield and Liverpool, rediscovered urban politics. Consequently, the community was to remain an important, if controversial, focus for service development and delivery of welfare provision in general, as well as being clearly evident in much sports development activity. At various times over the following twenty-five years, most notably with the Action Sport programme in the early 1980s, sport was identified as a focus for community development, integration and, if the rhetoric was to be believed, community creation.

The tensions over values, the role of the voluntary sector, the perception of professions and the significance of community provided the context within which sport policy emerged. However, sports development was not yet a recognised element within broader sport policy, although, as will be explored in the next section, the roots of sports development were securely in place. Against the backdrop of the emerging tensions surrounding the welfare state, there were three areas of activity that were to prove influential in shaping the emergence of sports development activity. The first was the dominant discourse around physical education and sport in schools; the second concerned the attitude of the youth service to sport; and the third, and by far the most important, was the lobbying of the CCPR and the Wolfenden Report that the Council sponsored.

Precursors of sports development

PE and sport in schools

Young people are a logical focus for sports development activities whether the primary aim is to promote sport for all or to foster young talent. The influence of school sport and physical education in shaping sports development is indirect, through the recruitment of physical education teachers into the ranks of sports development officers, rather than direct (see chapter 6 on sports development in rugby union). Indeed the involvement of schools and the education service in defining and contributing towards sports development objectives is poor, as exemplified by the modest level of co-operation between schools and sports clubs despite sustained encouragement from the Sports Council. Part of the explanation for the reluctance of schools and local education authorities to embrace sports development lies in the history of insecurity of PE and sport in the school curriculum. Despite confirmation of the value of PE by the 1933 Spens Report and the 1944 McNair Report the position of sport, games and PE in the curriculum has always been contested and the status of PE teachers insecure.

The 1933 Physical Training syllabus typified an approach to physical education that Musgrove referred to as 'a kind of military service on the cheap' (1975: 1). It was modernised in 1952 and greater discretion given to the PE teacher regarding curriculum content and delivery (Whitehead and Hendry 1976). Although the discretion was welcomed as an indication of the growing maturity of the PE teaching profession, change in practice was slow, reflecting the general uncertainty and under-confidence among PE teachers. The period from the early 1930s to the late 1960s was one of redefinition of PE and also marked the transition of school physical activity from a form of drill and physical training to a recognised subject within the school curriculum. The period also marked the resolution of the competition between different traditions in PE resulting in consolidation around competitive team games for both boys and girls and the steady marginalisation not only of drill but also of a variety of forms of gymnastics. The domination of competitive games in the PE curriculum was the product of a number of pressures, not least of which was the demand from older pupils for physical activities closer to those available to adults. Other pressures included the strongly held belief among politicians that games were a solution to a range of social problems such as juvenile crime and national confidence.[2] What was of especial significance was the increasing perception of sport as 'a common denominator and a unifying medium in society' (Kirk 1992: 99) and an acknowledgement of the importance of an early introduction to competitive games if sport was to fulfil the role of restoring Britain's flagging international prestige. The re-entry of the Soviet Union to Olympic competition in 1952, the startling success of the Australian swimming team at the 1956 Olympics and a series of defeats in soccer heightened the sense of alarm reflected in the growing calls for government intervention in the administration, organisation and funding of sport. By the end of the 1960s the discourse within which PE was debated was formally grounded in sport, social welfare and international prestige – education through the physical rather than education of the physical – a discourse which was to be echoed in the influential Wolfenden Report.

The youth service: flirting with sport

Along with education, the youth service, with its responsibility for the early post-school years of adolescence, is a significant element of the administrative and policy environment that has helped to shape sports development. Of especial importance was the influence of the youth service or, more accurately, those shaping the post-war revival of the youth service in helping to define the welfare context within which sport would operate in relation to young people. In 1939 the government established the youth service by giving the Board of Education responsibility for co-ordinating the work of local education authorities and the large number of voluntary bodies that had been active in youth work for well over fifty years. Among the most prominent organisations were the Boys' Brigade, the Boy Scouts Association, the Girl Guides Association, the National Association of Boys Clubs and various church-based youth organisations. The years of the Second World War and the economic problems that followed its conclusion meant that the momentum that existed in 1939 had been largely dissipated by the early 1950s. The establishment of the Albemarle Committee in 1958 to review the youth service came at a time of growing concern with the 'problems of youth', the 'gap between what is provided for the social and recreational life of young people so long as they are in formal education, and what is provided thereafter' (Albemarle Report 1960: 41), and the growing awareness of the frailty of the infrastructure of the service. The policy context for the service emphasised a dual function of 'social and physical training' with the aim of bringing 'young people into a normal relationship with their fellows and to develop bodily fitness' (Albemarle Report 1960: 8). The tension between 'bodily fitness' and 'self-government and citizenship' is one that has been evident throughout the history of the service and still persists. This tension had a number of sources, the first of which was the perception held by youth workers that teachers, followed by social workers, were their closest professional reference groups and role models: a perception reinforced by the Albemarle Report which declared that the youth service was 'an integral part of the education system [though it] shades off into the welfare and social services' (1960: 103, 104). The second source was the view that physical fitness through sport was a means to achieve attitudinal change, and the third was an often extreme wariness that an undue emphasis on sport would obscure the other objectives of the service. Despite these concerns the Albemarle Committee argued strongly for additional investment in facilities for sport and recreation, and for investment in coaching, thereby adding weight to the similar case made by the Wolfenden Committee when its report was published later the same year. But it was also clear that the Committee saw sport and physical recreation in instrumental terms: first, as a way of attracting adolescents to the youth service and its broader social agenda; second, because it was a set of activities that cut across lines of social stratification in society; and, third, because it was a convenient way of satisfying 'the increased physical energies of many young people' (Albemarle Report 1960: 57).

The experience of the youth service was not only important in relation to the evolution of substantive policy in sports development, it was also significant in shaping attitudes towards the administrative arrangements for the service. The Albemarle Committee had to wrestle with two difficult issues: the first (also an issue for the Wolfenden Committee) concerned the respective roles of government and the voluntary sector, and the second concerned the desirability of encouraging a professional core of youth workers and their subsequent relationship with volunteers. Like the Wolfenden Committee, the Albemarle Committee favoured an arrangement whereby government provided grant aid to the extensive voluntary sector, but qualified the independence of the voluntary bodies by recommending that the service would benefit from the appointment of a larger number of professional youth workers. Interestingly, the Committee saw existing teachers as the primary source of professional youth workers and recommended a structure of training and qualification that would enable youth workers to 'move across to other professional work in education or the social services' (1960: 72). However, the most important effect of the debates within the youth service was to confirm the perception of sport as a vehicle for moral development and social engineering: development *through* sport rather than development *of* sport.

Sport: expanding the definition of welfare

The period of stability over welfare policy was also the period during which sport and recreation were accepted as legitimate interests and responsibilities of government. Although the Conservative government of the early 1960s was reluctant to respond to the suggestion in the Wolfenden Report (1960) that the government should be more closely involved in the funding and organisation of sport, the Labour government of 1964 was more receptive. The willingness of the Wilson government to establish an advisory Sports Council in 1965 was less a reflection of its particular interest in sport and recreation than of its general willingness to expand the boundaries of the welfare state and move beyond the core of personal services such as housing, health and education to include a broader range of community services such as the arts and sport.

Moreover, the increasing willingness of governments to accept sport and leisure as legitimate areas of public policy was not simply due to the momentum generated by the welfare state ideology. Crucial to government involvement was the successful application of pressure by the sport lobby in which the CCPR was a key organisation. By the early 1960s the CCPR, partly funded by government grant, had established itself as the primary advocate on behalf of sport. Not only was it the body to which governments turned to for advice on sport policy, but it had also on some occasions organised sports festivals on behalf of the government. Established in 1935 as the Central Council of Recreative and Physical Training (CCRPT), the Council was initially concerned to stimulate the provision of recreational opportunities for the community and particularly school leavers. Within a short period the CCRPT became an umbrella organisation for a wide span of sports bodies and was involved across a range of sports-related activities, including the training of PE teachers and coaches. During the 1950s the Council played an important role in shaping the government's nascent youth policy. In truth it would be accurate to say that the government adopted the youth policy of the CCPR as there is little evidence that the government had given much serious independent thought to the issue. It was the perception of a policy vacuum concerning youth policy that prompted the CCPR to establish the Wolfenden Committee (Evans 1974: 91–4). While the CCPR was at the core of the sports lobby, other important organisations included the major governing bodies of sport and an emerging voice for teachers of, and advocates for, school PE, provided largely by Birmingham University's Department of PE (Kirk 1992: 108).

The report of the Wolfenden Committee was of profound significance, not only in raising the profile of sport with government but also, and more importantly, in shaping the context within which public involvement in sport was to be considered for the next generation. As Coghlan noted, the establishment of the Committee in 1957 'aroused no particular concern other than general broad interest and yet the results flowing from the fifty-seven recommendations were to alter the face of British sport within the decade' (1990: 8). While the primary stimulus for the establishment of the Committee came from a growing concern within the CCPR that youth sport was not being supported effectively by government, the immediate catalyst was the publication of a pamphlet (University of Birmingham 1956) bemoaning the inadequacy of support given to the country's elite athletes to enable them to prepare for international competition (Evans 1974). Even at this early stage the tensions between participation and excellence were clear.

The Committee was given very broad terms of reference: 'To examine the factors affecting the development of games, sport and outdoor activities in the UK and to make recommendations to the CCPR as to any practical measures which should be taken by statutory or voluntary bodies in order that these activities may play their full part in promoting the general welfare of the community' (Wolfenden Report 1960: 1). Although prompted by the concerns of elite athletes, the focus of the report was very strongly on the 'general welfare of the community'. Its many recommendations covered aspects of sport as diverse as coaching, Sunday sport, amateurism, and the shortage of facilities, reflecting the then current debates about the role of the state in welfare provision. In acknowledging the limits of voluntarism and, albeit tacitly, the advantages of professional administration and organisation, it supported, if somewhat warily, a positive role for the state in response to post-war social problems associated with juvenile crime, poor standards of fitness and health and the promotion of positive social values among the young. In framing its conclusions around the notion of a 'gap' between sports and games participation at school and participation in later adult life, the report not only echoed the Albemarle Report but also identified a concept that could be interpreted positively by those with a concern for the social development of young people and those with a narrower concern for the production of the next generation of elite athletes, thus uniting two significant elements within the sports lobby. The 'Wolfenden Gap' became an enduring theme of the sports development discourse throughout the next thirty years and the emphasis placed on the 'gap' represented, for the physical education profession, 'an opportunity to confirm their indispensability to the development of British sport' (Kirk 1992: 113–14).

The reticence of the Committee to endorse state intervention more enthusiastically was due to its concern to protect the voluntary infrastructure of sport with its 'rich and varied resources' (Wolfenden Report 1960: 53). Despite suggesting that there could be closer integration between sports organisations and acknowledging the benefits that professional administration could bring, the Committee strongly defended the voluntary sports structure as a cornerstone of sports organisation and provision in the UK. Yet the Committee also acknowledged the serious shortage of investment in sport, particularly in facilities, and was thus faced with the dilemma of reconciling the preservation of voluntary autonomy with the advocacy of greater public investment and the establishment of a Sports Advisory Council. As Coalter *et al.* pointed out, the report was located within the 'classic Beveridge tradition [where] state activity was only defensible as a framework for voluntarism. The concern of Wolfenden was to achieve reforms which would not introduce major structural change, but would assist existing organisations to perform more efficiently' (Coalter *et al.* 1986: 46). But the defence of voluntarism was modified by a recognition of the rise of a highly professionalised society and range of public services. The key proposal of the report – that a Sports Development Council (SDC) should be established – attempted to argue for the provision of public finance, but on terms which would enable the voluntary sports organisations to exercise discretion over its use, thus reinforcing the central role of the voluntary sector. It was suggested that the SDC should be given direct control over £5 million which it could distribute to sports organisations while being only indirectly accountable to Parliament. As Coalter *et al.* comment:

The concerns of the Wolfenden Report ... reflected the particular tran-
sitions taking place at this time. It was not based on the expansionist,
optimistic, social democratic, classless visions of (say) the later Cobham
Report (1973). Rather it reflected concerns for the possible consequences of rapid social change for traditional social institutions and
relationships.

(1986: 47)

Possibly because of the report's pragmatism, it had a substantial and long-
term impact on the shape of British sport. It both anticipated and gave
direction to the main features of the post-war prominence of competitive
games and sports, and provided the basis for the reorganisation of the
administration and funding of British sport over the next thirty years.

Despite increasing pressure from the sports lobby, and particularly the
CCPR, the Conservative government at the time of the publication of the
report remained suspicious of any expansion in the role of the state and
wary of undermining voluntarism, and consequently declined to take its
advice regarding the SDC. However, the Labour government elected in 1964
had fewer reservations, and in 1965 the Advisory Sports Council (ASC) was
formed with the brief to 'advise the Government on matters relating to the
development of amateur sport and physical recreation' (Advisory Sports
Council 1965). Among the particular subjects on which the ASC was to
provide advice were standards of provision of sports facilities for the
community, co-ordination of the use of community resources, the development of training and coaching and priorities in sports development. That
the Conservative government agreed in 1972 that the ASC should be
replaced by a Sports Council with executive rather than merely advisory
powers was as much a reflection of the success of the ASC and the growth
in confidence of the sports lobby as it was an indication of a change in attitude within the Conservative Party. Much of the success of the ASC was
due to its very close relationship with the CCPR, the sponsoring body of the
Wolfenden Committee. So close was the relationship that Evans remarked
that 'it became increasingly difficult to detach the work of the CCPR from
that of the [Advisory] Sports Council and the Regional Sports Councils'
(1974: 209). But in this close relationship lay both a strength and a cause of
friction for the future.

The acceptance by government that sport was now an area of public
policy and direct funding brought into sharp relief its relationship with the
voluntary sector and the CCPR in particular. The new Sports Council
worked within a public service culture that placed service planning and
professional assessment of need at the heart of public administration and
which was supportive, or at least tolerant, of voluntary effort as long as it
deferred to professional judgement. The preference of the Wolfenden
Committee that the government should provide funding but leave sport with
discretion over its use was an illustration of a persisting concern that the

voluntary sector constituted the organisational foundation of sport which government should aim to support but not dominate.

The priority of the Sports Council was the rapid expansion of the facility base by using its grant-awarding powers to pump-prime projects proposed by local authorities, and also by voluntary clubs. Although there had been some building of new swimming pools and leisure centres in the late 1960s, the period from the early 1970s to the early 1980s was to transform the opportunities for participating in sport. Between 1972 and 1976 the Council allocated £4.7 million in support of a broad range of voluntary sector facilities. Within the public sector, the Council helped to achieve the construction of over 500 new swimming pools and almost 450 new indoor sports centres between 1971 and 1981. The momentum achieved during the 1970s was maintained by a supportive report from the House of Lords Select Committee on Sport and Leisure in 1973 and two years later the publication of a White Paper on Sport and Recreation by the Department of the Environment.

Both documents endorsed the acceptance of sport and leisure as aspects of welfare provision and the broad quality of life of communities. The House of Lords' report was couched in language that reflected confidence in the role of the state to identify needs accurately and plan effectively to meet them. It supported strongly investment in the provision of recreation facilities, commenting that 'if the welfare state provides for education, health and social security but, by ignoring a shortage of recreational facilities, allows frustration to build up in non-working hours, then it has failed to provide adequately for the national welfare' (House of Lords 1973: ii). The Committee also supported the view of the Bains Committee on Local Authority Management that the new local authorities created by the forthcoming reorganisation in 1974 should consider establishing a separate recreation department to provide a strong organisational and policy focus for the emerging service. At national level, the Committee acknowledged the position of the voluntary sector as the 'lifeblood of sports provision' (*ibid.*: xxvi), but also stressed that co-ordination could only be achieved adequately through the resources and strategic planning capacity of national agencies such as the Sports Councils and the Countryside Commission.

The Department of the Environment White Paper reflected the optimism of the time in the capacity for positive state intervention and also reflected the priority of egalitarian principles. The paper recognised the importance of leisure for the 'general welfare of the community' (DoE 1975: 3) and the 'magnificent' contribution of the voluntary sector, but noted that 'voluntary bodies cannot achieve all that is needed' (*ibid.*: 4). Government, and especially local government, was identified as having a key role in the planning and co-ordination of recreation development. The White Paper highlighted recreational deprivation as an aspect of urban deprivation and indicated that the government would accord 'the highest priority for grant-aid … to suitable recreational projects in such areas' (*ibid.*: 16), but also drew attention to the needs of the disabled, the gifted and the young. In reference to youth sport, the government confirmed the relationship between teachers of PE, clubs and local government in sports development for the young. As regards the gifted, the White Paper expressed the government's concern to divert resources to meet their needs and suggested that centres of excellence be established at universities and colleges.

Conclusion

Although sports development was not to emerge as a recognised aspect of broader sport policy in its own right until the late 1970s, the policy and administrative framework within which sports development would operate had been fixed by the mid-1970s. Using the analytic framework outlined above, there was, at the level of deep structure, a set of taken-for-granted assumptions about the utilitarian value of sport that can be traced from the late Victorian period through the Wolfenden Report, to the report of the House of Lords Select Committee and the 1975 White Paper. Organised sport was promoted in the nineteenth century by the churches as a means of fostering Christian values, and, more recently, was advocated by those who saw in sport the answer to a series of social and health problems. As deeply rooted as the instrumental view of sport was, the attempt to preserve a distinction between amateur and professional sport persisted in some of Britain's major sports, such as tennis, athletics and rugby union, well into the second half of the twentieth century. The slow decline of amateurism prolonged the association between class and sports participation and affected the content of the physical education curriculum in state and public schools, with the emphasis in the former being on physical drill until the late 1950s. A third element was the deeply rooted gender order in both sport and physical education. Women and girls were either invisible or considered peripheral to mainstream discourse in sport, and women's and men's physical education developed separately. Even the youth service was male-defined with young women afforded little attention. One final element in the deep structure of beliefs and values was the long-standing disdain for international sports organisations, unless of course they were being run by Britons. All the elements of the deep structure – disdain, instrumentalism, gender and class – were still in place during the formative period of sports development from the mid-1950s to the mid-1970s (McIntosh 1987; Holt 1989; Birley 1995). What is conspicuous by its absence is any sustained attempt to defend the promotion of sport for its intrinsic benefits, thus creating a situation where the advocates of sports development were frequently those with little direct involvement in sport, but with a view as to how it could contribute to their own policy objectives. As a result, the voice of sports development is all too often the echo of those concerned with health, juvenile behaviour or international prestige. Also with its origins in the deep structure of society was the uncertainty and ambiguity concerning the role

of sport in schools and within the PE curriculum, which had the consequence of making PE teachers and schools wary of the emerging sports
development service.

At the level of the dominant core policy paradigm was the small number
of medium to long-term shifts in broad political orientations or operational
values. The gradual movement away from Keynesianism to a fuller acceptance of neo-liberal economics is one important example, while the equally
gradual decline in confidence in the beneficial effects of state planning and
intervention is another. Up to the mid-1970s, the commitment to Keynesian
economics and the belief in the positive value of state provision of welfare
services remained firm. Other important aspects of the prevailing policy
orientation that affected the emergence of sports development included the
attitude of government and wider society to social institutions, such as
voluntary organisations and professions, that may be either directly or indirectly involved in the policy process and especially in policy delivery. For
example, a commitment to a central role for the voluntary sector informed
early sport policy-making and remains a cornerstone of current policy,
whereas the fortunes of professional service groups associated with sport,
such as sports development officers, sports/leisure centre managers and
youth workers, have been far less secure.

A further dimension is the series of shorter-term changes in the salience
of particular policy areas to government which frequently reflects the interplay of structural interests. Election campaigns are one indicator of the
issues that political parties will give priority to, and in recent years trade
union reform, business competitiveness, welfare reform and education have,
at different times, moved to the top of the government's agenda. The shifting
pattern of policy salience may be due to other factors as well as the pursuit
of electoral advantage. Issues often move up the policy agenda as a result of
crisis, the sustained activity of interest groups, or the routine scanning of the
policy environment by civil servants. However, sports development is a
policy area that is less likely to be the direct focus of lobbying or scanning,
and it is therefore more likely that its salience to government will be the
consequence of changes in related but more politically significant policy
areas such as education, local government funding and health.

During the period up to the mid-1970s, the dominant feature of all four
key sets of interests, whether demand, provider, direct or indirect support
groups, was their general lack of political leverage. The weakness of demand
groups should come as no surprise as it is normal for the recipients of public
services to be poorly organised and marginal to the policy process. It would
therefore be unusual if the users of sports services were any more influential
in the policy area than their counterparts, such as patients, tenants, and
pupils and students were in other policy areas. Provider groups, including
leisure facility managers, physical education teachers and the small number of
sports development officers, were poorly organised and, during this period,
few in number and generally peripheral to local authority departmental

policy discussions. Direct support groups, such as national governing bodies and schools, were generally wary of the government's involvement in sport and of the new Sports Council and were concerned to ensure that their organisational autonomy was preserved while, at the same time (for NGBs at least), maximising their access to public resources. The exception was the CCPR, which had demonstrated its policy leverage following the publication of the Wolfenden Report.

As regards the dominant policy paradigm for the service, sports development was located within a broad welfare state discourse best reflected in the egalitarianism of what was later to be referred to as the 'Sport For All' campaign. Moreover, the acknowledgement of sport and recreation as elements of welfare provision brought the policy area within the established arrangements for service management and delivery. The professionalisation of PE teaching and the support for the professionalisation of the youth service given by the Albemarle Report established a model for recreation management and for the specialism of sports development. Along with the aspiration of professionalisation came the associated perceptions of service users as clients and service provision as a response to an identification and analysis of need rather than a response to market demand.

While association with the 'Sport For All' campaign provided a high level of security for much of the early facility development work of the Sports Council and local authorities, it disguised the underlying tension between the community welfare view of sports development (development through sport) and the perception of sports development as a synonym for talent identification and elite development (development of sport). The governing body-centred sports lobby which favoured this latter interpretation had little reason to challenge the current direction of policy that was providing much needed sports facilities and was also receptive to the pressure from elite sport for specialist facilities and the establishment of a network of centres of excellence. The elite sports lobby was given additional security by the focus and operation of the Council's Sports Development and Coaching sub-committee whose terms of reference, according to Coghlan, while making it 'clear that it was concerned with the general development of sport and participation across the board' (1990: 35) equally clearly saw clubs and national governing bodies (NGBs) of sport as its primary partners rather than local authorities or schools. The priority of the Council was 'to gain the confidence of the national governing bodies' and also to overcome the evident administrative weaknesses of most national governing bodies (Coghlan 1990: 35). To this end, between 1965 and 1970, the Council grant to NGBs to support headquarters organisation increased from £565,000 to £877,000. Once the Council was confident that NGBs possessed sufficient administrative and organisational capacity, it extended its grant aid to support the appointment of sports development officers.

Furthermore the endorsement of Sport For All by the Sports Council did not signal an unambiguous shift in policy from elite to mass provision. First, the definition of 'Sport For All' adopted by the Sports Council stressed that elite competitive sport was as much a part of Sport For All as the provision of community opportunities for participation, thus helping to protect the current primary policy emphasis. Sport For All was an extremely flexible policy. Early statements of the policy in the mid-1960s were constantly being amended and revised, and included objectives associated with social, sport, psychological, health and community benefits (McIntosh and Charlton 1985: 99–101). The initial enthusiasm for the policy generated a series of campaigns targeted at particular under-participating groups including the over-fifties, the disabled and families, but over the fifteen years from 1972 some fourteen different target groups were identified by the Sports Council or the regional councils (McIntosh and Charlton 1985: 114). As a result the diversity of target groups and objectives did little to help establish Sport For All as a coherent policy in its own right and perpetuated the impression of it being a convenient umbrella term for a diverse and constantly shifting set of objectives.

Second, the government and the Council moved to introduce the notion of recreation to their policy vocabulary. The House of Lords Select Committee report on Sport and Leisure gave clear support to the Sport For All campaign, but also endorsed a narrow definition of sport as focused largely on 'encouraging the development of excellence among sportsmen and urging people to take up sport' (1973: xxv). The Committee suggested that the Sport For All campaign needed to be complemented by a parallel policy designed to meet the needs of informal recreation under the slogan of Recreation For All. The Select Committee's identification of recreation as a policy priority was supported by the White Paper published two years later. The concept of areas of recreational priority was endorsed and the government encouraged the new Regional Councils for Sport and Recreation to take account of recreational deprivation when distributing grant aid (DoE 1975: 16). While the distinction between sport and recreation had little immediate impact on policy, it echoed and reinforced the emerging tension between foundation, performance and excellence, on the one hand, and participation, on the other. The advocates and sponsors of emerging sport policy were faced with a considerable difficulty in establishing a sense of common endeavour among partner organisations, especially local authorities and NGBs, which moved beyond an enthusiasm for new sports facilities. Participation that is casual rather than organised and where the motives are oriented towards social rather than sports outcomes has always been the most problematic aspect of Sports Council policy. The combined effect of the dilution of the Sport For All policy and the introduction of recreation as a conceptually distinct policy area had little immediate effect on broad policy direction within the Sports Council. However, it did have a longer-term effect of making it more difficult to conceptualise sports development as an integrated set of activities and objectives.

Finally, policy areas are affected by changes in management fashion. Over the last thirty years there have been a number of reconfigurations of the machinery of government including: the replacement of specialist departments at both central and local level with larger 'giant' departments; the expansion in the use of quangos which prompted a brief period of retreat in the early 1980s only to be followed by a prolonged period of steady expansion through the rest of the decade; the introduction of performance measurement, and budget and service planning models; changes in the pattern of relations between central and local government; and, finally, the expansion of the regional tier of administration. All these, mainly exogenous, changes in the policy environment alter the prevailing pattern of resource dependencies, thus shaping the evolution of policy and the context within which the endogenous pressures that arise – for example, from the experience of policy implementation – are addressed.

There were four aspects of the administrative infrastructure that affected sports development between 1960 and the mid-1970s. The first was the decision to establish the Sports Council as an 'arm's-length' body with a royal charter. Not only did this have the effect of distancing the new policy area from the mainstream policy concerns of its parent department, but it also had the effect of establishing a set of expectations among Sports Council staff regarding the autonomy of the organisation that proved difficult to alter when, in the mid-1970s, government became more concerned to utilise recreation and sport as elements of a broader welfare strategy. The second aspect concerned the decision to locate strategic responsibility for sport and later sports development within the Department of the Environment (DoE). Location within the DoE linked sport strongly to the department's core responsibility for local government, but also distanced sport from education and the youth service. The third aspect of the administrative infrastructure was the privileged position of the CCPR within the new Sports Council. Not only did the relationship prove to be a financial burden on the Sports Council, but it also created a deep tension on a number of strategic issues and slowed the pace at which the Council balanced its commitment to elite athletes with a greater concern with the opportunities available for mass participants. The final aspect concerns the respective roles of the voluntary and local authority sectors as vehicles for service delivery. In the 1960s and early 1970s government roundly endorsed the view of the Wolfenden Committee that the role of the public sector was to support voluntary providers. This view was reflected in the pattern of distribution of funding of the Sports Council, but sat less easily within the culture of direct service provision that existed among local authorities.

It was during the period from the mid-1970s to the end of the 1980s that sports development had the opportunity to become more sharply defined and to consolidate its position as an element within broader sport policy. As has been demonstrated the policy environment for sports development in the mid-1970s was mixed. On the one hand, the expansion of the welfare role of the state was supportive of the new service, as was the strength of the sports lobby; on the other hand, the internal provider lobby was weak and the welfare policy paradigm was about to be subject to an abrupt and sustained challenge.

2 The mid-1970s to the early 1990s

Sports development comes of age

Introduction

The period from the mid-1970s to the early 1990s was one of rapid expansion in sports development, paralleling the increasing availability of facilities and the first signs of a nascent sport and recreation services profession. With the growing interest of government in the utility of sport as an instrument of social policy and the greater willingness and capacity among national governing bodies of sport (NGBs) to plan effectively for the future of their sports, those involved in sports development had the opportunity to sharpen the public profile of the service and consolidate its position as an integral part of broader sport policy. Yet while many aspects of the policy environment for sports development were positive, there were also a number of aspects that were far less so. Of particular importance was the variability of government attitudes towards sport. Although from 1974 to 1979 Denis Howell proved an energetic champion of sport, he was a member of a government that rarely treated sport as anything more than a peripheral concern. From 1979 there was a succession of Conservative governments, led by Margaret Thatcher, whose perception of sport varied from it being a quick fix solution to urban unrest to it being a source of national embarrassment through soccer hooliganism. In general, the Conservative governments of the Thatcher period displayed little interest in sport and had few ministers or senior politicians who had any empathy with the policy area. The clearest reflection of the governments' prevailing attitude to sport was in the succession of ineffective politicians who held the post of Minister for Sport and for whom the post was the high point of their political career. An exception was Colin Moynihan, a former Olympic rowing cox, who actively promoted work on sport for people with disabilities and those in inner city areas, which proved to be precursors of later work on sports equity.

The environment for sports development during the years of the Thatcher governments was particularly difficult for, just at the time when advocates on behalf of sports development were attempting to move its consideration from the fringes of government, British politics was entering a period of sustained turbulence prompted by a series of major issues including the restructuring of the machinery of government, limitation on the powers of trade unions, reform of the powers and responsibilities of local authorities, and changes to the organisation and curriculum of schools. The focus of this chapter is on the interaction between the broader debates, largely of the Thatcher years, and the evolution of sports development, and it begins with an examination of the breakdown of the dominant welfare policy paradigm.

Welfare politics: the breakdown of consensus

In the early 1970s the edifice of the welfare state not only looked secure from political challenge but seemed set to continue to expand. What is most surprising is not that such a comprehensive attack on the welfare state emerged so rapidly, but that it met with so little resistance. The inadequacy of the defence of welfare services was due, in large part, to the fact that the challenges were coming from both the right and the left of the political spectrum. Although there had been some formidable academic critiques of the welfare role of the state as early as the mid-1940s, it was not until the economic crisis of 1976 that the range of disparate academic and political critiques coalesced into the powerful challenge that was to lead eventually to a substantial restructuring of welfare provision. The economic crisis that led to the Labour government borrowing £2.3 billion from the International Monetary Fund provided confirmation of the end of Keynesian economics, which had been heralded at the previous year's Labour Party conference when James Callaghan announced that the government could no longer spend its way out of recession. As Timmins notes, 'It was the moment which marked the first great fissure in Britain's welfare state' (1995: 315).

The late 1970s witnessed the gradual refinement and consolidation of the right's challenge to the welfare state: first, in the formulation of monetarism as a coherent alternative orthodoxy to Keynesianism, and, second, in an increasingly forceful and persuasive neo-liberal critique of the role of the state in providing welfare. In essence, the right argued: that the cost in taxation of the pursuit of the chimera of equality had undermined economic competitiveness; that welfare had undermined self-reliance; that the preoccupation with the redistribution of wealth distracted attention from its creation; and that the growth of the welfare state had created a series of self-seeking welfare professions whose primary interest was to act as an internal lobby for greater government expenditure (Niskanen 1973; Buchanan 1978; Minford 1984).[1]

That the left failed to defend the welfare state more robustly is an indication of the depth of ambivalence felt towards the operation and impact of welfare services. Thus, although the critique from the left was more muted, it carried considerable political significance. At the heart of the left's concerns was the apparent failure of the welfare state to make any noticeable impact on disadvantage and inequality over the period since 1950 in areas such as health, education, housing conditions and employment security (Timmins 1995: ch. 15; Higgins *et al.* 1984). The left also shared with the right the general concern that the welfare state was not responsive to the needs of the individual due to the professionalised, centralised and remote character of the welfare bureaucracy.

The late 1970s was a period of declining confidence in current welfare policy, but it was not until the late 1980s that the radical reshaping of welfare began. For Wilding, the period between 1988 and 1990 was a defining moment in the evolution of the welfare state as the legislation introduced during the period 'fundamentally reshaped British social policy' (1997: 716).[2] Four aspects of the reshaping of the welfare state are of especial significance for the future evolution of sports development. First, the effect of the radical critique undertaken by the Conservative government was to undermine confidence in state action and to redefine the welfare professions as 'producer interests' which could be justifiably pushed to the margin of policy debate. Most notably, professions were substantially excluded from the NHS Review and from the debates that led to the 1988 Education Reform Act. Second, the Conservatives also confirmed their commitment to a mixed economy of welfare provision and emphasised the role that the family, and the private and voluntary sectors, should play in provision. The voluntary sector was supported by a substantial increase in public funding, much of it channelled through the Manpower Services Commission. Third, the government also promoted the adoption of private sector management practices, such as performance measurement and strategic planning, introduced compulsory competitive tendering for the provision of public services, and constructed a series of internal markets. Finally, the Conservative government drastically reduced the role and capacity of local government, particularly in education, taxation and personal social services, and, possibly more importantly, sought to reshape the culture of local government and make it more comfortable with an enabling and facilitating role rather than that of primary service provider.

While the catalogue of the legislative and administrative restructuring of the public sector by the Thatcher governments is convincing evidence of the scale of the change achieved, it runs the risk of disguising the most significant consequence of that period of reform: namely, the extent of the reordering of the political context within which welfare policy was discussed. The Conservatives changed the terms of the debate about welfare – first, to give greater priority to international economic competitiveness and abandon any pretence of a commitment to full employment, and, second, to absorb the benefits regime within a framework of social discipline (Wilding 1997; Klein and Millar 1995; Jessop 1994). The Conservatives sought to challenge and overthrow the dependency culture and the poverty lobby that promoted it, and argued that the aim of social policy should be to 'remoralise' recipients so as to encourage greater self-reliance and a greater awareness of responsibilities rather than merely rights (Deakin 1994;

Deakin and Edwards 1993). These dramatic shifts in the ideological, administrative and financial context of welfare provided the dynamic background against which sports development emerged, and were complemented by a series of particular reforms and policy innovations of especial significance to sports development, most notably those in education and the allied area of youth work and the introduction of compulsory competitive tendering.

Education was one of the most consistent targets of reform for the Conservative government, and it is not surprising that physical education was affected by the changes to the funding and curriculum of schools. What is surprising is that the Conservative government should have paid such close and sustained attention to PE. Part of the explanation was that 'PE could be used to signify all else that was wrong with State secondary educational provision' (Evans 1988: 6). However, interest in PE was not limited to its symbolic value as it was subject to an intense critical review in its own right before its inclusion in the national curriculum. The public, and frequently the parliamentary, debate centred on the issue of the alleged decline in competitive team sports, but this was a clear distortion and simplification of a debate that had been under way for some time within the PE profession. The established curriculum, and particularly the role and significance of competitive team sport, was challenged first by those who argued that, while it produced pupils with requisite sports skills, it was less successful in producing strategic understanding of particular sports (Bunker and Thorpe 1982). The proposed solution was to introduce modified forms of adult sports better suited to the needs of the learner and better able to develop motor skills in parallel with strategic understanding. The existing curriculum was also challenged by those who argued that school sports were ineffective in improving the health of pupils, especially in relation to cardiovascular fitness and obesity. The emphasis of the proponents of health-related fitness was on activities that were not necessarily competitive or conducive to the development of sports-related skills. Both critiques challenged the emphasis on conventional team sport, both stressed the importance of meeting the individual needs of children rather than the collective needs of the class, and both favoured a less prescriptive curriculum and one that gave the child greater control (Evans and Clarke 1988; Kirk 1992).

Throughout the 1980s, but particularly from the mid-1980s onwards, there had been a steady stream of attacks on the perceived decline of competitive school sport. Despite the paucity of evidence, the PE profession drew criticism from the professional education press, the popular press, television and politicians (Kirk 1992). According to Kirk, 'the demise of school sport was equated with Britain's poor showing in international sport' (*ibid.*: 5). This round of public debate became part of the context for the consideration of the national curriculum. Although there is no evidence that the sports lobby had precipitated the debate on school sport, the raised public and political profile of the issue prompted sports interests, the CCPR and the major NGBs, in particular, to take steps to ensure that their voice was heard during the subsequent discussion of the content of the national curriculum. Not only did the sports lobby successfully support PE teachers in their campaign for the inclusion of PE as a foundation subject, it also influenced the content of the PE curriculum by achieving an increased emphasis on the practice of, as opposed to the study of, sport. The outcome of the debate on the national curriculum was better than many PE teachers had feared, especially as their professional voice had been marginalised by government. Talbot explains the survival of PE in the national curriculum as being due to the strength of the sports lobby and the health lobby, which she referred to as 'the rugby union Mafia of Harley Street' (1995: 27). The overall effect of the review was to leave the place of PE and sport in curriculum stronger, but the influence of PE teachers, as the provider group, much weaker. More importantly, the outcome reinforced a view of school sport as an element of the sports development strategy of the governing bodies, confirmed the importance of school PE and games in skills acquisition, and attempted to reduce the role of PE teachers to little more than coaches and talent scouts.

While the sport lobby took a keen interest in the debate on the curriculum, it had been less interested (and less successful) in influencing the debate concerning the place of sport in the Youth Service. As Swain noted, 'the Youth Service has a love–hate relationship with sport' (1987: 10). On the one hand, sport featured prominently in the range of activities offered by the service but the value of sport received little acknowledgement from youth workers. The 1987 review of youth work published by the National Youth Bureau made no mention of sport, and Swain also noted a reluctance among youth work training agencies to include sport in their curriculum. Stead paints a picture of a youth service that is suspicious of sport for a number of reasons: first, because of its potential to overwhelm the broader agenda of youth work; second, because of the perception that youth programmes built around sport are examples of 'lazy' youth work; and third, because many youth workers saw sport as a 'controlling device' (Stead 1987: 23). Furthermore, the wariness of youth workers was fuelled by a lack of confidence in their professional status and a concern that too close an association with sports development would undermine their already fragile organisational autonomy.

Despite these concerns, there were some examples of youth SDOs working closely with the Youth Service. Professional and volunteer youth workers were involved in a number of Action Sport projects as well as schemes funded through the Community Programme in the 1980s. Unfortunately, the number of examples is small and, in general, the relationship between the Youth Service and sports development was, and indeed remains, poor. One consequence of the weak relationship was largely to exclude SDOs from an established network with strong links to young people. A second consequence was to reinforce the belief among many

SDOs that their primary role was direct service provision rather than the construction and management of a network of service providers.

The changing relationship between sport policy and welfare

Throughout the 1970s the emphasis in sport policy was on facility development. In 1973 the Sports Council remarked that 'it is now time for provision of facilities for recreation to be given a higher priority in the national economy' (Sports Council 1973: 7). Annual reports made constant reference to facility development and extending the utilisation, through dual use schemes, of existing facilities. Even as late as 1981, the Council still referred to facility development as the 'greatest single need for sport in this country' (Sports Council 1981: 9). An emphasis on facility provision served to retain cohesion between a series of overlapping interests in sport. For the governing bodies of sport, whose primary concern was sport at the performance and excellence levels, increased facility provision was essential, particularly as most facilities were designed in a way that closely matched their requirements. For example, swimming pools were designed for the minority that used them for training and competition, rather than for the majority who used them for social, exercise and recreational purposes. The traditional rectangular design with a shallow end of about 1 metre and a deep end of 2–3 metres met the needs of the confident, or at least competent, swimmer much better than those of the young non-swimmer or the under-confident swimmer. Among those groups who were less involved with elite level sport, there was little opposition to the current pattern of facility design and development. Certainly not from physical educators, themselves often active competitive sportsmen and women, nor from the new leisure services departments within local authorities. For the latter, the combination of Sports Council subsidy and a lack of an alternative model of facility development made them equally enthusiastic supporters, irrespective of the consequences for the promotion of mass participation.

However, the consensus on sport policy began to break down once the first wave of facility development passed and the emphasis shifted from simply meeting latent demand for sport to attempting to promote wider participation. By the early 1980s there were clear signs of a shift away from facility provision and to a strategy of concentrating resources on particular sports or sections of the community. The strategy document *Sport in the Community* stated that the deficiency in facilities identified by the Wolfenden Committee in 1960 and by the Cobham Committee in 1973 had been overcome:

> The Council's new strategy … [is] to concentrate its efforts on selected targets … focusing particularly on people passing through two changes in lifestyle – from school and college to adult work and family life for

the 13–24 age group and those passing from parenthood and full-time work to retirement between 45 and 59 years of age.

(Sports Council 1982: 6)

As the Council summed up in the 1983 annual report, 'The strategy for the next ten years starting in 1983–84 shows an emphasis on participation. In these terms the year can be described as a watershed' (Sports Council 1983: 8).

Yet the emphasis placed on targeting under-participating groups did not mark a dramatic shift away from previous policy objectives. Throughout the period of facility development there was an acknowledgement on the part of the Sports Council that its Royal Charter left it 'with the difficult task of delicately steering a course which would serve both the elite and the wider community' (Sports Council 1982: 4). There were frequent references in annual reports admonishing those who 'see a marked difference between leisure sport ... and competitive sport ... and would wish to separate them' (Sports Council 1976: 12), as well as reminders that 'the Sports Council's responsibility is to sport overall ... to encourage participation ... "in the interests of social welfare" ... as well as to "encourage the achievement of high standards"' (Sports Council 1980: 9). However, by the early 1980s it was clear that the Council was coming under increasing pressure to give greater weight to its welfare responsibilities, which, as was noted in the 1981 Annual Report, 'had become more important than ever' (Sports Council 1981: 6). By 1983 the Council was claiming that 'if the work of the Sports Council can be summed up in one word it would be participation' (Sports Council 1983: 8).

Consequently, in the early 1980s the dominant definition of participation was one that continued to take the identification of under-participating groups as central, but which increasingly targeted groups that were also perceived to constitute social problems and where sport could be seen as fulfilling an ameliorative function – for example, in relation to young people. For much of the 1970s the dominant attitude within the Council towards young people was informed by the Wolfenden view that the decline in participation after leaving school should be tackled, in part at least, because participation would enhance the quality of life of young people. 'Youth, in particular, needs the challenge and adventure of sport, an outlet for energy and for a natural desire to excel' (Sports Council 1977: 4). However, within a few years participation for youth was being promoted increasingly as a solution to the problem of those young people 'who would otherwise be attracted to delinquency and vandalism' (Sports Council 1979: 6). The focus on youth was reinforced by the greater emphasis given to urban areas and ethnic minorities. 'The Council's work in this area of special need and in the concrete jungle of inner cities has begun' (Sports Council 1978: 3). It was against this background of a shift away from facility provision to participation, leadership and motivation that the Action Sport initiative was introduced.

Action Sport: sports development comes of age

The series of urban riots in the summer of 1981, most notably in Liverpool's Toxteth area and in the Brixton district of London, occurred just two years after the Conservative Party's election victory that was to result in the party remaining in office for eighteen years. Although the successive Conservative governments were to reshape much of the machinery of government and leave a lasting impression on most policy areas, the actions of the new government in the early 1980s in many areas of social policy reflected continuity rather than disjuncture with the policies and style of the previous Labour administration. This policy continuity arose partly because Margaret Thatcher's early priorities focused on the supply side of government policy, industrial competitiveness, trade union power and taxation, in particular, and partly because she was doubtful whether the government could manage the political costs of welfare reform (Timmins 1995). The 1981 riots therefore prompted what was in many ways a conventional policy response from the new government. Despite the prime minister's expressed dislike of quangos,[3] the government approved the co-operation between the Manpower Services Commission (MSC) and the Sports Council[4] to provide the resources for Action Sport. Action Sport was therefore introduced into a well-established policy framework. The MSC was already financing a number of schemes directed towards tackling the problem of inner-city unemployment, such as the Community Programme which was to fund a number of posts to support Action Sport activities. The alacrity with which the Sports Council adopted Action Sport was due as much, if not more, to financial opportunism than to conscious policy reorientation. Although there were some precursors to Action Sport, a focus on inner city welfare issues was still marginal to Council policy. However, there was a growing acceptance within the Council that their budgetary strategy of bidding for incremental growth in annual treasury grant on the basis of expanding existing programmes was generally failing to persuade and that some innovation in policy was required if significant additional funding was to be forthcoming. The willingness of the government to use sport as an instrument of urban policy provided the Sports Council with an opportunity to attract additional funding that would have been remiss to ignore.

As Coalter *et al.* remark, the establishment of an executive Sports Council marked a move away from a concern to 'develop a social policy for sport' to an emphasis on 'the role of sport in social policy' (1986: 53). The obligation on the Council to meet the needs of the mass participant and to take account of the contribution of sport to social welfare was clearly stated in the Royal Charter. Coming nine years after the formation of the Sports Council, Action Sport should have been informed by an established set of values and practices which reflected the Council's perception of the role of sport in social policy. Unfortunately, there is little evidence of debate within the Council over the interpretation of its new responsibilities. Although annual reports acknowledged the obligation of the Council to support the social objectives of the government, as expressed, for example, in the Department of the Environment 1975 White Paper, there was little evidence of a shift in resources. The domination of the Council by staff transferred from the CCPR reinforced a service culture that was deferential towards the needs of the elite athlete, prioritised the provision of organised sports opportunities for young people, and which considered the partnership with national governing bodies as the organisational cornerstone for the achievement of these priorities. The strength of the link between the CCPR and the Council also meant that there was no significant internal lobby on behalf of a broader conceptualisation of the Council's responsibilities more in line with the rhetoric of the charter. 'Despite growing political pressures to concentrate on encouraging mass participation and to address issues of recreational deprivation, [the Council] could continue to represent the economic interests of the elite sector' (*ibid.*: 56).

The broadening of Sports Council policy beyond the token acknowledgement of the role of sport in the achievement of wider social objectives was the result of two developments. The first was the alteration by government of the Council's funding arrangement by introducing an element of specific grant in 1978 to support the Football in the Community initiative designed to combat the growth of soccer hooliganism. The second was the realisation that other agencies were rapidly expanding their funding of sport and that the Council ran the risk of losing leadership on the facility development strategy. In 1981, for example, the Department of the Environment was channelling £18 million into facility provision through the Urban Aid programme, a sum only slightly smaller than the entire Sports Council budget. The Action Sport programme not only provided an opportunity to raise additional funding for sport, but was, more importantly, an opportunity for the Council to reassert its central position within debates on sport policy.

Action Sport proved to be one of the defining moments in the evolution of sports development. The government, somewhat grudgingly, supported the Sports Council in introducing the Action Sport programme which was funded by the Council at £1 million each year from 1982 to 1985, and focused on fifteen local authorities in the cities of Birmingham and London. The focus of the programme was the appointment of ninety sports leaders and motivators (the title 'sports development officer' had not yet gained common usage). The original intention of the Council to employ the sports leaders directly was thwarted by the government's determination to prevent any addition to the central government payroll. The leaders were therefore employed by their host local authorities although their salaries were fully covered by the Council. In many ways this (expensive) fiction proved fortuitous,[5] as it ensured a closer relationship between the sports leaders and local government which, due to the perceived success of Action Sport, gave the expansion of the programme additional momentum. Such was the success of the programme that by mid-1987 there were some 300 sports leaders/motivators employed by local government. The significance of the introduction of Action Sport lay less in its novelty, for there were a number of precursors of the programme, but rather in the fact that it helped to promote sports development as a legitimate local authority activity. However, Action Sport is also of interest because it draws attention to varied roots of sports development within broader welfare policy and, more importantly, because it is a useful point of reference when assessing current sports development activity.

At the time of the 1981 riots, the Sports Council had already introduced a number of smaller programmes with the co-operation of the local authority and the Manpower Services Commission aimed at areas of high unemployment. Pilot schemes were initiated in Derwentside District Council, Leicester and in Birmingham. The aims of the Leicester scheme, which was directed towards young people and ethnic minorities, were typical and were to reduce boredom, improve the quality of life through leisure, encourage and develop natural leaders, encourage more people to take coaching qualifications and provide an opportunity for sampling adventure activities (Coghlan 1990: 218). Similar welfare objectives associated with the urban young, ethnic minorities and unemployment can be found in the Action Sport programme, except on a grander scale. Of the fifteen Action Sport schemes, nine were in London and the other six in the West Midlands. The objectives of the London schemes were to:

- encourage the development of positive attitudes to sport and recreation among the low participant groups and to develop a concentrated programme of recreational activities appropriate to inner city dwellers;
- monitor the effects that such programmes may have on the social attitudes and behaviour of the client groups;
- encourage the development of self-help recreation projects in neighbourhood, tenant and community groups to build upon the work undertaken in the initial three-year programme;
- encourage existing agencies (local authorities, local education authorities, commercial interests, industries, etc.) to continue to support the programme following the three-year initiative; and
- create a Sports Leadership training programme in years 2 and 3.

(Rigg 1986: 9–10)

The aim of the West Midlands schemes was to 'provide leaders/motivators in a variety of typical urban situations in order to demonstrate the belief that leadership is crucial to increased participation in sport and recreation in deprived urban areas' (*ibid.*: 10). The various associated objectives emphasised similar themes to the London schemes, such as the importance of networking between voluntary, statutory and commercial agencies, but differed in specifying particular target groups, namely, 'teenagers, ethnic minority groups, Asian women, [and] the 55 year old plus age group' (*ibid.*: 11).

The identification of target groups of under-participating sections of the population was already a well-established strategy within the Sports Council by the late 1970s. The 'Sport For All' policy was based on the belief that participation in sport was a source of individual and social welfare and, as such, the role of the professional sports leader or SDO was to identify those groups whose participation was low and meet their, often unexpressed, need. Action Sport encouraged the shift to more proactive policy intervention away from a 'response based on publicising and promoting the benefits of sport to those in target groups to direct intervention at a face-to-face level' (*ibid.*: 45–6). This model of professional intervention overlapped significantly with established practices in community work. Although community workers would claim that their objective is to empower a community so that it might articulate its own interests, in contrast to the presumption of the Action Sport scheme that sport is a need of under-participating groups externally defined by professional sports leaders, there is much common ground in terms of using the community as a resource and as a source of future sports leaders, and also, in the West Midlands at least, the attempt to create self-sustaining programmes that would outlive the period of external intervention.

The aims and objectives of the Action Sport programme were a mix, and at times an uneasy mix, of broad welfare concerns associated with the alleviation of the consequences of unemployment and urban deprivation and sports-specific objectives associated with increasing participation. However, it is not just in terms of objectives that the programme appeared to be divided. The process by which the objectives were to be achieved also reflected the influence of different policy traditions. On the one hand, emphasis was placed on community self-help through the identification and training of community sports leaders, while, on the other, there was a strategy of professional intervention, especially in London, whereby full-time sports leaders ran sports/recreational sessions rather than devoting most of their time to motivating and training others to take care of delivery.

The establishment of the Action Sport programme broadly coincided with the reorientation of Sports Council strategy heralded in the publication of its 1982 strategy document *Sport in the Community: The Next Ten Years*. Satisfying the dual requirements of the Council's Royal Charter towards elite sportsmen and women and mass participation had been, during the 1970s, relatively easy insofar as facility construction supported both objectives. The 1982 strategy signalled a shift in policy towards a greater concern with the quality of the sports experience and the particular services required for both elite and mass sports development. It was at this point that the tensions between those whose primary concern was elite achievement and those concerned with increased participation began to surface. Encouraged by the early enthusiasm for Action Sport and the achievements of the pilot sports development schemes launched just prior to Action Sport, the Council sought to raise the profile of sports development as a process of active intervention in society designed to increase the participation levels of target groups. However, it was keen to reassure its partners from the national governing bodies that 35 per cent of resources would still be earmarked for 'encouraging excellence' (Sports Council 1982: 42). Tentatively and deferentially the Council disclosed that it was interested in discussing 'with the governing bodies the role they wish to play' in promoting participation (*ibid.*: 34). The Council's approach fell on deaf ears. As Coghlan remarks:

> The response from the governing bodies of sport was virtually nil as was that from the CCPR; not that this demonstrated a lack of interest but rather the sober fact that there is still today … a lack of understanding as to the part sport plays in the social field, or … there still exists a belief that this is not really their concern.
>
> (1990: 153)

If the Council was seeking an endorsement from the government for its embrace of sports development it was disappointed again as Coghlan pointedly remarks that a response 'from HM government was even more emphatically not forthcoming' (*ibid.*: 153) with the announcement of the next award of grant aid to the Council taking 'no account of the strategy' (*ibid.*: 153).

With the marked lack of enthusiasm shown by government and the governing bodies it is not surprising that the promotion of sports development by the Council was hesitant. Indeed it is to the credit of the Council that it persisted when a more politically comfortable response would have been to have applauded the achievements of Action Sport, but then quietly let the impetus behind socially oriented sports leadership/development dissipate. However, the Council launched an ambitious series of demonstration projects linked to a wide variety of partners and targeting a broad range of social problems and groups. Although the projects involved a variety of partners the most lasting effect was on local authorities.

National demonstration projects: redefining sports development

The national demonstration programme was launched in 1984 and was clearly focused on the promotion of mass participation in line with the 1982 strategy. The fifteen projects fell into three categories: first, those that sought to develop sports participation through outreach work (e.g. women in rural areas in conjunction with the Women's Institute); second, those more experimental schemes directed at particular target groups (e.g. health and exercise promotion in Liverpool in conjunction with the regional health authority); and, third, those that were linked to the education system (e.g. the Active Lifestyles Project in Coventry schools). The projects were undoubtedly successful in building on the achievements of Action Sport and did much to embed the notion of sports development within many local authorities. But the projects were also important in helping the Sports

Council to refine their conceptualisation of sports development and in identifying where some of the most substantial barriers to further expansion lay.

In the review of the demonstration projects conducted by the Sports Council much attention was devoted to the problems of managing the wide range of partnerships necessary for project implementation and the challenge of reconciling sports development objectives with those of the partner body. One central problem was the failure of many partners to ensure that the sports development officers that they were employing were incorporated within their organisational structures. The Council bemoaned the 'problems faced by the project leaders in developing appropriate line management structures', a situation which, on occasion, 'led to projects drifting from their initial objectives with "non-sporting" objectives being allocated a higher priority' (Sports Council 1991b: 14, 31). Not surprisingly, these problems were most evident when working with health authorities and the probation service where sport and sports development were unfamiliar activities. The Council showed a clear recognition of the problems of working with non-sports organisations and stated that 'If we in the sports world wish to use other organisations as a resource to further our own objectives, we must fully understand the aims and objectives of our new partners' (*ibid.*: 31). Yet this view of sport and health or the probation service as equal partners is undermined by an assessment, perhaps more realistic, of the relationship in which the Council noted that 'to get the maximum benefits from the partnerships, sports development objectives must try to fit in with the objectives of the partner organisation and not vice versa' (*ibid.*: 31).

More positively, the Council reported that since 1986, when it concluded that 'the large majority of local authorities remain conservative, hierarchical, and blinkered' (quoted in Sports Council 1991b: 31), there had been a significant shift in local authority perception of sports development such that 'many now see sports development, partnership initiatives, and target group promotions as a fundamental part of *their* role' (*ibid.*: 32, emphasis added). Undoubtedly the shift in perception was due more to the success of the government's campaign to force local authorities to accept the role of enabler not just service deliverer than to the success of the demonstration projects and Sports Council pump-priming finance. A similarly positive assessment was made of the relationship between sports development and the governing bodies of sport and clubs. As with local authorities, an earlier critical assessment of the willingness of individual sport clubs to incorporate community sports development objectives into their plans was revised, with the Sports Council noting the 'marked change in the attitudes of all our traditional sporting partners in the intervening five years' (*ibid.*: 41). One important indication of the growing complementarity between the development plans of clubs and their governing bodies, on the one hand, and that of the Sports Council, on the other, was the discussion in the report of a need to revisit the conceptualisation of sports development encompassed in the model of the sports development continuum.

The model of the sports development continuum was first used in a report authored by Derek Casey in 1988 (Scottish Sports Council 1988) and subsequently became widely used by sports organisations throughout the UK. It was an important, and generally successful, attempt to give coherence to the concept of sports development at both the intellectual level and at the practical level. The initial model was composed of four relatively discrete levels (Figure 2.1). The first level was *foundation*, where the emphasis was on the acquisition of 'physical literacy' – those basic motor and perceptual skills that underpin most sports. The assumption was that these would be acquired and developed within the primary school system. The second level, *participation*, was concerned with the provision and fostering of opportunities to participate in sport and physical activity whether casually or through clubs. Participation was seen as being the key concern and priority of the local government sport and recreation service. *Performance* referred to the improvement in a participant's existing level of skill and also the maintenance of a competitive structure for practice. As such, the central provider would be the governing bodies of sport and their networks of clubs. *Excellence* was the final level where the emphasis was on preparation to compete at the highest levels in sport. The value of the continuum was that it demonstrated the integration of the different forms of involvement and reinforced the view of the Sports Council that it was not possible to treat participation at the level of the local authority leisure facility, school sport and PE and international and Olympic participation as discrete policy areas, rather, it was important to acknowledge their interdependence.

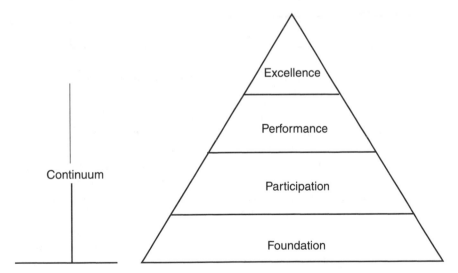

Figure 2.1   The early model of the sports development continuum
Source: Sport England

The early version of the continuum presented the relationship between levels as hierarchical with the implication that individuals moved upwards through the continuum until they found their preferred level or the limits of their ability. The research conducted for the review of the demonstration projects suggested that the continuum needed to be revised, particularly with regard to the relationship between participation and performance. While it had been acknowledged for some time that there was a need for ladders of performance to enable individuals to improve, receive training and broaden their competitive experience, there had been an implicit assumption that participation was more homogeneous, both as an experience and as a set of needs. The review stressed that there was a 'need for a "participation" structure which complements the performance ladder' (Sports Council 1991c: 7) which would enable individuals to shape their pattern of participation to meet changes in lifestyle, family and employment circumstances. The revised model of the continuum is shown in Figure 2.2.

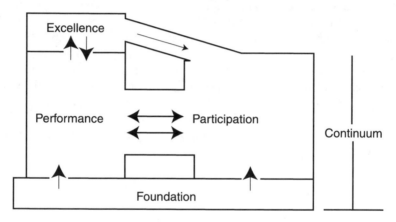

Figure 2.2   The modified model of the sports development continuum

In general, the demonstration projects were judged a success, but the review did identify a number of issues which were to prove to be significant impediments to the consolidation of sports development. The first concerned the shift in emphasis from 'an original concentration on target groups towards projects which are addressing contemporary issues' (Sports Council 1991c: 1). At the heart of sports development was uncertainty over the proper focus of activity and whether it was particular social issues or the level of participation that identified the target group. The importance of this point is apparent from another conclusion of the review which stressed the need for continuity of provision. All too often sports development interventions stimulated interest only for it to subside once the period of project funding ended. Much of the time this was due to the three-year cycle of funding, but it was frequently compounded by the instability of policy objectives which were often dictated by the dominant social problems of the day. For many under-participating groups, and especially those in rural areas, the introduction to sport was only a small part of the sports development activity. More significant was the need for continuing support to ensure that long-term barriers to participation, such as family responsibilities, poor transport links and poverty, were not re-established once the project was terminated. Yet the report identified a number of factors whose implications, at the time of publication, were far from clear. Among those identified were the introduction of local financial management of schools and compulsory competitive tendering for local authority facility management. It was the latter, CCT, that was to prove the most disruptive of attempts to establish a coherent and stable conceptualisation of sports development.

Compulsory competitive tendering and sports development

The introduction of compulsory competitive tendering for leisure services in the late 1980s as part of the government's general commitment to privatisation and marketisation had a significant impact on the immediate context of public sector sports development activity. As applied to leisure services in 1988, CCT legislation required that the management of facilities above a minimum size should be submitted for tender. The government anticipated a 20 per cent cost saving (Audit Commission 1989: 17). Despite the fact that the vast majority of tenders were won by in-house management teams and that many local authorities were exempt due to the small size of their facilities, the advent of CCT did have significant implications for the fledgling sports development service. Not only did the preparation for CCT dominate strategy discussions in the larger authorities to the disadvantage of sports development, but the introduction of contract-based service specifications often left sports development marginalised within sport and recreation services. More positively, the imminence of CCT did reinforce the encouragement being given by the Sports Council to local authorities to prepare strategic plans. However, many of the plans were inadequate guides to service delivery as they were often poorly specified and consequently sufficiently vague for contractors to safely ignore. Even when the local authority, as client, used its strategy to set explicit targets regarding particular priority groups and sports development activity, the targets were simply ignored by many contractors who gave priority to income maximisation, often with the tacit support of both client-side officers and elected members. It has been suggested that, in general, CCT had the effect of undermining the establishment and consolidation of sports development activity. 'In many cases sports development objectives are becoming irrelevant to what local authority facilities are actually delivering' (Centre for Leisure Research 1993: 46). Part of the problem lay in the failure (or inexperience) of many authorities to specify sports development objectives with sufficient clarity:

> Although many of the sport and leisure management contracts
> contained specific reference to a range of types of user and use, fewer
> were accompanied by specific methods of implementation and measur-
> able performance targets – throughput, time allocation, provision of
> coaches and so on.
>
> (*ibid.*: 47)

Many contracts did specify types of user with 85 per cent mentioning people
with disabilities, 80 per cent young people and 64 per cent women, but only
one in five specified throughput targets. A similarly large number of authorities specified a pricing policy with regard to particular target groups. Indeed,
references to price were the most common evidence of the incorporation of
sports development objectives into tender documents. Overall, the study
concluded that

> in sports participation terms, the contract specifications could be
> regarded as largely 'non-developmental'. This is because there was a
> much more limited attempt to move beyond general statements of
> service objectives and to specify methods of implementation and
> specific, measurable, social policy performance targets. The non-devel-
> opmental nature of contract specifications is emphasised further by the
> fact that only 6 per cent of contractors have sole responsibility for
> sports development, although in a further 16 per cent of contracts this
> was shared between client and contractor.
>
> (*ibid.*: 55)

It might be assumed charitably that the remaining 78 per cent of local
authorities deliberately took advantage of the right available under the legislation to retain sole responsibility for sports development, but the study
concluded that few respondents in local authorities 'referred to sports development, indicating its lack of consideration in the largely facility-oriented
CCT process' (*ibid.*: 67). It is much more likely that for many authorities
sports development was still peripheral to most strategies and that those
involved in sports development within authorities were not sufficiently influential to affect either strategy preparation or contract specification.

An optimistic interpretation of the Sports Council study of the introduction of CCT would highlight the overwhelming proportion of local
authorities that gave priority to some under-participating social group and
the relatively high proportion that supported that priority with concessionary charges and/or a specific time allocation. Yet this form of sports
development is largely passive and relies on members of the target population taking the initiative in visiting the sports/leisure facility. A less
optimistic assessment is that the survey highlighted the low number of local
authorities that had produced a sport and recreation strategy. While the exis-

tence of a strategy would by no means guarantee that sports development goals, as opposed to those associated with income maximisation, for example, would be included and given priority, there was a view within the Sports Council that the strategy preparation process was likely to result in a clearer recognition of sports development activity (Sports Council 1994a). Yet the Council was asking a lot, and probably too much, of the nascent sports development function. It suggested that local authorities should take a strategic decision regarding the incorporation of sports development within the contract, but argued that such a decision should not be at the expense of a client-side sports development capacity. '[F]or many authorities, only a client side SDO will be able to co-ordinate sports development across the district including dual-use facilities, clubs and other non-CCT facilities' (*ibid.*: 15). While this is true, it assumed an unrealistic degree of influence within local government for sports development officers. Only in a small number of authorities were there sufficient sports development officers at an appropriately senior level to have an impact on service-wide strategic direction; in a large number of authorities, sports development in the early 1990s was treated as a self-contained, time-constrained and project-specific activity.

Sports development and national governing bodies of sport

By the early 1970s national governing bodies (NGBs) were receiving about £900,000 annually from the Sports Council with almost all grant aid being directed towards improving the quality of central management services and coaching. Although it could be argued that improved central administration and, especially, a more extensive and better trained coaching staff were important developmental assets, there was a growing realisation within the NGBs that they needed to be active in attracting a new generation of athletes into their various sports. Rugby union, in the late 1980s, was the first sport to appoint development officers whose function was to assist clubs in recruiting players and setting up junior sections (see chapter 6). However, NGBs in general were extremely conservative organisations and were slow to generate momentum in sports development. For example, it was only in the 1970s that many major NGBs began to treat coaching as a necessary, if not yet central, aspect of their responsibilities. As Coghlan observes: 'There has always been in British sport a somewhat schizophrenic attitude to coaching and coaches' (1990: 46).

The recognition of the importance of coaching and the increased number of coaches was reflected in the formation of the British Association of National Coaches in 1966, though 'not without misapprehension in some national governing bodies' (*ibid.*: 46). The understandable preoccupation with addressing current weaknesses in the coaching structure dominated the relationship between the NGBs and the Sports Council for much of the

1970s with the consequence that consideration of broader development issues tended to be pushed to the margin. During the 1970s and early 1980s the NGBs and the Sports Council gradually established an acceptable framework for elite coaching and development. The establishment of a series of centres of excellence around the country in the late 1970s to focus on high-level coaching and support across a range of Olympic and non-Olympic sports was a major landmark. A second important landmark was the formation of the National Coaching Foundation in 1982 to promote and co-ordinate the burgeoning range of coaching courses and sports science programmes around the country.

The lack of interest and understanding of broader and, particularly, social aspects of sports development was evident in the absence of any significant response from NGBs to the Sports Council's major policy strategy, *Sport in the Community: The Next Ten Years*. It was only towards the middle of the 1980s that broader issues of sports development received more sustained attention in discussions between the governing bodies and the Council.

Sports development in the early 1990s

A survey of sports development in the local authority sector jointly commissioned by the Sports Council and ILAM in the early 1990s painted a vivid picture of the state of the service (Collins 1995). The survey was based on data collected in mid-1991 from English local authorities and described a youthful and junior occupational group with 63 per cent of district SDOs in post less than two years. In addition, 60 per cent of posts had no previous incumbent and a further 25 per cent had only one previous post-holder. On a more positive note, SDOs were a relatively well-qualified group with a quarter possessing a degree and almost 60 per cent holding a coaching qualification. However, not only were the majority of SDOs new to their post, they were often members of small teams. Only 9 per cent had six or more SDOs in the team, while 26 per cent had only one SDO in the local authority and 35 per cent had none at all. Moreover, just under three-quarters of district and metropolitan authorities relied on external grant aid to fund between 25 per cent and 50 per cent of partic-ular posts or projects. It is often the case in local government that when service costs are not part of the mainstream budget the service is unlikely to feature prominently in departmental strategies. As Collins concluded: 'While the SDO coverage of district and metropolitan authorities has grown rapidly in the 1980s it is still patchy at best and far from being a universally accepted function for local authorities ... despite strong Sports Council advocacy and substantial regional grant aid' (1993a). Moreover, Collins's findings highlight the lack of policy leverage possessed by SDOs: 'Their sphere of influence is limited and as junior client-side officers, [are] in no position to negotiate from strength with either contract managers, other service heads or key personnel in education, such as headteachers or governors' (1993b: 1).

Conclusion

The 1980s was not a good time for the promotion of a service as innovative and labour-intensive as sports development. The financial pressure that most local authorities were under made many reluctant to incorporate additional staffing and programme costs into their mainstream budgets. Furthermore, many authorities were distracted from a consideration of sports development issues by the need to prepare for CCT and the range of more salient issues that it raised for local elected members. Nevertheless, the period was important in helping to define what did and did not constitute sports development. It was no longer possible to claim that sports development could be defined in terms of current facility management practice where developmental objectives could be achieved through the pattern of pricing for facilities, the scheduling of activities and the general promotion of the sport and leisure service. This approach was more acceptable in the 1970s when participation grew rapidly without any outreach work or community intervention. However, the explanation of this phenomenon was that the facility building programme simply released latent demand and, when that demand had been satisfied, growth in participation slowed, then levelled off. Indeed participation data indicated that from about the beginning of the 1990s there has been very little increase in participation. Consequently, sports development needed to be defined as an interventionist strategy and not as a passive exercise in the provision of facilities. Moreover, it may be suggested that had such a model been better established in the 1980s, the momentum of growth in participation might not have declined so abruptly. Unfortunately, Collins's conclusion that, by the early 1990s, SDOs had had only a marginal impact on the ethos of recreation management and that recreation management remained 'solidly non-developmental' is depressing but fair.

In those local authorities where sports development was becoming established there was a heavy reliance on external, usually Sports Council, funding. While pump-priming or start-up funding is often essential in order to promote service innovations such as sports development, there is inevitably the awkward stage at which ownership of the programme and service is incorporated into the mainstream of the authority. Two factors militated against a smooth integration of sports development within local authorities. The first was the limiting of start-up funding to three years, which was often too short for individual programmes to demonstrate their value. Although rapid impact is the policy-makers' aspiration, it rarely matches reality where policies, especially those that seek to alter social behaviour, normally have a long lead time. The second factor was the instability of Sports Council priorities during the 1980s. As the report on the national demonstration projects noted, 'Over the seven years of the programme, the emphasis has shifted from an original concentration on target groups towards projects which are addressing contemporary issues' (Sports Council 1991c: 1). But as the Collins report showed, even in 1991 the vast majority of local authorities with a sports development programme continued to define their programme in terms of target groups rather than issues. Fifty-eight per cent identified 'target groups' as either their first or second priority compared with 26 per cent who mentioned 'community' and only 4 per cent who referred to 'health and fitness'. As Collins suggested, the attraction of targeting is that it makes the management and marketing tasks more easily defined and more easily measurable – a factor of some importance when SDOs were in need of indicators of performance of sufficient clarity and simplicity to support bids for further funding.

Finally, at the start of the 1990s sports development was still in its infancy, struggling to gain acceptance both within the turbulent local government environment and among the conservative and generally resource-poor national governing bodies. However, the characteristics and contours of contemporary sports development were already evident. Within local government, sports development was organisationally marginal, focused on specific target groups, particularly the young, and bedevilled by a short-term planning framework. Within the Sports Council, sports development marked a substantial reorientation away from capital projects and towards the strategy of injecting leadership and motivation in the form of SDOs into communities as a way of improving the quality of the sports experience and stimulating interest in sport. The National Coaching Foundation was also finding its feet, but was already responding to a substantial growth in interest in the training and advisory services it was beginning to develop. Yet there was also within the Council an uncertainty about the preferred focus of sports development, and particularly whether under-participation alone should be the criterion that identified target populations or whether sports development should seek to contribute to the amelioration of more complex social problems. Although there was a clear shift in rhetoric and funding from the former to the latter during the 1980s, it was not accompanied by a comparable shift in enthusiasm.

In part, the Council was influenced by its relationship with the national governing bodies who had initially been lukewarm towards the concept of sports development, particularly if it required use of their resources. However, during the 1980s the major sports had accepted that a number of factors had combined to make a development strategy more urgent. The broadening of the school PE/sport curriculum, the decline in extra-curricular sport, the growth in popularity of newer sports and the steady decline in the numbers within the 14–20 age group prompted many governing bodies to accept that they needed to pay more attention to the identification and coaching of young talent. Among national governing bodies, sports development was only slowly being accepted as a legitimate activity, and then only in terms more akin to marketing and recruitment than to any wider community-related definition.

While sports development in the early 1990s could still largely be located within the conceptual unity of the sports development continuum, there were signs that the practice of sports development was producing distinct variations in approach. Three policy themes or approaches can be identified: the first, targeted at young people, focused on a single sport and overseen by a national governing body; the second, concerned to promote mass participation, targeted a variety of under-participating groups, and located within local authorities; and a third, overlapping substantially with the second, focused on social problems such as crime, juvenile delinquency and poor health located within local authorities, but was heavily reliant on the co-operation of non-sports agencies, such as the police and Youth Service.

In summary, the fifteen years or so from the mid-1970s was one that is best described as significant expansion, but limited consolidation. While the number of sports development officers increased and the number of funded projects grew, they still remained marginal to mainstream strategies of both local authorities and national governing bodies. Table 2.1 provides an overview of the shifts in the environment of sports development using the variables identified in Table 1.1 in the previous chapter. As is only to be expected there was little discernible change at the deep structural level.

Although constrained by the fabric of deeply embedded values within the social formation, it is the pattern of interaction among structural interest groups and between interest groups and the state that not only determines the character of the policy community, but also gives the policy area its dynamic. The period from the mid-1970s to the early 1990s was one which witnessed the steady differentiation of structural interest groups, but not, it must be said, a strengthening of their influence over policy. During this period, the various direct support groups, particularly national governing bodies, were defining and refining their relationship with the Sports Council, but mainly in terms of grant aid for high performance sport and not as yet in terms of a concern with wider sports development. Moreover, the tetchy relationship between the Sports Council and the CCPR, which claimed to be the 'voice of sport', coloured the attitude of the NGBs towards the Sports Council. Provider groups were also more sharply delineated by the early 1990s and were slowly beginning to contribute to sports-related policy debates. That their influence was not especially prominent was due as much

Table 2.1 Changes in the environment of sports development policy, 1960 to the early 1990s

Variables	Changes from 1960 to the mid-1970s	Changes from the mid-1970s to the early 1990s
Shallow: more vulnerable to change		
Administrative arrangements	'Arm's-length' Sports Council; service delivery by local authorities and sports clubs.	Increase in the number of specialist leisure services departments in local authorities.
Pattern of inter-organisational resources dependencies	SC dependent on CCPR (and ex-CCPR staff) for expertise and on grant aid from central government for finance. LAs dependent on SC grant aid to pump-prime facility development projects.	Attritional relationship between the Sports Council and the CCPR; steady growth in Sports Council Treasury grant; growth in local government expenditure on sport and leisure services.
More stable: change over the medium term		
Interaction between structural interest groups:	In general interest groups were, at best, emergent during this period.	Period dominated by the tension between the CCPR and the Sports Council.
demand groups (consumers of service outputs);	Demand groups of negligible importance.	Still of marginal importance with the exception of some elite athletes who have influence through players' unions and bodies such as the BOA Athletes Commission.
provider groups (facility/club managers, sports development officers and leisure services managers);	No unified voice. Multiplicity of professional bodies but some discussion of the need to rationalise professional representation in sport and leisure management, but little, if any, recognition of sports development officers as a distinctive service group.	ILAM and ISRM beginning to provide a voice. Sport and leisure beginning to reach the agenda of the various local government associations. But no specific voice for sports development or SDOs.

Variables	Changes from 1960 to the mid-1970s	Changes from the mid-1970s to the early 1990s
direct support groups (e.g. national governing bodies, CCPR and schools)	Direct support groups better organised and almost all wary of the new Sports Council, especially the NGBs who were content to receive grant aid but suspicious of Council direction on policy.	CCPR emerging as an important advocacy group, but most major NGBs dealt directly with the Sports Council. Little or no discussion among structural interest groups of sports development or of sport for school-age children until late 1980s.
indirect support groups (related local authority services, e.g. land use planning, community development and non-Sports Council sources of funding)	Sport services, particularly sports development, were peripheral to their main responsibilities.	For some district councils sport and leisure was a major service as measured by expenditure, but sport was rarely central to corporate strategy. However, cross-department issues were beginning to emerge such as the sale of school playing fields and urban regeneration.
Service-specific policy paradigm	'Arms-length' government involvement; amateurism; voluntarism; sport emerging as an element of welfare provision.	CCT and greater emphasis on cost recovery and the concept of 'user pays'. Highly variable level of salience to government, but general government indifference. Shift in focus from facilities to people and from welfare service to sport as a tool of social engineering. Sports development continuum a unifying concept.
Dominant core policy paradigm	Keynesian and post-war welfare consensus; activist state; service planning; professionalisation.	Retreat from Keynesianism and embrace of neo-liberal economics. Increased criticism of the role of the state. Assertion of welfare state 'failure'. Increased emphasis on the reform of the machinery of government and privatisation.
Deep: entrenched Embedded structural values fundamental to the social formation	Patriarchal attitudes to participation in sport. Deference. Class-based pattern of participation reflected, for example, in the persistence of the distinction between amateur and professional participation. Voluntarism preferred to state intervention.	No discernible change.

to the absence of a receptive government as it was to their structural weaknesses (for example, the continuing competition between the Institute of Leisure and Amenity Management and the Institute of Sport and Recreation Management). Not surprisingly, demand groups, such as local sports councils, were still of only marginal significance to local decision-making let alone national policy.

The period up to the early 1990s was significant in terms of changes to the service-specific policy paradigm for sport and sports development. On the one hand, the early 1990s saw the formulation of the sports development continuum as a unifying conceptualisation of Sports Council policy and one which placed development activity at the heart of policy. On the other hand, the introduction of CCT and the parallel emphasis on cost recovery and income maximisation within local authority service providers created significant problems for the fledgling sports development service. In addition, the governments of the period were generally unenthusiastic about an expanded governmental role in sport, and at times, such as following the Heysel disaster, openly hostile. The introduction of CCT reflected the shift in the dominant core policy paradigm, which was defined by the embrace of privatisation, the rejection of Keynesian economics and a scepticism (though often more rhetorical than substantive) towards state involvement in public service provision.

At the level of organisational and administrative arrangements, the period up to the early 1990s had seen a steady increase in the number of specialist leisure services departments at local government level, and consequently an increasingly clear administrative home for sports development activity. At national level, the Sports Council was firmly established under the oversight of the Department of the Environment although the series of reviews and threatened reorganisations were hardly conducive to policy stability. The tension between the Council and the CCPR provided a further distraction and source of policy inertia.

Overall, the period from the mid-1970s to the early 1990s was one when there was a marked lack of sustained political interest and direction in sport and sports development and when the modest consolidation in sports development that took place was despite, rather than because of, governmental support. However, it was also a period during which lobbying interests began to become more sharply defined and coalesced around the particular cluster of policies, agencies and resources that demarcated their primary policy concerns most accurately. From the appointment of John Major as prime minister, when the political salience of sport increased substantially, policy debates took place within a much more contested political environment in which NGBs, school sport and PE interests, and local authorities were much more aware of the significance of increasing or losing access to public resources, and of the capacity of government policy to affect their ability to achieve their particular goals. Sport policy generally, and sports development policy in particular, was about to enter a period of sustained increase in public investment in sport, but also one of sustained governmental interest and debate about the role of sport in society.

3   The early 1990s to 1997
Welfare restructuring and Major's sporting glory

Introduction

Throughout the 1980s the nascent sports development function experienced periods of substantial promotion, support and encouragement, but also periods of uncertainty and neglect. Promotion and encouragement came not just from the momentum generated by the Action Sport programme and the series of national demonstration projects, but also from the increasing, though still small, number of local authorities, such as Nottinghamshire County and Birmingham City. They were developing policy for sport and recreation which drew upon a model of the sports development continuum that stressed the breadth of opportunity and pathways for high performance sports participation and which accepted a strongly interventionist strategy. The uncertainty and neglect came from a pattern of funding that encouraged local authorities to view sports development activity as time-limited and project-specific. In consequence few local authorities gave serious and sustained consideration to the appropriate location of sports development within the organisational fabric of the authority. However, the emergence and consolidation of sports development was also affected by a series of policy shifts both within wider sport policy and also in the parameters of welfare policy.

If the advocates of the fledgling sports development service were frustrated by the policy turbulence that hampered their efforts at consolidation, it should be borne in mind that mainstream sport policy, reflected in the activities of the Sports Council, the governing bodies of sport and those of local government, were hardly firmly established elements of welfare policy. Mention has already been made of the significance of the imposition of compulsory competitive tendering for leisure services, but, while CCT was undoubtedly a major change in the environment of leisure services, it was not the only change, nor indeed the most significant. Of greater long-term importance was the rapid increase in commercial providers of sport and recreation services for the mass market and the increasing commercialisation of elite sport.

In the mid-1980s the conventional wisdom was that the provision of opportunities for mass participation was economically unattractive to the commercial sector. Such was the cost structure of service provision that the public could only be attracted to facilities such as pools and sports/leisure centres if substantial user subsidies were available. In addition, the fact that the rapid expansion in sports facilities was underpinned by public subsidy of both the capital costs and the continuing revenue costs was seen as a major deterrent to entry to the market by commercial providers. The commercial sport and recreation sector was generally limited to the long-established areas such as racquet sports and golf, where niche market position was frequently based on social exclusivity that was maintained by costly joining and annual membership fees. However, by the early 1980s this situation had changed radically with the commercial leisure industry moving rapidly into the mass participation market and increasingly overlapping with and competing directly against public and voluntary providers. Perhaps the most dramatic expansion has been in health and fitness clubs. By the middle of the 1990s it was estimated that there were approximately 1,300 clubs with over 500 members and a further 2,000 clubs with fewer than 500 members. The pioneer companies in the field, such as David Lloyd, Curzon Fitness clubs, and Living Well Health and Leisure, were rapidly being bought out by the large leisure conglomerates such as Whitbread and Stakis. Although the expansion of the commercial sector is significant, it is still largely confined to a limited range of sports. In outdoor sports, the commercial sector is prominent mainly in golf and tennis and some newer quasi-sporting areas such as paintball, trekking and a range of activity holidays; in indoor sports, in addition to the health and fitness area, the sector is important in water-based activities (Waterworld), tenpin bowling and in some quasi-sports, such as Quasar (an indoor electronic version of paintball). While the impact of the commercial sector might be narrowly focused, it is not insignificant and in the area of fitness gyms and aerobics classes, in particular, it has made a significant contribution to the increase in participation levels, especially among women. However, local authorities and governing bodies have generally been slow to acknowledge the contribution that the commercial sector can make to broader sports development objectives and rarely make reference to the sector in local authority or sports-specific development plans outside the limited areas of tennis and golf.

A further change in the environment of sport and recreation services was the previously mentioned slowdown in the growth in participation. From around 1990 the rise in participation faltered, then levelled out broadly coinciding, ironically, with a period of sustained growth in sports development activity by both local authorities and national governing bodies. Additional pressure came from the pattern of demographic change with the most active age group, 16 to 24 year olds, declining in numbers throughout most of the 1980s and not recovering until the late 1990s.

In addition to the series of factors that impinged directly on sports development and broader sport policy, there were also, in the late 1980s and early

1990s, some shifts in wider welfare policy that were to have a profound and continuing impact on the context for the policy area.

From welfare state to welfare pluralism

The phrase 'the welfare state' has a particular meaning and resonance in modern Britain. On the one hand, it signifies a range of services designed, in general at least, to support individuals and groups in society; on the other hand, it emphasises the centrality of the state and its benign and key role in service provision. In areas such as education, health, housing, and sport and recreation, the state has been the defining, if not always the dominant, provider. As was discussed in the previous chapter, the neo-liberal critique of welfare and the failure of the social democratic left to mount a robust defence not only ushered in a period of sustained challenge to the then current range of welfare assumptions, but also, and much more importantly, undermined the prevailing assumptions about the central role of the state in welfare service provision. 'What has been disrupted in the 1980s is the apparently inextricable connection between the words "welfare" and "state"' (Clarke 1996: 15). As a result alternative descriptions of the pattern of welfare provision have been sought with 'privatisation', 'welfare pluralism' and 'a mixed economy of welfare' being some of the more common.

Much of the discussion of welfare reform has focused, with obvious justification, on the impact of policy change on the individual, redefining citizens as either welfare recidivists – unable or, in the eyes of some, unwilling to break the pattern of dependence – or as active, confident consumers. Rather less attention has been devoted to the consequences for the role of the state and the relationship between the state and the institutions of civil society. The dominant metaphor that has shaped perceptions of the changing role of the state is that of the 'hollowing out' of the state (Rhodes 1994, 1997). According to this view, there has been a transfer of traditional state functions, especially in relation to direct service delivery, to organisations in the private or voluntary sectors and a growing number of arm's-length public agencies. The role retained by the state was increasingly that of the determination of the strategic direction of policy and the use of resources, particularly legislation and finance, to manage the activities of its partners and agents. Whereas emphasis tends to be placed on the transfer out of service responsibilities through CCT, delegation and decentralisation, less attention has been paid to the potential expansion of the state's sphere of influence. As Clarke observes, 'What from one angle can be viewed as the diminution of the state's role can be seen from another as the extension of state power, but through new and unfamiliar means' (1996: 17). Thus, the emergence of welfare pluralism or a mixed economy of welfare may be seen as referring only to the pattern of service delivery underpinned by an expanded capacity of the state to give direction to policy change.

The provision of sport and recreation services in the 1990s was not immune from these broad trends. The impact of CCT was the most obvious example, but others included the increasingly contractual relationship between the Sports Councils and NGBs regarding the use of World Class Performance funds, and the agreements that were entered into prior to the release of National Lottery funding. Rather than the state reducing its involvement in service delivery in sport and recreation, its reach had grown substantially. Similar examples may be drawn from other areas of welfare provision, including housing, care of the elderly and the protection of children. In the first two of these areas, service responsibility has been transferred to voluntary housing associations and private care homes, and in the third the responsibility of the family has been made more explicit. In each case the shift in the boundaries between the state and the voluntary or private sector had been accompanied by an extension in the state's right to scrutinise the work of the latter and also its right to intervene. However, the image of a 'surveillance state' is weakened by the problem that the state had in accumulating the resources necessary to exercise effective monitoring, evaluation and intervention. While it would be seriously misleading to accept the rhetoric of the Conservative governments of Margaret Thatcher that the state was being 'rolled back' and that greater responsibility and choice was being returned to citizen-consumers and civil society, it would also be unwise to accept the ' "rolling out" of state power in new, dispersed, forms' as suggested by Clarke (1996: 31) without clearer empirical evidence of the state's organisational capacity. As was shown with regard to CCT, one of the major problems for the pursuit of sports development activities was that, even when sports development objectives were included in the tender specification, local authorities rarely had the resources to monitor compliance.

The changing character of the state and its relationship to welfare provision dominated academic discussion of social policy for much of the 1990s. While it is not necessary to rehearse all the various strands of what is frequently a labyrinthine and unilluminating debate, there are aspects that are central to an understanding of sports development within what is frequently referred to as the post-Fordist welfare state. Loader and Burrows summarise, in an idealised form, the dichotomy between Fordist and post-Fordist welfare as the contrast between Fordism which is

> represented by a homology between mass production, mass consumption, modernist cultural forms and mass public provision of welfare [and post-Fordism which] is characterised by an emerging coalition between flexible production, differentiated and segmented consumption patterns, post-modernist cultural forms and a restructured welfare state.
> (Loader and Burrows 1994: 1)

Leaving aside for the moment the problems of applying the post-Fordist analysis of welfare to sports development and returning to the broader

debate about the reshaping of welfare policy, one important, if not fundamental, question is whether the restructuring of welfare, and by implication
sports development, is being imposed from above or is the outcome of a
more negotiative, pluralistic process. Jessop, arguing from a neo-Marxist
perspective, explores the implications for social policy of changes in the
form of capitalist production and accumulation, which laid increasing stress
on the need for labour flexibility, shorter product life cycles, rapid techno-
logical innovation and the continuing globalisation of markets (Jessop 1992,
1994, 1999). The role of the state is to facilitate the establishment of post-
Fordist labour processes and accumulation regimes: the post-Fordist state is
not less interventionist than the Keynsian welfare state but simply intervenes
in different ways to achieve different ends. For Jessop, the fundamental
strategic reorientation of the capitalist state is away from social policy goals
of domestic full employment and resource redistribution and towards social
policy designed to enhance international competitiveness and productivity.
According to this argument, neo-liberal governments, such as those of
Margaret Thatcher, were less intent on cutting the cost of welfare services
than identifying new modes of regulation that supported and complemented
more effectively the post-Fordist pattern of capital accumulation.

It should be emphasised that Jessop is aware of the vagueness and ambi-
guities in the attempts to conceptualise post-Fordism, but his work is based
on an assumption that there is a base–superstructure relationship between
the prevailing pattern of capital accumulation and social policy. Providing
empirical support for the base–superstructure assumption is fraught with
difficulties, but what is easier to demonstrate is the extent to which Fordist
methods developed in the productive sphere were applied to the production
and delivery of social policy. The principle of universality of welfare rights
often led to a standardisation in the design of homes, schools, new towns
and financial welfare benefits. The lack of variety was justified in terms of
equality of provision and also in terms of the need to maximise economies
of scale. As Williams suggests, the dominant characterisation of modern
welfare as bureaucratic, hierarchical, centralised and remote from users is
illustrative of Fordist organisation (Williams 1994). The argument that
follows from this is that in a post-Fordist welfare regime one would expect to
find evidence of a retreat from universalism and an embrace of bespoke
benefits.

In relation to sports development, evidence of Fordist policy would be
the emphasis on Sport For All with its underlying assumption of sports
participation as a universal good, the associated emphasis on equality of
access to sport, the physical similarity of much facility design reflecting a
largely uniform and professionally defined conception of sport and recreation, and the conceptual unity of sports development reflected in the sports
development continuum model. By contrast, post-Fordist sports development may be reflected in the casualisation of sports participation at the
expense of sports clubs, the growth in popularity of individual activities

such as weight training, aerobics, jogging and swimming, the growth of private sector provision and public–private partnerships, and, finally, the introduction of the series of 'Active' programmes which reflect a more segmented market.[1] Examples of post-Fordism from within wider sport policy would include the increased selectivity in the award of Sports Council's grants to governing bodies, the encouragement of differential emphasis on sport in schools through the National Junior Sports Programme, the promotion of schemes such as Sportsmark and the proposal to designate a series of specialist sports colleges, and the decision by the Conservative government that applications for National Lottery funds were to be assessed on their individual merits and not necessarily in relation to local, regional or national strategic plans. However, any attempt to produce neat dichotomies is always open to challenge and, while the listed examples fit closely within the post-Fordist ideal type, there are many current policies which would be more comfortably placed within the traditional Fordist category; these include the National Curriculum for Physical Education, the TOPS programmes and Sport England's encouragement to local authorities to adopt a formulaic approach to strategic planning, the identification of facility need (through the proposed Facility Planning Model) and playing pitch needs (through the Playing Pitch Methodology), and the insistence that national governing bodies produce development plans as a condition of grant aid.

What is less convincing in neo-Marxist analyses of welfare is the assertion that change in the welfare regime is determined by structural changes in forms of capital accumulation. While it would be foolish to ignore the significance of the economy for social policy, the evidence suggests that change in broader social policy and more narrowly in sport policy is the result of a much more complex process that reflects a greater plurality of interests beyond the economic. While it is plausible that the welfare regime of the 1970s may well be inappropriate for the needs of the early twenty-first century economy, it would be unwise to ignore the impact of internal lobbies within the various welfare services (professions and unions in particular) and the increasing number of external interest groups and social movements. The greater emphasis on issues of gender, race, disability and location within welfare policy is indicative of the construction of an agenda for debate beyond narrow class interests. Furthermore, there is at least an equally persuasive argument that the replacement of local authorities with housing associations as social housing landlords, the replacement of institutional care for many with mental health problems with 'care in the community', and the increasing diversity in forms of management of public leisure facilities (trusts, private contractors and local authorities) constitute a positive change towards greater choice and diversity. Any reservations about greater diversity of provision leading to a diminution in accountability should not be exaggerated, particularly when it is remembered just how weak accountability was under the traditional welfare state regime.

The debate over the source of change in the contemporary welfare state is set to continue for some time, but there is far more agreement that, even in the relatively short period from the late 1980s, there has been significant, even if not seismic, change in both the objectives of the welfare regime and in the way in which services are delivered. Changes in objectives include the greater emphasis on the benefits system as an incentive to seek employment (or to make unemployment as unpalatable as possible) and achieving social inclusion (or treating welfare as socialisation). As regards the organisation of welfare, the emphasis has been on decentralisation and dispersal of modes of service delivery, though not necessarily of strategic responsibility, and a retreat from universalism in favour of selectivity and targeting.

Sports development in the early 1990s: a period of government neglect and indecision

The period from the early 1980s to the early 1990s was one during which, for the most part, sport languished in the margins of government interest. On the rare occasions when government did remember sport it was to create doubt and uncertainty about the future of the British Sports Council. Although the creation of the Department of National Heritage in 1992 went some way towards giving sport policy a clearer strategic purpose, it was not until the publication of the policy document *Sport: Raising the Game* in 1995 that a firm statement of government priorities was made. Unfortunately the message it sent to sports development officers, especially those in local government, was discouraging.

The late 1980s saw the beginning of a significant and long-term reorientation of British Sports Council priorities away from a broad focus on development and implementation of policy designed to benefit the sports development continuum as a whole to a much greater degree of selectivity. In 1989 the Council agreed to prioritise the long-term funding of Olympic sports with the sum of £40 million allocated over the following four years. Not only did this introduce greater selectivity regarding the sports that the Council would now support, but it also gave 'high performance athletes a greater share of the Council's resources than had ever previously been the case' (Pickup 1996: 20).

On the one hand the Sports Council was attempting to use its modest resources to support its increasingly performance and excellence oriented objectives and on the other hand new funding bodies such as the Foundation for Sport and the Arts (FSA) and the National Lottery sports distribution board were not required to take a broad or synoptic view of sports development. In the Council's 1990–4 corporate plan it was made clear that there would be a 'progressive switching of resources towards activities at the Performance and Excellence end of the spectrum' and that foundation level work would receive 'relatively few resources' (Pickup 1996: 58). This shift in funding priorities was reinforced in 1992 when the Council was considering the implications of Lottery funding and the prospect of an elite institute along the lines of the Australian Institute of Sport. Pickup comments that 'We began, on our return to London, to spread the thought that, once the UKSC [United Kingdom Sports Council] was established, it too should concentrate its resources for high performance sport on a much more selective group of governing bodies' (1996: 100). An additional emerging priority within the Council was to redefine its relationship with its governing body partners on a more contractual basis.

It is interesting that at the time when the Council was seeking to clarify its focus on high performance sport it was also beginning to involve itself in sport for school-age children. Following a joint Department of the Environment and Department of Education and Science initiative, the School Sport Forum was established with Audry Bambra, a Sports Council member, as chair. Its report, published in 1988, gave the Council the opportunity and encouragement that it needed to address the increasingly problematic areas of school sport in particular and sport for young people generally. More importantly, it led to a reinvigoration of sports development activity through a more rapid diversion of regional resources away from capital projects and towards 'providing encouragement for those local authorities prepared to appoint sports development officers whose role was to ... promote participation in active games, especially by young people' (Pickup 1996: 24). By early 1991 the Council estimated that the number of SDOs had grown to 2,000 supported by approximately 23 per cent (c.£3 million) of the Council's regional office budget.

The strategic reorientation by the Sports Council took place despite the absence of a strong political lead and in the face of a series of external reviews and enquiries. While the latter were time consuming and often unproductive, the former was a continuing cause of concern. Pickup reports that not only were the periodic strategy plans, such as *Sport in the Community: The Next Ten Years* and its interim review in 1988, *Sport in the Community: Into the '90s*, met with a 'studied lack of any specific endorsement – or even rejection – by the government', but so too were annual action plans (1996: 53). It was during this period of political neglect that the Council attempted to reconcile the scope of activities implicit in the sports development continuum model with the increasing calls on its largely static resource base. Anticipating the dual focus of *Sport: Raising the Game*, the Council, in 1990, acknowledged 'two distinct shifts in the organisation's work – an increased emphasis on sport for school-aged children and the concerted development of the Council's provision of support services within the performance and excellence sectors' (Sports Council 1991a: 6). Although Council officers and members were sensitive to the likely political response to the shift in policy, the reorientation was in large part the outcome of internal debate and the increasing recognition by members of the problems of reconciling the objectives of increasing participation with international sporting success. The sense of neglect that pervaded sport policy in the early

climate of the time. A second important development of, and difference from, the earlier target group approach was the idea that sports equity should apply throughout the sports development continuum, rather than just seeking to increase participation among target groups. Sports equity implied a mainstreaming of equity principles through both the client and organisational sides of service delivery (White 1997). The Council adopted the principle of sports equity in 1990 and then went on to develop specific policies and frameworks for action for the women, people with disabilities, and black and ethnic minorities, which were published after consultation in 1993. All were underpinned by the two core concepts of sports development (as defined in chapter 1) and sports equity (as defined above).

The three policy statements were based on an analysis of the current position that included an audit of activity taking place and a selective review of research literature. Although equality issues were on the agenda in most Labour-controlled local authorities at the time, the vast majority of the sports development community had limited understanding of the issues. While most would subscribe to 'Sport For All' in the sense of encouraging more people to participate, few acknowledged the barriers that existed as part of the culture and fabric of sport itself. The policy statement on black and ethnic minorities (Sports Council 1993a) contained a section on institutional racism, a concept that was to feature prominently on the political agenda in the late nineties but which was not acknowledged in most sports organisations or was part of sports discourse in the early nineties. All of the policies attempted to link the current position with policy objectives and action required of different agencies to achieve the objectives. The women and sport policy (Sports Council 1993b) contained a set of seven 'Frameworks for Action' addressed to governing bodies, local authorities, sports facility managers, education, the voluntary sector, the mass media and the Sports Council itself. The policy for people with disabilities (Sports Council 1993c) focused on action that the Sports Council would take in conjunction with governing bodies and specialist disability sports organisations. The policy for black and ethnic minorities set an agenda for the Sports Council itself and urged all organisations to develop racial equality policies and plans with anti-racism and community development initiatives. Like the *New Horizons* strategy, the equity policies had limited impact on the sports development community, partly because of the weak influence of the Council at the time, and partly because the ideas they contained did not fit with the immediate priorities and concerns of governing bodies or Conservative-controlled local authorities. Those local authorities that were Labour-controlled considered themselves well ahead of the Sports Council on equity issues, regarding the Council as a conservative and somewhat inequitable institution itself in both its membership and operations.

The statement concerned with gender equity, though having limited impact in Britain, did have a significant impact on international sport policy through the work of a number of feminist activists who formed an effective international pressure group with colleagues from Commonwealth and European countries. The Sports Council took the lead in facilitating the development of what was to become a worldwide movement to promote gender equity in sport by organising an international conference in Brighton in 1994. It was attended by 280 delegates from 82 countries representing governmental and non-governmental organisations, national Olympic committees, international and national sports federations, and educational and research institutions. One of the main outcomes of the conference was the Brighton Declaration (Sports Council 1994b), an agreed statement of principles for developing a sporting culture that enables and values the full involvement of women in every aspect of sport. The ten principles in the Brighton Declaration cover equity and equality, facilities, school and junior sport, participation, high performance sport, leadership, education, information and research, resources, and domestic and international competition.

Not only comprehensive in its content, the Brighton Declaration was also ambitious in its scope. It was addressed to 'all those governments, public authorities, businesses, educational and research establishments, women's organisations and individuals who are responsible for ... the conduct, development or promotion of sport'. In order to ensure the fine ambitions and words in the Declaration did not fade from consciousness after the conference, an international strategy for promotion of the Brighton Declaration was developed and a working group set up to drive the strategy forward. The essence of the strategy was to use the Brighton Declaration as a tool to raise awareness of gender equity issues in sport and secure the commitment of international and national government and non-governmental organisations to creating a more equitable sporting culture by persuading them to formally endorse the Declaration. Between 1994 and 1998 over 200 governments and major international and national organisations endorsed the Brighton Declaration (UK Sports Council 1998), including the International Olympic Committee, Commonwealth Heads of Government, European ministers of sport, Arab ministers of youth and sport, the Supreme Council for Youth and Sport in Africa, the International Council for Sport Science and Physical Education and many other sport-specific and national organisations. The international women and sport movement has become firmly established with regional organisations set up in Africa, South America, the Arab States and Asia (a European group had existed since the early 1990s) and a second World Conference held in Namibia in 1998 to follow up and take forward the work started in Brighton four years earlier.

It is interesting that while the UK's leadership on gender equity policy was extremely effective internationally, it was not welcomed by the government of the day in the UK. Ian Sproat, the then Minister for Sport, when asked by Tom Pendry (the opposition spokesperson on sport) if the government would endorse the Declaration, refused, describing it in the House of Commons as 'political correctness in excelsis' (*Parliamentary Debates* 1994). It was not until May 1998, on the eve of the second world conference in

Namibia, that the Labour government adopted it with the following statement from Tony Banks, Minister for Sport:

> Our decision to adopt the Declaration further indicates our determination to improve opportunities for women at all levels in sport, whether as participants, competitors, coaches or administrators. Through our policy of Sport For All we shall continue to work with the Sports Councils and others to promote and develop opportunities for women regardless of where they live, social background, age or ability.
>
> (DCMS 1998a)

A fourth policy statement *Young People and Sport: Frameworks for Action*, also published in 1993, was one of the more immediately influential statements as it informed existing debates within the physical education and sports development networks and was also more in tune with government priorities. It helped to consolidate the Sports Council's central position in the series of important policy debates around the issue of youth sport policy, including those concerned with the physical education curriculum, extra-curricular sport and the youth development responsibilities of the national governing bodies. It was welcomed by practitioners because it addressed shared concerns about the quantity and quality of physical education and school sport and the importance of the foundation stage of the continuum for the development of sport. The Sports Council was able to position itself as an honest broker between physical education and sport in the face of a good deal of ill-informed public rhetoric about the state of school sport as the cause of the demise of national team performances in major sports. More significantly, the statement anticipated the policy emphasis to be given to young people and school sport in the Department of National Heritage's strategy document *Sport: Raising the Game*, the first national government policy for sport in twenty years.

Sport: Raising the Game: from the margins to centre stage

The publication of *Sport: Raising the Game* in 1995 confirmed, but also reinforced, many of the emerging trends in Sports Council and DNH policy. Indeed, in the year prior to publication, Ian Sproat, the then Minister for Sport, stated that the Sports Council would 'withdraw from the promotion of mass participation and informal recreation' (DNH 1994: 4, quoted in McDonald 1995). The minister also rejected the pursuit of Sport For All as 'laudable … but secondary to the pursuit of high standards of sporting achievement' (*ibid.*). The explicit focus on high performance sport and school sport provided the central theme of the policy statement. However, the statement also contained a number of more implicit policies which were at least as significant in shaping sports development. Of particular importance was the marginalisation of local government and the heavy emphasis on a relatively narrow range of traditional sports within schools. For the government, the context for preparing *Sport: Raising the Game* had been set in the earlier debates over the National Curriculum for Physical Education when the emphasis on the practice of traditional competitive team sports had been given strong political endorsement. In the introduction to the policy statement, John Major made clear the centrality of school sport to broader sport policy. The statement re-emphasised the priority of competitive team sports within the National Curriculum, noting that 'The focus for this policy statement is deliberately on sport rather than on physical education' (DNH 1995: 7).

As regards high performance sport, the centrepiece of the policy statement was the commitment to establish an elite sports training centre, a British Academy of Sport, modelled on the successful Australian Institute of Sport at Canberra. Underwritten by Lottery funds, the academy was intended to provide top-class training facilities coupled with a concentration of supporting services such as coaching, sports science and sports medicine. In addition, the statement prompted the Sports Council to require governing bodies to become more actively involved in talent identification and development. While governing bodies were strongly encouraged to develop closer links with schools, it was not in order to support schools in delivering their physical education objectives, but rather to help governing bodies deliver their objectives of elite success. In stressing that 'stronger links between schools and clubs will ensure that all those with an interest in sport have every opportunity to develop and maintain that interest', the statement concluded with the observation that 'Sporting competition exists to encourage sports men and women to excel and we want to ensure that talented competitors at every level have the support necessary to allow them to exploit their talent to the full' (DNH 1995: 34). Thus school sport was to be integrated into a process of talent identification and a ladder of competition designed to meet the needs of governing bodies. The conventional rationalisation of an emphasis on elite success, intended to assuage the concerns of the advocates of 'sport for all', was that elite achievement had a demonstration effect for the rest of the population and would encourage higher levels of participation. Dubious though this justification was, it at least maintained a strong link between the interests of the national governing bodies, schools and the local authorities and maintained the notion of a unified sports development policy. However, the Department of National Heritage failed to take the opportunity to reinforce the connection between elite and mass sport and referred blandly to the capacity of sport 'at the highest level to engage the wider community' and 'because people care about the performance of our national teams and sporting superstars' (*ibid.*: 34). High performance sport was thus progressively being separated from the practice of sport at other levels of the continuum and fast becoming the preserve of highly specialist agencies (NGBs and elite academies), whereas school physical education and sport were valued only insofar as they could be integrated into an elite development strategy and ladder of progression.

The primary message of *Sport: Raising the Game* was to endorse the Sports Council's twin emphasis on school sport and excellence. Furthermore, the document promoted very narrow and self-contained definitions of the various elements of the sports development continuum, re-defining it as sport in schools, sport in clubs and the development of excellence. Sport in clubs was about offering opportunities to young people to develop their talent, and a challenge fund to promote school club links, administered by the Sports Council, was introduced. There was no acknowledgement of the wider community participation promoted by local authorities, though there was a short section on further and higher education. Whereas in the early 1990s the Sports Council had been at pains to stress the overlap of interest and responsibility among organisations for the various elements of the continuum, *Sport: Raising the Game* tended to emphasise a model according to which different elements of the continuum were more closely associated with particular organisations. For example, schools, which were always seen as having a central responsibility regarding the foundation level, were now given an almost exclusive responsibility for ensuring the introduction and promotion of traditional sports among young people. Similarly, governing bodies, which at one time were strongly encouraged to become more closely involved in supporting the achievement of community sport objectives, were now being encouraged to focus exclusively on supporting objectives related to elite achievement.

The statement made little reference to participation or to the main agents of its promotion, local authorities. The assumption was that participation was now the central, if not sole, responsibility of local government – a policy lead that the governing bodies of sport were content to follow as they always had considerable difficulty accepting that they had a broader community responsibility. However, at the time when central government was marginalising local government, the Sports Council was attempting to integrate local authorities into a network of partnerships focused on sport for young people through the formulation of the National Junior Sports Programme (NJSP). In *Young People and Sport: Frameworks for Action*, the Council stated that it would 'take the lead in encouraging the approval and adoption of its policy for young people and sport' (1993d: 3). The advocacy and leadership role of the Council resulted in it establishing a Young People and Sport Task Force which promoted the NJSP. The programme focused on the needs of the 4 to 18 years age group and aimed to achieve greater coherence and direction to the current disparate range of schemes, funding opportunities and providers (see Figure 3.1).

As well as linking the range of organisations identified in Figure 3.1, the programme also provided a structure that would retain the strong links between foundation, performance and excellence reflected in the sports development continuum model. Assessing the success of the NJSP is diffi-

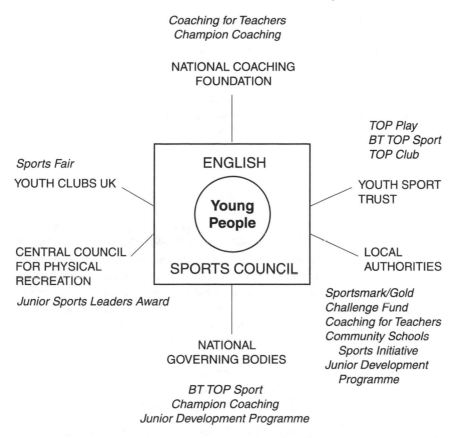

Figure 3.1 Organisation links supporting the 'Young people and sport' policy

Source: English Sports Council, Information sheet 15, *Young People and Sport*, 1998

cult. On the one hand, it can be argued that it established a network of organisations on which later partnerships could be built, led to a number of successful and innovative schemes and consolidated the position of the Sports Council in a leading role in what was fast becoming a policy priority for government. On the other hand, the NJSP had a variable take-up around the country and the degree of integration between participation and performance objectives was limited, and the NJSP was soon overshadowed by the Active and World Class programmes which were launched in 1998. In addition the Youth Sport Trust, which had been established in 1994, soon emerged as an extremely influential organisation, primarily in youth and school sport but also through its director, Sue Campbell, in other areas of sport policy.

The Trust was established as a charity with a donation from John Beckwith, a wealthy businessman, and, led by Sue Campbell, it moved swiftly to attract additional resources from a variety of sources including the

Sports Council and the Department for Education and Employment. The subsequent success of the series of TOP schemes aimed initially at improving the quality of physical education teaching in primary schools enabled the Trust to challenge the Sports Council for policy leadership in this increasingly politically salient area. The growing influence of the Trust was due to three factors: first, the success of the TOP schemes, which was based partly on effective marketing and partly on the fact that the various schemes were clearly meeting a perceived need among teachers and head teachers; second, the complementarity between the objectives of the Trust and the emerging priority on school sport given by the government of John Major and reflected in *Sport: Raising the Game*; and third, the capacity of the Director of the Trust to fulfil the role of policy entrepreneur particularly with the Labour government of 1997.

After much delay and prevarication, the Sports Council was restructured during 1996 into a UK Sports Council and an English Sports Council. While the logic of the restructuring was to eradicate the anomaly of the former Sports Council having both British and English functions, the outcome of the split was the bifurcation of sports development, and, for British governing bodies, the frustration of having to deal with two organisations rather than one. The UK Sports Council was charged with developing excellence at UK level, international relations and doping control, while the English Sports Council (ESC) was charged with the development of sport in England, from foundation through to excellence. The English Sports Council emerged as the bigger and stronger organisation, retaining 80 per cent of the human and financial resources, as well as the network of ten regional offices and six national centres. It moved quickly to establish its mission as 'leading the development of sport in England by influencing and serving the public, private and commercial sectors' (English Sports Council 1998a). Its three main aims, which also became the basis for its programmes and work organisation, were: 'More people involved in sport; More places to play sport; More medals through higher standards of performance'.

While some people may have interpreted the new mission and strap line as a move away from the old sports development continuum and principle of working in partnership with local authorities and governing bodies, in fact it was a reaffirmation of traditional sports development philosophy and practice. The difference was that, with the uncertainties over restructuring finally resolved, new leadership and the advent of the National Lottery within which the ESC was the distributor of the lion's share of the funds for sport, the ESC had a new-found confidence to try to establish itself as the leading sports development agency in England. The new aims of the ESC also positioned facility development as an essential aspect of sports development, with facility provision as necessary to achieve the aims of 'more people' and 'more medals'.

In mid-1996, when the restructuring of the Sports Council had been finalised, it was announced that the new English Sports Council, when established in January 1997, would concentrate its resources on a selected group of twenty-two sports and also require them to enter into service agreements 'identifying what services the Sports Council can provide, either directly or indirectly, so that expectations are clear on both sides' (White 1996: 7). Selection as a priority sport was based on an analysis of ten criteria, including the public profile of the sport, participation levels, achievement at excellence level, potential for international success and governing body administrative infrastructure. However, particular weight was given to the extent to which the sports supported the English Sports Council's twin priorities of young people and the development of excellence. Sports which contributed to both priorities were graded category A status while those that contributed to only one priority were placed in category B.[2] In many respects the ESC was following the government–NGB model established in Canada and Australia, where the grant of public funds was conditional upon a greater professionalism in management, especially in relation to elite squad development and achievement in international competition. The pressure on NGBs to think strategically, particularly with regard to talent identification and development, was reinforced in subsequent years with a renewed emphasis on the production of development strategies as a condition of grant aid. However, while, on the one hand, requiring sports governing bodies to plan strategically, on the other hand, the Sports Council found itself operating within a funding environment where its capacity to influence the strategic deployment of Lottery funding was greatly restricted. The Conservative government of John Major thus perversely established a funding regime for sport which deliberately ignored a fundamental principle of good business practice: namely, that of strategic planning of resources.

The Foundation for Sports and the Arts (FSA) was established in 1991 in an attempt by the football pools industry to undermine support for the proposed National Lottery. The FSA would receive approximately £60 million each year, two-thirds of which would be allocated to sports projects. The Foundation was established without reference to the Sports Council, which was kept on the margins of its decision-making, although it did have representation on the panel that would advise the Foundation on sports-related bids for grant-aid. Eschewing the establishment of clear strategic priorities, the FSA, over its first year or two, gave priority to the applications from individual clubs and governing bodies for capital projects, thus, in David Pickup's words, 'facilitating the Council's relative withdrawal of support in these areas' (1996: 91). The impact of the FSA was substantial but also short lived. In its first three years it distributed over £40 million each year to sport, a figure which fell to under £10 million following the introduction of the National Lottery in late 1994. Although much of the FSA's grant was of general value to sports development, very little helped fund, even indirectly, SDO posts. Although the financial impact of the FSA was modest and short lived, its decision-making parameters, especially the rejection of any strategic dimension, was important as a model for the distribution of National Lottery funds.

Although lotteries, as a source of funding for sport, were well established in most European countries, it was not until the late 1980s that the idea was seriously considered in the UK. Undoubtedly part of the attraction of a Lottery to the Conservative government was that it provided a means of generating additional finance that was under the control of government but technically not public expenditure. As the financial pressures on public services intensified throughout the 1980s, the advent of a National Lottery was eagerly awaited, particularly by local authorities who were being significantly affected by the gradual reduction in direct funding from central government, the refocusing of Sports Council funding priorities and their limited access to FSA finances.

The introduction of the National Lottery in November 1994 offered the prospect of around £300 million for sport each year. Given that local authorities had powers to smooth the way for Lottery bids due to their role as the planning authority, usually possessing considerable land holdings and being better able to absorb costs of feasibility studies (which the Sports Lottery Board would not support), it might be assumed that the prospects for sports development receiving direct, or at least indirect, benefit from the Lottery were good. However, the optimism that Lottery funding would reinvigorate participation-level sports development was dampened because the priority given to capital projects was of only limited value to an essentially revenue-based service. The government was quite explicit in its directions to the Sports Council that Lottery funding should not be used to support coaching, training and sports development. The advent of the Lottery also had some indirect effects which affected the prospects for sports development, foremost of which was the impact on local government leisure services spending. Evans and Smeding (1996) report that, based on 1996–7 data, while spending on all local government services had risen by 1.1 per cent since the previous year, leisure services had recorded a decline of 1.7 per cent, with the decline in sports spending in Outer London districts estimated at 3 per cent. More significantly, the contraction in spending was greatest in service levels (staffing and opening hours) and maintenance of existing facilities, whereas new facilities (often Lottery funded) received increased funding. The Lottery thus appeared to be resulting in a redistribution of local authority funds away from existing projects and towards meeting the revenue costs of Lottery-funded capital projects, an effect which, according to Evans and Smeding, was particularly evident in sport. Given the tenuous status of sports development in many local authorities, there was a real danger that current sports development programmes would be squeezed to fund the long-term financial liabilities arising from Lottery-funded capital projects.

Sports development was also affected by the exclusion of bids intended to cover the increasingly pressing need for refurbishment because applicants had to demonstrate that the investment would result in a widening of participation. However, a growing proportion of existing facilities built in the

1970s or earlier, particularly pools and synthetic surfaces, were in such a state of disrepair that managers were imposing limitations on use. A further criticism was the requirement to provide matching funding of 35 per cent or more. Such a requirement, designed to demonstrate substantial local support, clearly put those sports that attracted more affluent participants (such as cricket, hockey, rowing, tennis and golf) and the clubs in the more affluent areas at a clear advantage. An additional problem for poorer sports and areas was the cost of preparing their bid, which was often an insurmountable hurdle in itself. These concerns notwithstanding, the most significant issue as far as sports development was concerned was the lack of any strategic co-ordination of the distribution of Lottery funds between areas and also between sports.

Not surprisingly, when the Sports Council undertook an analysis of the distribution of Lottery funds, the skewed distribution of funding was clearly evident. Consequently, a number of changes were announced in 1996 – the first of which was to identify a series of priority areas where the matching funding requirement could be as low as 10 per cent. A second change also involved a reduction in the level of matching funding, but to 20 per cent, in relation to bids from schools under the School Community Sport Initiative, which was designed to reinvigorate the long-standing strategy of dual use. The third change, and the one of greatest potential interest to sports development, was the decision to allow the use of Lottery funds for revenue grants. Although revenue funding was only available to support the training costs of elite athletes, the acceptance of bids for the funding of revenue projects created some optimism that both the revenue and capital costs of participation-level sports development might soon be acceptable.

The early years of the National Lottery placed local authorities in a difficult position. With around 40 per cent of Lottery funding allocated to local authorities, there was substantial pressure to build funding strategies around the Lottery guidelines. However, the guidelines, such as they were, excluded a service strategy. Consequently, although the Sports Council had devoted considerable resources to encouraging local authorities to think strategically about sport and recreation, there was little incentive for local authorities to respond as bids for Lottery funding based on analysis of need and levels of participation, or on goals such as the reduction of deprivation or community regeneration, were explicitly prohibited. As Buchan observes, there was a 'latent sympathy' within the National Lottery Sports Distribution Board for 'strategically relevant projects', but it was far removed from the strategic use of Lottery funding (1998: 6). However, while many local authorities bemoaned their lack of influence over the funding of projects in their areas, many national governing bodies of sport were receiving a level of funding that, for the first time, was enabling them to improve the level of club facilities, and, more significantly, support their high-performance development plans with a facilities development programme.

Conclusion

Sports development was an activity that emerged largely under a series of Conservative governments and was defined and redefined through the 1980s and 1990s. An attempt to take stock of sports development on the eve of the election of the first Labour government since 1979 was hampered by the very youthfulness of the 'service', for it assumed that there had in the past been a period of stability during which the features of sports development had been allowed to set. With hindsight, the definitions of sports development provided in chapter 1 might more accurately be seen as aspirations for sports development rather than descriptions of the then current practice. As time progressed sports development, within local authorities at least, changed from being a form of remedial social work intervention in selected urban areas (Action Sport), through a generalised ambition to target under-participating sections of the population, to a situation in the mid-1990s where it was increasingly a bifurcated activity both in terms of objectives and organisation. Within governing bodies, sports development was slowly coalescing around talent identification and youth development, on the one hand, and support for high performance athletes, on the other.

As Lentell notes, sports development within local government had come a long way from its roots in community recreation and was increasingly defined in terms of 'the development of specific sports and sporting performance' and increasingly dependent on market factors (1993: 44). In terms of objectives, the selective targeting of under-participating groups had largely given way to a focus on young people, a policy shift signalled by the NJSP and later endorsed by the government in *Sport: Raising the Game*. The other strand of sports development, that of talent identification and development, focused on the work of the national governing bodies and was reinforced by the increasingly selective allocation of resources to elite sports by the Sports Council. It is a moot point whether the pattern of policy in the mid-1990s reflected a refinement and maturation of policy or whether the concept of sports development had become so flexible or vague that it could safely be used as a synonym for sport policy in general.

Change at the level of socially formative values is normally slow, but the brief period from the early 1990s to 1997 saw clear signs of lasting change in some of the most persistent values affecting sport (Table 3.1). Most significant was the public acknowledgement, in *Sport: Raising the Game*, that success at the elite levels of competition could no longer be achieved without the systematic application of the highest standards of sports science and coaching to a squad of athletes who trained full time. John Major finally put the myth of the inspired British amateur to rest. Complementing the demise of the dilettante approach to preparation of elite athletes was the public acknowledgement that international sporting success matters. The long history of British, and especially English, disdain for international sport and its organisations was finally abandoned.

Table 3.1 Changes in the environment of sports development policy, mid-1970s to 1997

Variables	Changes from the mid-1970s to the early 1990s	Changes from the early 1990s to 1997
Shallow and more vulnerable to change		
Administrative arrangements	Increase in the number of specialist leisure services departments in local authorities.	Establishment of the Department of National Heritage (1992) gave sport a voice in the Cabinet, but removed the Sports Council from its link with the DoE; establishment of English Sports Council and UK Sports Council (1997). Both changes increased complexity in the sports policy area.
Pattern of inter-organisational resources dependencies	Attritional relationship between the Sports Council and the CCPR; steady growth in Sports Council Treasury grant; growth in local government expenditure on sport and leisure services.	Sports Council–CCPR relationship less abrasive. Introduction of the National Lottery and establishment of Foundation for Sport and the Arts increased funding influence of government at the expense of Sports Council and local government. Local government expenditure under increasing pressure.
More stable with change over the medium term		
Interaction between structural interest groups:	Period dominated by the tension between the CCPR and the Sports Council.	Period dominated by the introduction of the National Lottery, the debate over the National Curriculum for PE and competition for resources.
demand groups (consumers of service outputs);	Still of marginal importance with the exception of some elite athletes who have influence through players' unions and bodies such as the BOA Athletes Commission.	Still of marginal importance with the exception of some elite athletes who have influence through players' unions and bodies such as the BOA Athletes Commission.

Variables	Changes from the mid-1970s to the early 1990s	Changes from the early 1990s to 1997
provider groups (facility/club managers, sports development officers, PE teachers and leisure services managers);	ILAM and ISRM beginning to provide a voice. Sport and leisure beginning to reach the agenda of the various local government associations. But no specific voice for sports development or SDOs.	*Sport: Raising the Game* did little to encourage local government interest in and lobbying on behalf of sports development work. SDOs getting more organised via an annual conference and regional meetings, but still a limited influence on policy.
direct support groups (e.g. national governing bodies and schools);	CCPR emerging as an important advocacy group, but most major NGBs dealt directly with the Sports Council. Little or no discussion among structural interest groups of sports development or of sport for school-age children until late 1980s.	Intensive lobbying around the content of the NCPE from NGBs and CCPR. NGBs and BOA influential regarding the content of *Sport: Raising the Game.*
indirect support groups (related local authority services, e.g. land use planning, community development and non-Sports Council sources of funding)	For some district councils sport and leisure was a major service as measured by expenditure, but sport was rarely central to corporate strategy. However, cross-department issues were beginning to emerge such as the sale of school playing fields and urban regeneration.	Sport more marginal due to cuts in local government public expenditure. The exceptions were the issue of the sale and development of school playing fields.
Service-specific policy paradigm	CCT and greater emphasis on cost recovery and the concept of 'user pays'. Highly variable level of salience to government, but general government indifference. Shift in focus from facilities to people and from welfare service to sport as a tool of social engineering. Sports development continuum a unifying concept.	*Sport: Raising the Game* stressed national sporting heritage, the moral value of sport and tradition. Increasing acceptance that international success requires investment and systematic preparation. But suspicion of 'state planning'. Heavy reliance on National Lottery for funding. Emergence of a 'bidding culture' among local authorities.

Variables	Changes from the mid-1970s to the early 1990s	Changes from the early 1990s to 1997
Dominant core policy paradigm	Retreat from Keynesianism and embrace of neo-liberal economics. Increased criticism of the role of the state. Assertion of welfare state 'failure'. Increased emphasis on the reform of the machinery of government and privatisation.	Dominance of neo-liberal economics reflected in privatisation and managerialism, but also partial return to 'one-nation' Conservatism on some aspects of social policy.
Deeply entrenched		
Embedded structural values fundamental to the social formation		Mythology of British amateurism dispelled and replaced by an acknowledgement of the need for greater professionalism in the preparation of elite athletes. Concept of equity introduced into the sports discourse.

The changed attitude of society and government to sport was reflected most significantly in the introduction of the National Lottery, a funding vehicle that enabled John Major to maintain his monetarist economic credentials while at the same significantly increasing the amount of uncommitted money available for allocation to sport. More significant than the increased funding available for sport, which was partly offset by the steady cuts in local authority sport and leisure budgets and the standstill in Sports Council funding during much of the 1990s, was the fact that Lottery resources altered the pattern of resource dependencies between the main organisations responsible for sports development. Of particular importance was the weakening of the, albeit modest, strategic direction to sports development from local government as a result of pressure on local authority budgets and the growth in importance of bidding to external funders, who might have different strategic goals (job creation and training within the European Union) or a scepticism towards the strategic role of local government (as with the National Lottery Sports Distribution Board). Policy influence during this period at first became more diffuse but, following the publication of *Sport: Raising the Game*, then became more centralised within the DNH and the Sports Council Lottery Distribution Board, and also within the DfEE as a result of its control over the physical education curriculum.

The administrative arrangements for sport were also radically altered in the early 1990s. Sports long-established location within the DoE had ended in 1990 when, following the appointment of John Major as prime minister, he moved responsibility to the Department of Education and Science. Two years later the sport portfolio was moved again: this time to the newly created Department of National Heritage. One effect of the transfer away from the DoE was to weaken the link between sport and the other range of community-focused services and thus facilitate the refocusing of the Sports Council on the emerging twin objectives of school sport and elite achievement. The subsequent restructuring of the Sports Council to create the English Sports Council and the UK Sports Council further reinforced the change in strategic direction of sport policy and the increasing priority of elite achievement.

The early 1990s was certainly a turbulent time for the sport-specific policy paradigm. The decade started with the Thatcher legacy of neglect and disdain for sport in general and a suspicion of local government and state planning. Within five years that attitude had been replaced by a much more positive policy climate for sport and a set of much more specific policy objectives. *Sport: Raising the Game* not only reasserted the 'one-nation' strand within Conservative philosophy, with its acceptance that a common tradition, heritage and culture, of which sport was a part, was an important integrative force in British society, but it also reinforced that perception of the role of sport, thus signalling the abandonment of the more reticent attitude towards intervention in sport policy that had typified previous Labour and Conservative governments.

One result – and, to a much lesser extent, cause – of the steady rise of sport up the national political agenda was that it stimulated greater activity among sports-related structural interest groups. National governing bodies, in particular, were successful in protecting the major team sports in the drafting of the National Curriculum for Physical Education and were also influential in shaping the policy towards elite sports development, not only in the drafting of *Sport: Raising the Game*, but more significantly in shaping policy on the distribution of Lottery grants to elite athletes and, subsequently, the details of the implementation of the proposal for an elite sports institute. The growing prominence of the voice of NGBs and the British Olympic Association threw the continued marginalisation of local authority interests in sports development into sharper relief. The main professional bodies representing local authority level sport had little influence over policy. The Local Government Association had more important services to defend from Conservative government expenditure cuts than sport, and sports development officers were still a largely unorganised occupational group. By the end of the period there were, however, some signs that the participation lobby was becoming more effectively organised. Of particular importance was the re-invigoration of the Chief Leisure Officers Association (CLOA), which provided local authority sport with a potentially authoritative voice. In addition, SDOs were establishing a more formal organisational structure, based around the annual conferences held since the early 1990s and the existing pattern of regional associations. Despite these promising signs of more effective organisation, the voice of sports development for mass participation was still weak at the time of the 1997 election.

Overall, the period from the early 1990s to 1997 was crucial for sports development in particular and sport policy in general. Yet even acknowledging the significant benefits of policy changes to elite sports development, there is the strong impression that sports development policy was still not being shaped in conjunction with sports interests. A fortuitous coincidence of interests between John Major and other senior Conservatives, such as David Mellor and Kenneth Clarke, is a much more persuasive explanation of policy change than one based on a more deeply embedded process of discussion and negotiation within a well-established policy community.

4 New Labour
The reinvigoration of sports development

The policy infrastructure for sports development

The Labour Party victory at the 1997 election coincided with the emergence of significant tensions within sports development. As mentioned in chapter 1, sports development is at best a series of overlapping policy objectives and associated processes. Mass participation/Sport For All objectives had an uneasy relationship with goals associated with high performance sport and international achievement; sports objectives had similar tensions with broader welfare goals; and investment in community facilities was, at times, at odds with the demands to meet the specialist needs of the elite athlete. For the first thirty years or so of significant government funding for sport and involvement in policy, these tensions were largely subsumed initially by the common interest of all sports groups to maximise government investment in the building of a range of basic facilities, which, at a time when training was both less intense and less scientific, met not only the needs of those interested in foundation, participation and performance activities but also many of the requirements of the elite athlete. When the initial phase of facility building had passed, by about the middle or end of the 1970s, the uneasy coalition of sports interests was maintained by the common concern to protect the modest gains for sport in the face of a series of Conservative governments that, for the most part, alternated between hostility and indifference towards sport. However, the Conservative government of John Major provided a policy and funding environment which was markedly more positive and one where the mutual interest in defending sport and papering over the conflicts within sport was replaced by a more aggressive competition for the substantial new resources available from the National Lottery.

The unity given to policy by the sports development continuum was strained by the emphasis provided by *Sport: Raising the Game* on school sport (the foundation level) and elite sport (the excellence level). Around these two increasingly dominant policy priorities was built an infrastructure of programmes, funding opportunities and organisational support that left other sports interests – particularly participation/Sport For All, but also performance – at a substantial disadvantage. While the incoming Labour government made it clear that it would redirect resources towards participation/Sport For All, it did so in a way that created a third cluster of interests rather than (re)established an advocacy coalition supportive of a more integrated conceptualisation of sport policy objectives.

Establishing common policy ground among the various sports interests was made more difficult because by 1997 the policy infrastructure for sports development was already complex and was set to become even more so over the following years. Mapping the range of organisations, programmes and funding vehicles associated with sports development poses a substantial challenge. Table 4.1 identifies the main sports development policy themes of the late 1990s and the environment within which they operated. Three relatively discrete themes can be identified focusing on sport for young people, participation, and elite sport. Although there is some overlap between these policies in terms of objectives, lead organisations and programmes, the extent to which these policies represent increasingly self-contained clusters of programmes, resources and organisations is striking.

Mention has already been made of the dominant core policy paradigm of the early years of the Blair government, with its concern to promote moral, urban and economic regeneration reflected in its commitment to address social exclusion and its support for economic modernisation and creative excellence. In terms of its orientation towards policy implementation, the government emphasised the importance of building partnerships and networks with voluntary and commercial organisations, the importance of co-operation between government departments and agencies, and regionalism and devolution. An emphasis on partnership and networking was broadly consistent with previous practice in the implementation of sport policy. Not only did the Sports Councils and the Department of Culture, Media and Sports (DCMS) (and its predecessor, the Department of National Heritage) have little capacity for direct service provision, they also had little inclination, having always relied heavily on using their resources to stimulate activity by national governing bodies, clubs, schools and local authorities. Co-operation between different branches of government has long been a goal of new administrations, and it is one that is potentially of particular value in relation to sport policy given that there is hardly a central government department that does not have some interest in sport. At the very least, achieving close co-operation between the DCMS, the DfEE – because of its responsibility for schools – and the DETR, with its responsibility for local government, would bring together the three most important departments concerned with sport policy. Finally, devolution of power to Northern Ireland, Scotland and Wales, and the more recent establishment of regional assemblies and regional cultural consortiums within England, added a further dimension to the infrastructure of the policy process.

Table 4.1 Sports development policy and its current environment

| Dominant core policy paradigm | • Social inclusion and stakeholding
• Work, employment and enterprise
• Moral and urban regeneration
• Excellence, creativity and 'cool Britannia' |
| Orientation towards implementation | • Partnerships and networking
• 'Joined-up government'
• Regionalism and devolution |

Variables	PE and school sport	Sports development policy themes Sports participation	Elite sport
General policy objectives	• Increased sports participation (curricular and extra-curricular) • Increased quality of school sport • Improved talent identification and development	• Increased participation • Community regeneration • Moral regeneration • Social inclusion	• International sporting success in sports deemed to be culturally significant and/or internationally prestigious
Key policy sources	• *Sport: Raising the Game* • *A Sporting Future For All* • *The Government's Plan for Sport* • Lottery Strategy 1998 'Investing for our sporting future' • Young People and Sport survey 1999 • National Curriculum for Physical Education • Active Schools programme • National Junior Sports Programme	• PAT 10 report to Social Exclusion Unit • Sport England 1998 Annual Report (More people, etc. ...) • Lottery Strategy, 1998 'Investing for our sporting future'	• *Sport: Raising the Game* • *A Sporting Future For All* • *The Government's Plan for Sport* • Lottery Strategy 1998 'Investing for our sporting future' • World Class Performance programmes
Specific targets	• Under 11 years in general • Talented children and adolescents in particular • 2 hours for PE	• Geographical areas of multiple deprivation • Youth at risk, women and ethnic minorities	• Success in the Olympic and Paralympic Games and other major international competitions • Success in major team sports, especially football and cricket

Variables	PE and school sport	Sports development policy themes Sports participation	Elite sport

Main programmes	• Specialist Sports Colleges
	• c600 School sport co-ordinators
	• TOP programmes
	• Sportsmark and Sportsmark Gold
	• Coaching for Teachers
	• Sportsearch
	• Activemark and Activemark Gold
		• Sports Action Zones
		• Priority Areas Initiative
		• Active Communities projects
		• Sporting Equals
			• World Class programme:
			  - World Class Start
			  - World Class Potential
			  - World Class Performance

Lead national agencies	• Youth Sport Trust • DCMS and DfEE • Sport England • Physical Education Association UK	• Sport England • CCPR	• UK Sport • Sport England • UKSI • National governing bodies • British Olympic Association
Lead local or regional agencies	• Individual schools	• Local authorities	• Regional sports institute centres • Clubs
Main sources of funding	• National Lottery (including the New Opportunities Fund) • DfEE • Sport England	• National Lottery • Sport England • Local government budgets • Minor funding from Football Foundation, Sportsmatch, Foundation for Sport and the Arts, etc.	• National Lottery • National governing bodies and clubs • Sports Aid • BOA

Social policy under New Labour

Labour won the election in May 1997 with a clear policy agenda. Education was the main service priority and was seen as a key to achieving the broader objective of social inclusion. Moreover, the new government's understanding of social exclusion was that its causes were multiple and cut across the functionally based responsibilities of government departments. The achievement of greater social inclusion could only be by way of 'joined up government', according to which each department and service agency, such as the Sports Councils, would be expected to overcome the traditional culture of departmentalism and make a contribution to the construction of a comprehensive policy response to a complex and multi-dimensional problem.

Social inclusion objectives were built on a distinctive perception of the balance between duties and rights of citizens, which had the effect of setting a limit on state support for the individual while at the same time attempting to ensure that citizens were also 'stakeholders'. Stakeholding was a defining element of Labour social policy and reinforced the reorientation of the Labour Party away from its traditional commitment to equality and towards the vaguer notion of social inclusion. Thus, the concept of stakeholding 'has been packaged as a new approach which challenges the inequality that was central to the economic neo-liberalism of Thatcherism, whilst simultaneously distancing itself from many of the redistributive ideals that ... are seen as synonymous with "old" Labour thinking' (Heron and Dwyer 1999: 98). The concept of stakeholding led the government to concentrate on the creation of opportunities to re-enter the social mainstream (essentially, re-enter the labour market) and to de-emphasise the provision of benefits to alleviate poverty. Moreover, the general thrust of social policy, modelled on the American 'workfare' programme, emphasised a further retreat from the principle of universalism of social provision and benefits and endorsed the language of targeting, selectivity and personal responsibility. At the heart of the New Labour discourse on 'social inclusion' was an emphasis on the importance of 'resocialisation through work' (Stepney et al. 1999: 110). New Labour's approach to social policy was complemented by an economic policy which stressed modernisation, as reflected, for example, in its enthusiasm for e-commerce initiatives, and which sought to place British creativity and Britain's creative industries at the heart of economic development and achieve the rebranding of Britain as 'cool Britannia'. The emphasis on achieving excellence in the creative industries had a clear resonance in the area of elite achievement in sport. These themes were explicitly endorsed by the DCMS in its comprehensive spending review published in 1998 in which it stated that the Department's concerns were the promotion of access, the pursuit of excellence and innovation, the nurturing of educational opportunity, and the fostering of creative industries.

The initial impact of New Labour policy was muted due to the Labour Party's pre-election promise not to exceed the spending commitments of the then current government of John Major. It was not until mid-1999 that the

Labour government was able to commit significant additional resources to support more effectively its policy objectives. However, even in the years from 1997 to 1999, it was possible to identify the partial reorientation of sport policy away from the priorities of the Major government.

Sport for young people

In the pre-election policy statement, *Labour's Sporting Nation* (Labour Party 1996), there were some areas of clear continuity with the outgoing government, particularly in the emphasis placed on the provision of sports opportunities for young people, 'the most crucial aspect of our strategy of sport for all' (*ibid.*: 6), competitive sport in schools which 'should continue to be the mainstay of school sport provision' (*ibid.*: 8) and in the priority given to high performance sport 'to enable Britain to become a successful sporting nation once more' (*ibid.*: 6). The endorsement of competitive school sport had a ritual feel to it and reflected the extent to which the Conservative government had fabricated a populist issue about which they could express indignation and at the same time imply that the Labour Party was a threat to the competitive sport ideal. More significant, and certainly more intriguing, was how the Labour government could reconcile its commitment to fostering school sport with its election slogan of 'education, education, education'. The almost immediate suspension of the curriculum requirements for physical education in primary schools in order to make time for specific classes on literacy and numeracy did not augur well for the claimed priority for school sport. However, despite this inauspicious start, the publication of the DCMS strategy, *A Sporting Future For All*, in 2000 confirmed that school sport in particular, and sport for young people in general, was indeed to hold a central position in Labour's conceptualisation of sports development.

As Tony Blair noted in his foreword to the strategy, 'It is in school where most of us get our first chance to try sport. It is here that children discover their talent and their potential' (DCMS 2000a: 2). The strategy outlined a five-part plan, the first element of which was to 'rebuild school sport facilities' (*ibid.*: 7) with an emphasis on primary schools supported by Lottery and Exchequer funds and, if the governing bodies of sport could be persuaded, a proportion of broadcasting income. The second element was the commitment to create 110 specialist sports colleges by 2003, a target later raised to 200 by 2004. The colleges would be secondary schools which would receive additional funding and would concentrate on physical education and sport. The colleges would also work with other schools in the neighbourhood to disseminate good practice and raise standards. Third, there would be greater encouragement and support for after-school sport for which some funding would be available. Fourth, the previously announced 600 school sport co-ordinators were to facilitate inter-school sport and promote a broadening of the range of opportunities for competitive sport outside the school curriculum. Finally, the strategy promised coaching support for the most talented young people focused on the network of specialist sports colleges and linked to the regional centres of the UK Sports Institute, thus contributing to the development of 'a clear pathway for those with special talents that allows them to fulfil their sporting and academic potential'. The strategy was thus attempting to deliver sports development defined as more people playing more sport by encouraging a sports habit in young children, but also sports development defined as talent identification and performance pathways. Improved facilities and physical education teaching, especially in primary schools, were the keys to the former, while specialist sports colleges, school sport co-ordinators and more extensive and effective school–club links would deliver the latter. *A Sporting Future For All* certainly returned schools to the heart of the sports development process, but, at the same time, hardened the emerging bifurcation between sports development as participation and sports development as talent identification and elite achievement.

The commitment of the government to the successful implementation of the strategy was reinforced by the establishment of three working groups to refine implementation and ensure progress. The report of the working groups was published in March 2001 and placed the development of partnerships, the encouragement to seek community benefit of school-based projects and the establishment of pathways for talent development at the centre of the implementation strategy. The School Sport Alliance, comprising the DfEE, DCMS, the Youth Sport Trust, Sport England and the distribution board for the New Opportunities Fund, was established in November 2000 to bring 'together the key stakeholders … [and] … ensure that there is a co-ordinated approach' (DCMS 2001: 11). The overall thrust of the strategy was to improve the quality of data on the geographical distribution and condition of school sports facilities, including playing fields, and to enhance access to provision through additional investment largely, but not exclusively, from Lottery sources, and the establishment of effective partnerships – for example, between independent and state schools and between schools and clubs.

Funding from the Space For Sport and the Arts scheme would make available up to £130 million for the 65 most deprived local education authorities, and a further £750 million from the National Lottery New Opportunities Fund would be available over ten years for school facility development and improvement, particularly for those projects which offered access to the local community. Indeed, part of the role of the School Sport Alliance was to 'develop an incentive scheme for schools and colleges wishing to adapt their facilities, or open them up, for community and club use' (DCMS 2001: 13). While the scale of resources directed towards the improvement of school facilities reflected the government's belief that an enjoyable and effective sports experience at school was crucial to lifelong involvement in sport, it also reflected the degree of neglect that they had suffered over the previous twenty years.

The many innovations in the government's strategy, especially in the area of funding, supported the recent Active Schools programme launched by Sport England in 1999. The development of the Active programmes (Active Schools, Active Communities and Active Sports, see Figure 4.1) was intended to complement the World Class Performance Programme initiated in 1996 and also to enable the ESC to reposition itself more closely in relation to the new government. The ESC, in its 1998 Corporate Plan, decided to organise its work around three broad objectives, summed up in the slogan 'More People, More Places, More Medals', and also within the framework of the Active programmes.

The Active programmes were not designed to supplant the model of the sports development continuum, but were a part of the rebranding of the English Sports Council that included the adoption of the title 'Sport England' as its marketing name. The Active Schools Programme consequently incorporated a number of schemes and programmes already well established within the National Junior Sports Programme, such as Coaching For Teachers, TOP Play, TOP Sport and Sportsmark, and would also be the umbrella programme for proposed schemes such as the talent identification mechanism, Sportsearch and the School Sport Co-ordinators. However, a more significant motive for the repackaging was the perceived lack of clarity within the NJSP regarding which ESC programmes and products were within its scope and, more importantly, where ownership lay. It was intended that Active Schools would be a brand that would be clearly associated with the ESC and with schools with, by implication, local authorities being less central. Doubtless the steady decline in the significance of

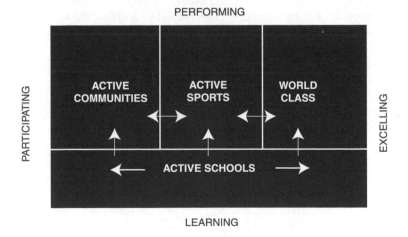

Figure 4.1   The ESC Active programmes
Source: English Sports Council

local education authorities also encouraged the ESC to target its products more directly at individual schools, much in the same way as the Youth Sport Trust (YST) had done so successfully with TOPs.

The government strategy also built upon the success of the YST, whose director, Sue Campbell, was a joint policy advisor to the then Minister for Sport, Kate Hoey, in the DCMS and to Estelle Morris, the then Minister for Standards in the DfEE. The Trust was established in 1994 with the aim 'to develop and implement ... quality physical education and sports programmes for all young people aged 18 months to 18 years in schools and the community'. The various TOP schemes combine the provision of teaching/coaching resources with training. In many respects it is the training that is more valuable than the resource bags and cards with the offer of the latter being the incentive to undergo the former. Not surprisingly, many of the schemes are targeted at primary schools where very few teachers are PE specialists and where appropriately designed and imaginative activities are crucial to capturing the enthusiasm of the young.

The success of TOPs was clearly significant in shaping the government's thinking and provided Sue Campbell with a strong basis from which to fulfil an advocacy role on behalf of school sport. However, what was also important in influencing government thinking was the worrying picture painted of school sport and physical education, particularly within the primary sector, by the 1999 Young People and Sport national survey. The proportion of children in primary years 2–4 experiencing two hours or more of physical education had declined from 32 per cent in 1994 to 11 per cent in 1999, and those in years 5–6 had declined from 46 per cent to 21 per cent over the same period. In addition, 95 per cent of primary schools had no full-time specialist for PE and 86 per cent had no part-time specialist. Finally, fewer than one-fifth of primary schools had access to a multi-purpose sports hall. On a more positive note, there had been a modest increase in the number of young people joining sports clubs outside school, up from 42 per cent in 1994 to 46 per cent in 1999 (Rowe and Champion 2000).

The continuing pressure under which physical education functioned had also encouraged the government to broaden the scope of its policy towards young people's participation. Thus, rather than simply see the problem as primarily one of competition for curriculum control and timetable allocation, *A Sporting Future For All* put increased emphasis on the promotion of after-school sports opportunities (with money from the New Opportunities Fund and from the DfEE Standards Fund designed to support out-of-school learning and with the support of the 600 school sport co-ordinators) and encouraging national governing bodies, with the incentive of greater discretion over their grant aid, to contribute either through closer links with schools or through the creation of high quality junior sections in their clubs.

The encouragement to NGBs and clubs to contribute more to social policy goals and to the efforts of schools to deliver sport and PE was not new and, while the financial incentives might prove successful, a significant increase in the contribution of voluntary sports organisations to the goal of Sport For All for young people is unlikely in the short to medium term. Consequently, schools still remain firmly at the heart of the current strategy for increased participation among the young, both in terms of curriculum innovation and improved professional development of staff – through TOPs, for example – and also in terms of the school as a resource for extra-curricular sport.

Yet it is within the very centrality of schools to the sports development strategy that a significant tension lies, because schools will have to reconcile the pressure to meet the participation objectives that require a concern to deliver sports opportunities across the whole ability range, with a mounting pressure to fulfil an important role in the process of talent identification and development; this implies selection, targeting and a skewed distribution of resources to the most able. The tension is most evident in the continuing discussion over the role of specialist sports colleges. In many respects, the specialist sports colleges sit uneasily at the intersection of at least three distinct sectoral interests, the first of which is that of the national governing bodies of sport with their primary concern with talent identification and development. The DfEE stipulated that SSCs should commit themselves to

> becoming local and regional centres of achievement in their specialist subjects … [and] … provide enhanced opportunities to fulfil the potential of talented performers and … help prepare many young people for careers in professional sport, coaching, teaching and the leisure industry.
>
> (DfEE 1998a: 1, 14)

According to the Youth Sport Trust, 'it is hoped that the Sports Colleges will in time serve as feeder institutions to the government's proposed British Academy of Sport' (YST 1996: 3). The second sectoral interest is that of educationalists and their concern, inter alia, with the needs of all children, the promotion of life-long learning and the establishment of beacon schools. To this end the DfEE refers to the objective of SSCs to 'enhance self-esteem, interpersonal and problem-solving skills' (1998a: 3), sharpen the identity of the school and 'develop within the school characteristics which signal their changed identity and which are reflected in the school's aims' (1998b: 1). The final sectoral interest is that broader coalition concerned with a set of sports–community development interests. Here, the specialist school is seen as a resource for 'their local families of schools and their communities' (DfEE 1998a: 1). Moreover, SSCs 'will form a focal point for revitalising education in areas of socio-economic disadvantage, particularly in the new Education Action Zones' (1998a: 1).

Such incipient tensions are not necessarily destructive and may well be managed effectively as the specialist sports colleges mature, for it is certainly not impossible to manage the colleges in a way that produces benefits such as increased self-esteem and interest in sport for all pupils, while also attracting and providing for the specialist needs of talented young athletes. To a degree, much will depend on the response of the national governing bodies and their willingness to integrate SSCs into their talent development programmes. At present there is growing evidence that NGBs, such as the Football Association and Table Tennis Federation, are excluding the school system from their performance plans and removing their junior squads from the school sport system. The Football Association, for example, has strongly encouraged the establishment of centres of excellence and football academies by professional clubs designed to attract talented boys of school age and exclude them from the school sport system and also from the county schools football network.

A further policy strand in sport for young people was child protection. Public recognition of the issue of child abuse in sport was triggered by the Hickson case in 1995, when Paul Hickson, a former Olympic swimming coach, was convicted of fifteen sexual offences, including two rapes of teenage swimmers in his care. Celia Brackenridge charts the way in which the moral panic that ensued led to a build up of concern, education initiatives by the NCF and the NSPCC, and responses from sports governing bodies, the Sports Councils and the state (Brackenridge 2001). Brackenridge makes the point that the state was slow to acknowledge the issue of child exploitation in sport, leaving local authorities and governing bodies to take child protection initiatives in a policy vacuum. She suggests that, at the level of the state, there was a refusal by politicians – including the first Minister for Sport under New Labour, Tony Banks – to define sexual exploitation as a sport problem. A major breakthrough came in 1999 when a National Task Force on Child Protection in Sport was established by Sport England. It agreed the following key principles (Sport England 2000c):

1   Sport has a duty of care to safeguard all children from harm. All children have a right to protection, and the needs of disabled children and others who may be particularly vulnerable must be taken into account.
2   The implementation of a sports-wide Action Plan for Child Protection in Sport should be afforded the status, commitment and financial support commensurate with public concern in this area.
3   All organisations which provide sport for children should be able to demonstrate the existence, implementation and effectiveness of child protection policies. Public funding organisations should make this a condition of grant aid.

Brackenridge states:

> These principles reflect a major shift in the attitude of British governments towards the issue of child protection (if not sexual exploitation) in sport. The work of the Task Force led to the establishment early in

2001 of a permanent Child Protection in Sport Unit inside the NSPCC
... backed by Sport England ... and was the first tangible evidence of
'joined up' thinking and action on child protection in British sport ...
the original laissez-faire state response of the early 1990s gave way to a
developmental approach by the end of the decade and is now moving to
a more coercive approach.

(Brackenridge 2001: 172)

Developing participation

Although there was much continuity between the sport policy of the outgoing Conservative government and New Labour, as reflected in its
pre-election policy statement *Labour's Sporting Nation*, there were also signs
of an emerging sport policy that reflected many of the core concerns of the
new government. There was an emphasis on 'modernisation' of governing
bodies, on the morally improving potential of sport in relation to young
people, and on sport as a vehicle for social inclusion. Running through the
statement was a commitment to return the objective of Sport For All to the
heart of its sport policy. Labour promised to produce a national strategy
that would '[give] sport back to the nation' by '[increasing] the availability of
sporting opportunities (and) [improving] our national sporting performance'
(1996: 11) and by acknowledging the 'importance of participating in sport
for the sake of enjoyment' (*ibid.*: 6).

Yet the statement was unclear just what was meant by a return to the
priority of Sport For All. For example, the statement promised that a
Labour government would 'begin by taking three important steps to ensure
access: ... end the policy of selling playing fields; ... seek to ensure that
important national events continue to be available to the widest television
audience; and ... legislate against ticket touting' (*ibid.*: 6). The last two, in
particular, are concerned with passive involvement in sport rather than
'doing' sport: 'Spectating For All' rather than Sport For All. In addition,
much of the discussion of Sport For All was couched in terms of the contribution that the policy could make to the more specific goals associated with
high performance sport. Thus the emphasis on the establishment of wider
opportunities for young people to participate was so as to create 'a greater
pool of people from which talent can develop' (*ibid.*: 6). Similarly, the
encouragement of school–club links was to provide exit routes for the
talented, who could 'progress through its [the club's] ranks' (*ibid.*: 8), not
better coaching for the average. It was in the context of strengthening the
links between clubs and schools that the statement referred to the 'crucial
role played by local authority sports development officers' (*ibid.*: 9).
Although passing comment was made regarding community sports needs, it
was clear that SDOs were seen primarily as fulfilling a role defined more in
terms of performance and excellence objectives than those of community
development. Overall, the statement was much more coherent when

endorsing Conservative government policies, such as those designed to support elite athletes.

However, once in office the Labour government appeared to be granting Sport For All and sports development a greater priority in overall sport policy. As Chris Smith, Secretary of State for National Heritage, said in the first House of Commons debate on sport policy, 'We believe that the concept of sport for all should be wide-ranging, ensuring sporting enjoyment and opportunity for the public at large' (*Parliamentary Debates* 1997: col. 1059). He was at pains to stress that while 'some say that we have to choose between aiming for sporting excellence and aiming for sport for all ... the two concepts are complementary and reinforce each other' (*ibid.*). The Secretary of State also made supportive statements regarding the value of the work undertaken by SDOs within schools and clubs and drew attention to the government's concern with those who 'feel alienated, self-conscious, unrewarded or disinterested [*sic*] in sport' (*ibid.*: col. 1062). The growing significance of Sport For All was confirmed by the decision to use Lottery funding more strategically. In contrast to the Conservatives, who preferred a reactive Sports Lottery Distribution Board, the new government saw the Lottery as a central vehicle for strategy implementation. The early articulation of policy towards participation was generally endorsed by the comprehensive spending review established by the government soon after it took office. In the review, the Secretary of State for Culture, Media and Sport emphasised the refocusing of sport policy to embrace the priorities of access and opportunity and commented that 'The ESC [English Sports Council] has already adopted progressive policies which seek to engage the widest cross section of the community in sport and physical recreation and for the most part we are satisfied that their work is well directed and deserves continued support' (DCMS 1998a: para. 5).

The complementarity between ESC objectives and those of the government was reflected most clearly in the 1998 Corporate Plan, and particularly in the restructuring of ESC activities within the framework of the Active Programmes. As with the Active Schools programme discussed above, Active Communities was essentially a repackaging of existing ESC products designed to indicate a sharper focus and a clearer responsibility for implementation. While 'participation', defined in terms of the sports development continuum, was an accurate description of the functional orientation of ESC products, it was less successful in identifying the organisations with responsibility for implementation and policy leadership. Among the objectives of the Active Communities programme was 'a commitment to serve the needs of local communities across England based on effective consultation, planning and strategic investment in linked facility/sports development programmes' (ESC 1998a) and, as such, it clearly placed local authorities at the heart of policy implementation.

In formulating the Active Programmes the ESC was attempting to adjust its activities to the general social and sports priorities of the new government, and anticipate and, more importantly, also give a steer to the more precise delineation of policy that was expected in the promised DCMS strategy. Unfortunately, the strategy was slow to emerge, leaving the ESC and its partners in a policy vacuum that allowed a number of tensions to develop during the first two years of the new government. The most significant tension was that between the rhetoric of participation and the desire to provide 'the widest possible range of sports easily accessible to the entire community' (Department of National Heritage, press release, 27 June 1997), on the one hand, and a more tightly focused policy with school sport and the needs of elite athletes at its heart, on the other. However, Active Communities, along with the other Active programmes in the 'More People programme' of the ESC, worked under the shared vision of 'more people playing better quality sport', with the five principles of fairness, fulfilling the needs of individuals, contributing to wider social objectives, progressive practice and partnership working underpinning all the work (Sport England 2001: 5). The Active Communities projects addressed the third principle – contributing to wider social objectives – most directly. All the thirty-seven projects adopted the principles of the PAT 10 report, discussed below, and reflected the ESC's commitment to delivering sports equity. Most were being developed in close association with local communities and were pioneering new partnerships with 'non traditional partners'. They were seen as a testing ground for new approaches to developing sport in the community, addressing social issues such as community safety, crime, drug abuse, truancy, multicultural development and community health.

Active Communities had been launched by the ESC in 1998 and was given a timely boost in 1999 when the then Cabinet Minister, Mo Mowlam, and Trevor Brooking, Sport England's Chair, saw the opportunity of co-operating on what subsequently became known as 'Positive Futures'. The aim was to reduce anti-social behaviour, crime and drug misuse among 10–16 year olds in selected neighbourhoods through partnership between Sport England, the UK Anti-Drugs Co-ordination Unit and the Youth Justice Board. Local authorities were hastily trawled for existing activities that might make suitable Positive Futures projects and new projects were also established. In the first year of operation, Positive Futures was funded by the government's confiscated assets fund (£500,000), English Sports Council (£300,000) and £100,000 from the Youth Justice Board. The government's enthusiasm for the initiative was demonstrated by the Chancellor's allocation of £5 million over two years as part of the 2001 budget.

In this instance, the ESC responded swiftly to the policy thinking emanating from the government and were prepared to make a major shift from 'development of sport' to 'development through sport.' In many ways, the approach is reminiscent of the Demonstration Projects of the 1980s, though the emphasis on tackling social issues, as opposed to increasing participation among underrepresented groups, is much more explicit. As the Positive Futures initiative develops, it will be interesting to see if the projects do serve as a model for community sports development and are embraced by the local authority sector, or whether they are seen as politically expedient window dressing.

The Positive Futures experiment was one example of the gradual clarification of government policy towards sport in general and participation in particular that came mainly through the publication of three important documents: the report of Policy Action Team (PAT)10 in 1999, the review of the Lottery Strategy in 1998 and the policy statement *A Sporting Future For All*. PAT 10 was established to report to the Social Exclusion Unit on the contribution that the arts and sport might make to the achievement of greater social inclusion, especially with regard to 'disaffected young people and people from ethnic minorities' (DCMS 1999: 5). The success of arts and sport in contributing to community renewal was to be measured in terms of four 'key indicators' – health, crime, employment and education. The perception of the arts and sport was as contributors to the New Deal for Communities strategy reminiscent of the experimental community development projects of the 1970s. Consequently, the emphasis was on sports projects that would rely on local control, aim for sustainability and contribute to 'capacity building'. Local authorities were exhorted to ensure that 'the principles of the community development approach should underpin … local authority culture/leisure strategies' (*ibid.*: 50); Lottery distributors were required to 'specifically address issues of social inclusion and ethnic and geographical equity' (*ibid.*: 56); while Sport England was recommended to 'recognise that sustaining cultural diversity and using sport to combat social exclusion and promote community development are among its basic policy aims' (*ibid.*: 60).

While Active Communities was readily acknowledged and accepted through its contribution to the government's policy on tackling social exclusion, Active Sports was not as well understood or accepted and barely got a mention in the 'Government's Plan for Sport'. Active Sports, though mainstreaming sports equity in its operations, is more about the development of sport and was an attempt to bridge the gap between participation and excellence. In the parlance of the sports development continuum, it is located in the performance stage. With the increasing bifurcation between participation and excellence, the ESC recognised the gap that was opening up between participation programmes and the increasingly specialised World Class programmes and designed Active Sports to fill the gap and provide performance pathways for young people. The programme aimed to bring together local authorities and governing bodies from nine sports to work in forty-five local partnerships covering the whole of England. Local sports clubs working with schools are at the heart of the delivery of the programme, which will provide access to coaching, clubs and competitive opportunities for young people. It is too early to assess the effects of this programme, though some early reactions of local authorities and governing bodies are recorded in chapters 5 and 6.

The financing of sports participation: Labour and the National Lottery

Due to the Labour government's commitment to operate within the funding plans of the previous government for its first two years of office, it was no surprise that non-statutory services would be squeezed in order to free money for new projects and that the Lottery would become the primary source of funding for policy initiatives in sport. In opposition the Labour Party's primary criticism of the Lottery was that it did little for those most in need. As a result the government set about altering the criteria for eligibility to enable the funding of revenue costs, easing the requirements for matching funding and also introducing a new 'good cause' which would address its central priority of achieving greater social inclusion.

The 1998 National Lottery Act made a number of important changes to the organisation of the distribution of Lottery income. Of particular importance was the power given to distributing bodies to solicit applications coupled with the requirement from the Secretary of State that they should prepare a strategic plan. The use of Lottery funds could now be part of a service development strategy with bodies such as Sport England approaching clubs and local authorities in areas of under-provision. Part of Sport England's response to the New Labour agenda was the revision of two existing initiatives, the Priority Areas Initiative (PAI) and the School Community Sport Initiative (SCSI), which had been introduced in 1996 to stimulate more applications from the socially deprived areas and from the education sector. The revised PAI and SCSI, along with the creation of up to thirty Sport Action Zones in areas with inadequate community provision, were included in the Lottery Fund Strategy produced by Sport England in response to the 1998 Lottery Act. According to the strategy, Lottery income, estimated to be £200 million per annum, would be divided between a Community Projects Fund, which would receive £150 million, and a World Class Fund, which would receive the remaining £50 million. Of particular significance for sports development was that £25 million was allocated for revenue projects, at least half of which would be invested in areas of deprivation and aim to tackle 'social exclusion or ... under representation in sports participation; most especially [those] projects that will benefit ethnic communities, disabled people, women and those on low incomes' (Sport England 1999a: 41). In general, Sport England produced a politically astute strategy which sought to balance the longer-term developmental needs of sport with the current priorities of New Labour. Hence the details of the strategy were built around the five key themes of the government – education, health, regeneration of communities, social inclusion, and employment and economic growth.

The specific targets set by Sport England provided a considerable boost to the confidence of those seeking a reinvigoration of sports development. The introduction of revenue funding, the lowering of match-funding thresholds and the political priority given to social inclusion marked a clear and substantial break, not only with the immediate past of the Major government, but also with the longer-term drift away from the community focus of sports development activity. The scale of the problem to be overcome should not be underestimated as there remained deeply rooted barriers to successful policy reorientation. For example, in 1998/99 five overwhelming middle-class sports – tennis, cricket, sailing/yachting, hockey and rugby union – accounted for over half of all awards and 30 per cent of the total grants distributed. However, the data are not always transparent, especially if evidence is being sought to support the Labour view that the pattern of Lottery funding constituted a subsidy to the middle class at the expense of poorer income groups. As Table 4.2 shows the pattern of distribution of Lottery finance in 1998 and over the period from 1995 to 1998 does not suggest any substantial imbalance in the distribution between sports.

The six sports at the top of Table 4.2 are among those where there is a significant imbalance in participation as measured by social group, with sailing showing the greatest imbalance. The five sports at the foot of the table are those which have higher levels of social class E participation and where the imbalance between social groups is at its narrowest. The huge allocation to swimming not only reflects the substantial capital costs of pools and diving facilities, but also reflects the popularity of the sport and the fact that it is one of the more socially balanced sports. The most surprising figure is that for sailing, the most socially exclusive of the sports

Table 4.2 National Lottery allocations by sport and level of participation by social class

Sport	Percentage of male/female population participating in the sport, 1993*	Participation indices social groups AB: E male/female, 1993 (all = 100)*	National Lottery allocation, 1998 (£m)**	National Lottery allocation, March 1995–8 (£m)**
Cricket	6.1 / na	146: 36 / na	6.4	54.6
Golf	14.0 / 2.1	148: 41 / 213: 44	0.6	5.5
Sailing	2.3 / na	233: 43 / na	4.1	22.2
Squash	7.2 / 2.3	156: 34 / 148: 19	0.04	2.4
Rugby union	2.9 / na	148: 44 / na	5.3	20.8
Tennis	6.9 / 5.1	157: 54 / 186: 37	16.7	45.8
Basketball	2.5 / na	130: 69 / na	3.2	27.7
Bowls	4.4 / 2.7	109: 79 / 121: 91	1.4	24.1
Swimming	19.5 / 23.6	128: 66 / 140: 48	11.5	175.6
Keep fit / dance	4.0 / 18.1	120: 79 / 123: 48	0.09	4.6
Association football	10.6 / na	106: 62 / na	12.9	79.6

Sources: *Sports Council, BRMB / Central Policy Unit (February 1994); **Lottery Monitor* (February 1999: 4)

listed, which received only slightly less than bowls and basketball, both of which attract more participants and which are far more socially inclusive.

A more demonstrable and persistent problem with the Lottery has been the unevenness of distribution of Lottery grant between regions. Fuelled by the publicity accorded major projects, such as the refurbishment of the Royal Opera House and, more recently, the grant to rebuild Wembley Stadium/build a national stadium, there was a perception that there was a north–south divide in the distribution of Lottery funds with London bene-fiting disproportionately along with other regions in the south. However, part of the explanation for the imbalance lies in the fact that data on grant allocations are kept by the DCMS according to the postcode of the appli-cant organisation, not according to where the money is eventually spent. According to Buchan (2000), relying on the postcode of the successful organisation shows the following allocations per head in 1998: London £225.07, East Midlands £71.17 and West Midlands £91.51, compared with an average UK figure of £124.59. Once account is taken of where money is eventually spent, and if national facilities are excluded, the figures are: London £80.77, East Midlands £57.36 and West Midlands £74.81 compared with the UK average of £73.53. However, whether a national stadium, if it is to be built at Wembley, should be treated as a benefit to Londoners (or the residents of the local authority of Brent), or excluded because the whole nation benefits, is a moot point. Not surprisingly regional comparisons mask some substantial inequalities at the district level as Table 4.3 shows.

Whereas the East Midlands has nearly a quarter of its local authorities in the bottom 10 per cent, London has only three and Wales and Northern Ireland have none. This picture of pockets of low Lottery funding is confirmed by a DCMS-commissioned study of the proportion of Lottery

Table 4.3 Allocation of National Lottery grants by district, 1998

Region	No. of local authorities	LAs in the bottom 10%	LAs in the top 10%
East Midlands	40	9	1
Eastern	48	8	3
London	33	3	11
North East	23	0	3
North West	42	4	4
South East	68	4	6
South West	45	3	5
West Midlands	34	5	2
Yorks and Humberside	20	1	1
Scotland	32	1	5
Wales	22	0	2
N Ireland	26	0	2

Source: *Lottery Monitor* (February 1999: 6)

funding received by the 'coalfield' areas, which in 1996 accounted for just under 10 per cent of the GB population (Gore *et al*. 1999). Both in terms of applications submitted (7.4 per cent) and successful awards (8.1 per cent), these areas underperform in relation to population. More seriously the financial value of successful awards is only 4 per cent, representing £30.12 per head compared with a figure for GB of £61.77 and £43.27 for the local authorities within which coalfield communities are located.

Further evidence of the difficulty of aligning Lottery funding with social priorities comes from the survey of the use of swimming pools and sports halls carried out in 1997 (Sport England 2000a). Forty-seven per cent of pool users were from social classes A and B (which comprise 29 per cent of the population); 39 per cent of sports hall users were from social class C1 (21 per cent of the population); and 7 per cent of hall users and 11 per cent of pool users were disabled compared with 22 per cent of the population who have some disability or long-term illness. Ethnic minority representation at 5.3 per cent of sports hall users compares favourably with a figure of 5.2 per cent for the population as a whole; the figure for pool use is much lower at 2.8 per cent. The survey suggests that progress in overcoming social exclusion is slow and, bearing in mind that swimming is the biggest beneficiary of Lottery funding, that the Lottery is still acting as a source of subsidy to the higher-income groups.

The changes introduced by the 1998 legislation made the National Lottery a more effective tool for achieving the policy objectives of the Labour government, which was undoubtedly welcomed by most local authorities. However, for a number of authorities, Lottery money was only a part of a larger funding package, and consequently what was crucial was the complementarity between the objectives of the various 'good causes' and other potential funding partners, such as the European Union. While an increasing number of authorities have local sport and leisure strategies, it is still the case that specific service strategies are subservient to an often implicit funding strategy according to which the primary aim is to maximise external income for the authority. Muter comments that 'Local authorities find themselves at the heart of a radical re-engineering of funding decisions' (Muter 1998: 6). He goes on to list the various Challenge funds, regeneration budgets and the increasing variety of EU funds aimed at specific areas of industrial decline that are available in Nottingham and suggests that the 'fit' between Lottery funding and the three main external sources of funding varies considerably between 'good causes' (see Table 4.4).

If an authority is planning to maximise external income it will focus its resources in preparing bids in those areas of greatest synergy and, particularly, where the opportunities for employment creation are most evident. It is in this area of employment creation that sport appears to be weaker compared with the other four good causes.

At the end of the third year of office of the Labour government there were signs that there was substance behind the immediate post-election rhetoric of

Table 4.4 Degree of strategic fit between National Lottery 'good causes' and three regeneration funding programmes in Nottingham

Good cause	EU Structural Funds	Single Regeneration Budget	Rural Development Funds
Arts	**	**	**
Sports	*	*	*
Heritage	**	**	**
Charities	*	***	***
New Opportunities	*	***	***

Source: Muter 1998

Note: * low degree of fit; ** medium degree of fit; *** high degree of fit

policy change. Although the government was pre-occupied with the needs of high performance athletes and the lengthy process of agreeing the location and structure of the UK Sports Institute, there was more evidence of progress towards fulfilling the commitment to restore mass participation as a central policy objective. Needless to say, the commitment of the government must be assessed by its success in achieving its target and in supporting the objectives set by Sport England's and the other Sports Councils' Lottery strategies. There are, however, two sources of concern, the first of which is whether the value of Lottery funding will be maintained. In part, this depends on the success of the Lottery itself and its capacity to generate the £200 million plus expected each year. Even if that target is achieved there is the more serious concern that the government will continue to erode the income from the Lottery by reducing funding on sport through local authorities and the Sports Councils. DCMS grant aid to Sport England, for example, fell in 1998/99 to £31.6 million from £32.9 million the previous year. Despite assurances, from the Secretary of State, that Lottery funds should only support initiatives additional to programmes funded from taxation, the government is gradually blurring the definition between core and additional funding. As Baring points out, the government has already defined 'additional' in a number of conflicting ways: as 'additional to mainstream/core statutory services', as 'additional to what is normally provided by the state' and as 'additional to what is currently provided by the state' (Baring 1999: 4–5).

The second concern relates to the attitude of local authorities, the key partner in the delivery of sports development. Even if Lottery funding is not seriously eroded by the government, there is the more serious problem of whether local authorities will see sports projects as the best way of optimising income from external sources and also of meeting local objectives such as economic regeneration and employment creation. While some authorities may be encouraged by the commitment in the recent Sport England Lottery strategy to provide funding for revenue costs, this commitment is limited to three years. Three years is far too short to judge the effectiveness of projects and places managers in the position of seeking continuation funding with little hard evidence of success.

A Sporting Future For All

Although the PAT 10 report provided sport policy with a general focus in relation to the government's overarching policy priorities and the 1998 Sport England National Lottery strategy, *Investing For Our Sporting Future*, established a funding framework supportive of mass participation objectives, sport policy still lacked detail and precision. Indeed there were times in the first two years or so of the Labour government when sport policy seemed to comprise little more than a generalised football populism and the intermittent output of policy statements from the Football Taskforce. During this period there was much talk of the forthcoming DCMS strategy but repeated postponements. In November 1998 Tony Banks, then Minister for Sport, announced to the annual conference of the CCPR that the strategy was imminent and that it would concentrate on five themes: access, improving health, lifelong learning through sport, higher achievement through sporting competition and a maximisation of the wealth-creating capacity of sport. As regards access, Banks linked sport to the government's concern with social exclusion and intended that sport should provide 'wider access for all – regardless of gender, ethnicity, age and ability' (DCMS, press release 290/98, 25 November 1998). Given the obscurity of some of these objectives, it is little surprise that no strategy appeared in 1999.

In the policy vacuum that existed, and the long wait for a Government Sports strategy to be produced, the new English Sports Council tried to fill the vacuum by producing *England: The Sporting Nation: a Strategy* in September 1997, a strategy addressed to all the major actors in the delivery of English sport policy. It was produced by a working group which represented the main interests in the sport policy network and sought to create a shared vision:

> for England to be a sporting nation providing equal opportunities:
>
> - For everyone to develop skills and competence for sport to be enjoyed
> - For all to follow a lifestyle which includes active participation in sport and recreation
> - For people to achieve their personal goals at whatever their chosen level of involvement
> - For developing excellence and for achieving success in sport at the highest level.
>
> (English Sports Council 1997: 4)

The strategy used the sports development continuum as its framework, using definitions of the four elements very close to those used in 1988. Under each of the four elements of the continuum strategic goals and measurable targets were set with timelines for the achievement of targets. These targets were based on available research and data and a careful analysis of trends. The approach was both systematic and scientific. The strategy emphasised both access and excellence and set a series of ambitious targets in relation to sport for young people: for example, to achieve a 20 per cent increase in the number of young people participating in extra-curricular sport by 2001; participation (where targets were set for various age groups and also for women's participation); performance (a 10 per cent increase in the number of adults who are members of sports clubs); and excellence (to be world champions in squash by 2005 and to win a bronze medal in badminton in the 2005 world championships). It was intended that the strategy should be updated annually to provide a series of rolling targets for English sport.

In contrast to earlier Sports Council strategies (and the subsequent Government Plan for Sport), it was short and succinct with the emphasis on outcomes rather than the means to achieve them. In common with earlier Sports Council strategies, it failed to have a lasting impact because the government finally wrested back the leadership and initiative for setting national policy and strategy when Kate Hoey succeeded Tony Banks as Minister for Sport and employed Sue Campbell of the Youth Sport Trust as her special advisor. This was symptomatic of deteriorating relationships between the English Sports Council and the minister/DCMS during the late 1990s and early part of 2000. In seeking to 'lead the development of sport', and in rebranding and developing its programmes and communication, the English Sports Council had gone a step too far for the minister's liking and she sought to rein the organisation back in a number of ways. Consequently, the strategy was quietly abandoned by the ESC in return for agreement from the Secretary of State that the ESC would have a greater input to the forthcoming DCMS strategy for sport.

It was not until May 2000 and the publication of *A Sporting Future For All* that the government provided the definition and sharpness of focus that made policy leadership possible. The prime minister's Foreword linked sport policy to the touchstones of New Labour policy. Sport was associated with community building, offering benefits to 'individuals, to families and in bringing people together for a common aim, to communities at every level' (DCMS 2000a: 2). The opportunity that sport presented for moral leadership was also noted. The 'sports champions of today have a responsibility to … set an example of integrity and fair play' (*ibid.*: 2). The need to ensure that opportunities for progression for talented athletes was identified, as were the health benefits of sports participation. Perhaps, most importantly, was the endorsement of the intrinsic merits of sports participation. 'Sport offers friendship, rivalry, challenge and enjoyment … sport isn't just about being healthy: sport is fun – one of the good things in life' (*ibid.*: 2).

As regards community participation, the strategy declared that the government wanted to see 'more people of all ages and all social groups taking part in sport' and set a target 'to reduce, over the next ten years, the unfairness in access to sport' (DCMS 2000a: 5, 11). In addition to making it more difficult to sell playing fields, the strategy recorded the government's intention to invest in the development of community facilities. To this end, and following a national audit of existing facilities, the government planned to support facility development with the £125 million allocated from the recently established New Opportunities Fund for green spaces. In addition, the government indicated that it would expect sports with a significant income from broadcasting to invest 5 per cent of that income in grassroots facilities. Agreement had already been reached with the football authorities, and, as a result, the Football Trust was re-established as the Football Foundation in order to act as the fund-distributing body. In marked contrast to the Conservative strategy, *Sport: Raising the Game*, local authorities were to 'play a lead role in ensuring fair access ... [and] ... in particular, we want to develop the role of sports development officers' (*ibid.*: 13). To facilitate fulfilment of the strategy three implementation groups were established which reported in Spring 2001, one of which focused on sport in the community.

Unlike the ESC strategy, *England: The Sporting Nation*, the DCMS strategy lacked any mention of measurable targets for increasing participation apart from the general ten-year time-frame for reducing 'the unfairness in access to sport' noted above. However, increasing participation in sport and achieving greater equity in involvement is likely to prove a formidable challenge and one that probably requires more sharply defined goals if momentum in implementation is to be developed and sustained. Evidence from the 1996 General Household Survey confirmed that participation across all age groups began to level off at the start of the 1990s (see Table 4.5) and in many sub-groups of the population has begun to decline.

Among 16–19 year olds participation declined from 61 per cent in 1993 to 56 per cent in 1996. Over the same period, participation by 20–29 year olds declined from 46 per cent to 43 per cent and that for 30–59 year olds from 32 per cent to 30 per cent. Only among the 60-years-plus age group did participation remain steady at 15 per cent. The decline in participation also affected all social classes with only those in the semi-skilled category registering a slight increase in participation (Table 4.6).

Table 4.5 Participation in sport on at least four occasions in the previous four weeks (%)

	1987	1990	1993	1996
Males	41	38	40	36
Females	21	23	23	24

Source: Rowe (2001)

Table 4.6   Social class differences in participation (%)

	1987	*1990*	*1993*	*1996*
Professional	65	65	64	63
Senior managers	52	53	53	52
Junior managers	45	49	49	47
Skilled manual	48	49	46	45
Semi-skilled manual	34	38	36	37
Unskilled	26	28	31	23

Source: Rowe (2001)

The framework for implementation

What marked *A Sporting Future For All* as a distinctive strategy, especially by comparison with *Sport: Raising the Game*, was the attention paid to implementation. *A Sporting Future For All* was followed by the establishment of a series of implementation groups drawn from three key sets of organisations: local education authorities, local authorities and national governing bodies. Six sub-groups were formed covering club and talent development, coaching and volunteering, community provision, education facilities and development, education teacher training, and world class, UK Sports Institute and devolved powers. The report to which the deliberations of the working groups contributed reinforced the principle of equity as underpinning the strategy stating that 'Fairness is at the heart of our action plan: ensuring that sport is accessible to all members of society, whatever their age, ability, gender, race, ethnicity, sexuality or socio-economic status' (DCMS 2000b: 4). The report, which was presented to both the DCMS and Department for Education and Employment, was structured as an action plan covering ten aspects of *A Sporting Future For All*, ranging from matters associated with education playing fields through to the devolution of power to national governing bodies. As one would expect in an action plan, the document was concise and made it clear what was to be achieved, by when and which organisation was to take the lead.

Those actors in sport policy area that had routinely bemoaned the lack of sustained government interest in sport and had criticised successive governments for publishing policy documents and then losing interest were taken aback by the prescriptive nature of the action plan. The action plan formed the basis of the subsequent document, *A Sporting Future For All: The Government's Plan for Sport* published in March 2001, which was equally prescriptive and set targets for all major partners in sports development, including government departments, the Sports Councils, and the clubs and national governing bodies of sport.

The redirection of the National Lottery and the publication of *A Sporting Future For All* and *The Government's Plan for Sport* provided both a relatively secure financial base and a strong policy direction for participation. Yet

Lottery resources and DCMS policy direction were only small, albeit significant, parts of the framework for policy implementation. One key resource for successful implementation which was acknowledged in the strategy was that of sports development officers. 'In order to achieve [lifelong participation] the role of sports development work in local areas is of the greatest importance – to promote, develop and manage opportunities for people in their local communities' (DCMS 2000a: 37). The strategy also declared that the government wanted 'to develop the role of sports development officers' and put in place 'the first ever national training scheme for development officers working across the country' (*ibid.*: 13). As well as providing a welcome acknowledgement of the work of SDOs, the strategy also tacitly acknowledged their marginal position in many local authorities. Perhaps most significantly of all, the strategy gave a clear steer to the type of work that SDOs should be involved in, namely, promoting, developing and managing, but not direct service delivery.

Sports development officers were clearly seen as a central resource in the government's strategy. In a survey of local authority sports development officers conducted for this study it was found that while many SDOs were well positioned to support policy implementation this was not the case with them all. The survey, conducted in 1999, found that SDOs were young (57 per cent were between 25 and 35 years old) and fairly new to their current post with 59 per cent having been in their present post less than three years and only 15 per cent in post longer than six years (Houlihan and King 1999). In addition, just under one-third of SDOs were on fixed-term contracts. Not surprisingly, few were in senior posts with the vast majority (61 per cent) being on grade SO1 or lower. The government's concern to enhance the training opportunities open to SDOs is endorsed by the survey which found little evidence that SDOs felt there was a clear career path which would keep them close to sports development work. Indeed, just under half (48 per cent) considered that their next logical career move would involve at least a partial move away from sports development and over a quarter responded that if they wanted to stay in sports development they would need to move out of the local government sector.

As regards the opportunities for SDOs to deliver the policy goals of the government's strategy, the evidence was mixed. While the vast majority of local authorities have one or more SDOs, few have sports development teams of any size. Forty-four per cent of local authorities have either one or two SDOs, although 31 per cent did report being part of a team of five or more. The high proportion of SDOs, just under 40 per cent, who were not funded by their employing local authority is significant. On the one hand, this might simply indicate that the authority is successfully exploiting external funding opportunities, but it might also suggest that there is a reluctance to treat sports development as a mainstream activity. More positively, over 90 per cent of respondents reported that their local authority had a sport and leisure strategy and 75 per cent agreed that the strategy set clear policy objectives for their area of work, although only 54 per cent reported that there was a separate sports development strategy. However, only half agreed that the strategy set 'measurable' targets for sports development and 45 per cent thought that the main value of the strategy was to support bids for funding.

The objective in *A Sporting Future For All* to strengthen the training base for SDOs found support in the survey. There was clear evidence that SDOs were keen to undertake training courses that linked sports development to the broader social policy objectives of the government and local authority. Almost half (47 per cent) ranked courses related to specific objectives, such as urban regeneration or social exclusion, as the most valuable with a further 24 per cent ranking such courses as their second choice. The most commonly selected second preference for training was courses linked to the work of services close to sports development, such as the Youth Service and social services. The third 'most valued' training opportunity also had a social policy dimension and concerned courses related to a specific target group such as ethnic minorities and young people. Interestingly, it was courses run by Sport England that were considered the most useful. Of those who had attended Sport England courses, 80 per cent had found them 'highly relevant'; 77 per cent also found courses offered by the National Coaching Foundation 'highly relevant'.

There is also some comfort for the government in terms of its objective to build partnerships and to achieve cross-service co-operation. When SDOs were asked to identify the partners with which they had the most frequent contact and with which they worked most closely, the most common answer was LEA schools (almost 90 per cent) followed by national governing bodies (88 per cent), sports clubs (80 per cent) and the National Coaching Foundation (79 per cent). The next cluster of organisations was those where the contact was high but the relationship less close and included FE colleges, grant maintained schools, the Youth Service and health/medical centres. With regard to the relationship with Sport England (SE), the conclusions were mixed and reflected an ambivalence towards the organisation. While almost 80 per cent of SDOs agreed that SE was 'supportive of local authority sports development objectives' and had a 'strong commitment to increasing participation', just under half also agreed that SE was 'more concerned with elite sport than mass participation' and 63 per cent agreed that SE was 'more concerned to promote its own objectives than support those of the local authority'.

At the local level, local authorities and the SDOs they employ play the key role in implementing participation policies. Yet, as has been shown, they operate within a funding environment dominated by the Lottery and within a network of programmes that tightly constrains their scope for service innovation. Following the policy lead of the government, Sport England, and especially the Sport England Lottery Board, which determines the approval of applications for Lottery funding, has established a series of

sports participation programmes that direct funding to particular geographical areas and to particular types of projects. Priority Areas Initiative,
School Community Sport Initiative (SCSI) and Sports Action Zones all
serve to direct funding to areas where participation is both low and where
intervention could contribute to the amelioration of other causes of social
exclusion.

The Priority Areas Initiative was designed to channel capital funding
to the 100 most deprived local authority areas and offered grants up to
90 per cent of cost. The SCSI was designed to encourage schools and
colleges to apply for funding for capital schemes which would benefit the
community. While there was some interest in the Priority Areas Initiative
and the SCSI, neither proved especially attractive. Up to 1998 there had
been 167 SCSI awards with a combined value of £78.5 million towards
capital projects. Interest in the Priority Areas Initiative was more modest
with, for example, only four awards being made in 1998/99. The capacity
of both programmes to address issues of under-investment in poorer
areas was hampered by the restrictive funding conditions that were
attached to the Lottery before the 1998 reform, by their largely reactive
character, and also by the geographical scope.

Sports Action Zones, introduced in January 2000, were an attempt to
overcome some of these shortcomings, as they promised a much more
geographically concentrated and proactive strategy to channel funding to
areas of low participation. More importantly, whereas Priority Areas and
SCSIs were largely capital programmes, the SAZs placed an emphasis on
the revenue funding of sports and community development officers,
coaches, sports leaders and other outreach workers. The first twelve SAZs
were designated in January 2000 with a further eighteen promised over
the next ten years. The first twelve included areas of rural deprivation
such as Cornwall and the Isles of Scilly, the coalfields area of north
Nottinghamshire and north Derbyshire, and urban areas such as Bradford
and south Liverpool. Each SAZ, which will have a life of five to seven
years, has a designated manager, part of whose responsibility will be
carrying out a needs analysis of the area and creating partnerships
between local authorities, sports bodies and community organisations to
overcome barriers to participation 'such as the costs of using facilities,
poor access to transport, lack of confidence and low self esteem' (Sport
England, press release, 17 January 2000). The clear expectation is that
SAZs will link sport with community development as identified in the
PAT 10 report. The emphasis is on 'trying to raise aspirations and
help[ing] local communities to help themselves', and the expected partners
include 'local authorities ... community groups, residents' and housing
associations, schools ... the police, social services [and] the health
authority', with the emphasis on traditional sports providers.[1] However,
what is less clear is whether the priority of the Zones will be to achieve
an expansion in sports participation which *might* have consequential bene-

fits for the community development and, by implication, contribute to social inclusion objectives, or whether the concern is to achieve community development through sport which *might* have an impact on sports participation. This is a tension of which Sport England is aware as it notes, on the one hand, that SAZs 'can help to alleviate some of the effects of poverty and deprivation', but also emphasises that 'Sport England is a sports development agency and, as such, we will expect over time all projects funded within a zone to make a contribution to increasing participation' (Sport England, press release, 17 January 2000). The early projects emerging from the first twelve SAZs include some with a primarily social engineering focus, such as working with young people involved in anti-social behaviour, others with a primary concern with health, but also others with a much clearer sports development focus, such as schemes to establish sports clubs where none currently exist and to make local sports centres more accessible.

The policy environment for the promotion of Sport For All has changed radically since 1997. Most significantly the policy has regained some of its lost prominence and is now firmly located in the mainstream of government policy and, perhaps more significantly, in the funding priorities of the National Lottery. Yet the renewed prominence of participation on the policy agenda has been, in part at least, due to the assumed potential for sport to contribute to non-sports objectives. It will therefore be a test of the lobbying capacity of supporters of Sport For All to ensure that sports development objectives are not marginalised in deference to broader objectives associated with social inclusion.

Local authorities, as the primary local agents of policy implementation for participation, are under similar conflicting pressures through being expected to contribute to the government's social inclusion objectives. One important development in recent years has been the loss of clearly defined sports development functions and, in a number of cases, the absorption of sports development sections and leisure services departments into more broadly based administrative units with a focus on community development. Moreover, mention has already been made of the increasing constraints on local authority finance and the growth of a bidding culture which has the effect of undermining the capacity of local authorities to define policy objectives independent of the various funding bodies on which they are increasingly dependent. Thus the capacity to sustain a strategy that reflects an analysis of local sporting needs is undermined by the requirement to prepare bids that help the European Union, the Sports Lottery Distribution Board and the Football Foundation achieve their various objectives. The environment of local government seems to be both more resource rich but also more tightly constrained than in previous years. Senior sports development officers are therefore faced with the challenge of maximising income while, at the same time, not compromising to too great a degree the leisure strategy of the local authority.

Elite sport

As the Cold War provided much of the impetus for government investment in sport on both sides of the ideological divide, it would have been a reasonable hypothesis that the post-Cold War peace dividend would not have been limited to reduced expenditure on the armed forces but would also have included a decline in state subsidy of high performance sport. Yet, in the ten years since the fall of the Berlin wall, state investment in elite sport has steadily increased in almost all developed countries, and especially among those in Western Europe. Britain was no exception and produced one of the more substantial increases in public investment in elite sporting success. *Sport: Raising the Game* made explicit the government's concern to 'bring about a seachange in the prospects for British sport'(DNH 1995: 1). Using income from the National Lottery, the government proposed to establish an elite training centre, the British Academy of Sport, as 'the key to top level performance' (*ibid.*: 36). Perhaps, most importantly, the Conservative policy document legitimised the explicit and systematic planning for high performance success: elite achievement ceased to be a mere policy aspiration and became a plan of action and a commitment of resources. The deeply rooted antipathy of successive governments towards acknowledging that elite sport development was a professional, resource-intensive and scientific process was overcome. The need for a systematic and professional approach to elite sports development was strongly endorsed by the Labour government of Tony Blair, which accepted that 'We need to learn the lessons of our competitor nations and have the most professional system for talent development and support of excellence' (DCMS 2000a: 15). To this end, NGBs were asked to 'create a national talent development plan' (*ibid.*: 15). 'The most talented 14 year olds will be identified and offered a place at one of the sports colleges [which] … will in turn be linked to the UKSI network' (*ibid.*: 16).

The Lottery provided the resources for the elite development strategy and the World Class Performance programmes provided the specific policy infrastructure. Most significantly, the World Class Performance grants were given, via governing bodies, to athletes to cover their living expenses while training – a recognition that to compete at the highest levels British athletes needed to devote themselves to training on a full-time basis. The deeply-rooted commitment to the myth of the gifted amateur was finally overcome. The World Class Performance programme was soon complemented by other schemes, including the World Class Potential, in 1998, designed to provide systematic and well-resourced support to those responsible for identifying and nurturing talented young people. World Class Start, also launched in 1998, completed the World Class Performance programme and provided funding to enable NGBs to search more systematically for young talent and to develop appropriate coaching systems and techniques.

Part of the World Class Performance strategy has been a far greater degree of selectivity by Sport England in its allocation of funds. Building on the designation of 22 priority sports by the Sports Council in 1996, 33 sports in 1999 were declared eligible for World Class funding with a further 23 eligible for World Class Potential and World Class Start funds. Not surprisingly, the move to a greater degree of selectivity provoked a substantial amount of criticism from those sports excluded from priority funding, but the confirmation of the policy by the new government provided further evidence of the change in attitude towards elite sports development and a recognition that concentration of scarce resources was necessary if Britain was to compete more effectively for international success.

By the end of the first Blair government, elite sports development had emerged as a distinct policy objective with its own, increasingly self-contained, set of facilities centred on the UK Sports Institute regional network and the specialist sports colleges, its own specialist medicine, science and coaching support services, and its own ring-fenced funding arrangements with the National Lottery. However, the government demonstrated an awareness of the tendency of NGBs to adopt an overly narrow focus on elite achievement and in *A Sporting Future For All* emphasis was placed on the need for NGBs to 'have a clear strategy for participation and excellence; and commit themselves to putting social inclusion and fairness at the heart of everything they do' (DCMS 2000a: 22). However, given that most NGBs have been, at best, lukewarm to devoting their limited resources to broader social objectives, it will be interesting to see how the government and Sport England will treat NGBs that achieve international sporting success, but prove reluctant to pursue social objectives.

Conclusion

By the end of the first Blair government, sport policy generally and sports development objectives in particular had received substantial reinvigoration. Many of the policies initiated by the government of John Major were endorsed by New Labour and pursued with additional enthusiasm and resources. The revival of the commitment to Sport For All brought local authorities back to the heart of sport policy, especially those that covered areas of deprivation. But the reinvigoration of policy has brought with it additional complexity in terms of the plethora of programmes, schemes and strategies produced by Sport England, the increase in the number of funding sources and also, and perhaps most importantly, in terms of the range of overlapping (and possibly conflicting) policy objectives that implementing organisations have to balance and operate within.

At the local authority level, the current policy environment raises a number of important questions about the direction of sports development. First, how and to what extent are local authorities able to determine and sustain a local sports development policy in the face of increasingly explicit national strategy statements from Sport England and from the DCMS? How have the shifts in the pattern of resource dependencies, Lottery funding in particular, affected local discretion? Second, is there evidence that local authorities are narrowing the scope of their sports development activity to focus more sharply on participation and retreating from their previous contributions to provision for competitive sport (performance level) and especially for excellence? As Taylor (1993) noted, local authorities provided more support for the achievement of excellence than the Sports Council and the value of local authority grants to excellent teams and individuals was twice that provided by the Sports Aid Foundation. Third, how are local authorities balancing sports development objectives with the broader requirements of social inclusion and Best Value? Fourth, what strategies do local authorities adopt to manage their increasingly complex network of relationships with partners, especially schools and clubs? Finally, what has been the impact of recent policy on the role of sports development officers?

A similar set of questions could be asked in relation to the national governing bodies. First, how do the NGBs view their evolving relationship with Sport England and UK Sport? Do they view the relationship as constraining, mutually beneficial, exploitative or supportive? Do they still feel in control of the direction of their development strategy? How do they react to the suggestion that there is a need for a 'modernising partnership' with government (DCMS 2000a: 22)? Second, how do NGBs view the expectation that they should contribute to social objectives as the price of Lottery funding? The next two chapters explore the interpretation and operation of sports development policies within a range of local authorities and national governing bodies in order to illuminate these and other questions.

5 Sports development in four local authorities

Introduction

Sport: Raising the Game was notable for its failure to discuss the contribution of local authorities to sport. If the omission was simply the product of the deeply embedded antipathy of successive Conservative governments towards local government, then it represented the triumph of prejudice over the realities of sports provision in Britain. If, on the other hand, the omission was based on the belief that sports participation could be developed successfully through improved physical education provision at school and the efforts of voluntary sports clubs, then it reflected an almost wilful naivety regarding the realities of British sports provision. Whatever the particular mix of motives, the fact that *Sport: Raising the Game* had such a muted impact, apart from the proposal to establish an elite training academy, indicated its misunderstanding of a pattern of provision of opportunities for sport and the central role of local authorities, not just in offering opportunities for casual sport and recreation, but also in supporting pathways for talent development and making a substantial contribution to the infrastructure of high performance training and competition.

A Sporting Future For All was, by comparison to its predecessor, a much more realistic strategy document insofar as it acknowledged that local authorities had a role to play across all elements of the sports development continuum. The acknowledgement of the importance of local authorities rested on a recognition of the importance of the resources they controlled, not just the range of sport facilities, but also the specialist sports development staff. Local authorities were consequently identified as making a central contribution to the achievement of social inclusion, but were also seen as important in co-ordinating the efforts of other partners. 'They [local authorities] are the catalyst that can ensure all the different partners are working together to a shared strategy' (DCMS 2000a: 13). In summary, the strategy identified local authorities as important in helping to build school–club links and helping to develop voluntary clubs, as well as fulfilling their traditional role in sports development and facility provision.

The Government's Plan for Sport noted the significant sums of public money that have been allocated for local authority public sports services, £412 million from the Lottery Sports Fund, a share of the £750 million from the New Opportunities Fund for PE and school sport and further finance from the Space for Sport and Arts scheme directed at improving facilities in primary schools. While the last two funds are directed towards schools, there is the requirement that their allocation should include provision for community use. *The Government's Plan for Sport* restates the policy objectives set for local government in *A Sporting Future For All*, but also emphasises the particular role of the local authority as a developer and manager of partnerships with many references to the centrality of inter-agency working and partnerships for the delivery of both sports development objectives and broader community regeneration benefits.

In contrast to the 1980s and much of the 1990s when local government was relegated to the margins of sport policy-making and implementation by central government, local authorities are now back at the heart of government strategic thinking and have a central role in policy implementation. Yet this is not the first time that central government has devolved responsibility for policy delivery to local authorities only to be frustrated by the reluctance of local authorities to be treated as the administrative agents for government policy initiatives. Local authorities have a habit of reminding central government and its quangos, such as Sport England, that, as democratically elected councils, they have some right to set their own policy priorities and that their co-operation may be sought but cannot be taken for granted. The government and Sport England therefore need to combine incentives and regulation with a degree of policy flexibility in order to generate co-operation.

The case studies that follow explore the way in which four local authorities have responded to the reorientation of sports development policy over the last four or five years. In particular, the cases examine the necessary compromise between central government and Sport England policy objectives and locally determined priorities. The four local authorities – Derbyshire County Council, Herefordshire Council, Kent County Council and Coventry City Council – do not comprise a representative cross-section of local authorities in England. However, an effort was made to avoid selecting an overly uniform set of cases. Thus Derbyshire County Council is a two-tier, predominantly rural authority with some pockets of severe economic deprivation; Herefordshire Council is a unitary authority, covering a sparsely populated rural area where access and relatively low income are significant issues; Kent County Council is a populous, economically diverse authority affected by its proximity both to London and to mainland Europe; and finally, Coventry is an urban authority with an industrial heritage where the predominant concern is economic regeneration and community development. However, while there was some concern to select authorities that reflected the variation in operating contexts of local government, the primary criterion for selection was that each authority had a reputation for treating sports development seriously and also had a reputation for service innovation. With this in mind, it is intended that the cases will not only provide a basis for drawing conclusions about the management of the relationship between central and local government in negotiating sports development policy, but that they will also provide examples of service innovation and good practice.

Derbyshire County Council

The County Council administrative area has a population of about 740,000 spread across eight district councils with a further 240,000 in the unitary authority of the city of Derby. The county has pockets of affluence, but the general profile is one of a relatively poor area. Across the county 39 per cent of dwellings are in the lower value bands A and B for Council Tax, which is twice the national figure, while the number of properties allocated to band E is half the national average. Approximately 30 per cent of the population is employed in manufacturing and a further 60 per cent in the service sector. Over the last twenty years there has been a steep decline in employment in the primary industries, especially coal mining. Levels of unemployment in the county (excluding the city of Derby) are close to both the national and regional averages, although these figures mask pockets of unemployment almost 50 per cent above the county and national averages, mainly in former coalfield districts such as Bolsover, Chesterfield and north-east Derbyshire. Unemployment in the city of Derby is also approximately 50 per cent higher than in the rest of the county. Such new investment as has taken place has tended to be in the south of the county, with the establishment of the Toyota factory at Burnaston being the best example. Finally, just under 2 per cent of the population is from an ethnic minority.

Not only has the economy of the county suffered as a result of structural economic changes, but it also faired particularly badly in financial terms during the last years of the Conservative government of John Major and during the early years of the 1997 Labour government, which had made a commitment to operate within the spending plans of the outgoing Conservative administration. As a result, the County Council claimed that it had suffered cuts of £240 million in the nine years to 1998 which had led to the loss of 4,500 jobs within the authority. However, for 1999/2000 the county council was able to present a revenue budget of £506 million, an increase of 7.5 per cent on the previous year, that allowed the administration to begin the process of rebuilding its service base. In 2001/2002 the budget increased again to £563 million, an increase of 9.3 per cent, which allowed a continuation of service rebuilding. Partly as a result of the contraction in its mainstream budget up to 1999, and partly due to increased availability of sources of alternative funds, the County has been active in pursuing external funding. In addition to general funds, such as the National Lottery, parts of the county are currently eligible for a variety of European Union funds including

RECHAR, RESIDER, RETEX[1] and Objective 2, 3 and 5b programmes, Rural Development Commission programmes in the west of the county and in coalfields areas, and the Single Regeneration Budget. Not surprisingly, the Council is staunchly Labour, with the results of the 2001 local elections leaving the political composition of the council virtually unchanged. Of the sixty-four seats on the Council, Labour control 43, the Conservative Party 13, the Liberal Democrats 7, and there is one Independent. Derbyshire has a varied and reasonably extensive sports structure ranging from first class county cricket and Premier League football to the Donnington Park race track and the extensive Peak District National Park. There is also a well-established infrastructure catering for participation and performance in a broad range of sport based on a network of clubs.

The County is organised along conventional departmental lines with there being six main service delivery committees (Education; Social Services; Libraries, Heritage and the Arts; Environmental Services; Fire Authority; Community and Public Protection) plus the Chief Executive's Office. Sports development is located within the Education Department and has twelve staff with a budget of approximately £360,000 in 2001/2002. In 1998 the department agreed a major review of strategic priorities stimulated by the recently elected Labour government and produced the Millennium Education Development Plan, which managed to avoid any reference to the potential contribution of sport to the achievement of its objectives, even those concerned with life-long learning and the achievement of social inclusion where the sports development section was already active. Consequently, the sports development section may be *in* the Education Department but it is not *of* it. The impression is that the Education Department is a convenient, but not particularly interested, home for the service with the department being content to allow the section to continue with its own activities so long as they do not distract attention from the broader and, one must admit, more politically weighty pre-occupations of the department of raising standards, reducing class sizes and achieving greater social inclusion. The organisational structure within the sports development section is shown in Figure 5.1.

The overall budget in 2000–01 for sports development was just under £360,000. Of this total, approximately £10,000 (contributions of about £1,500 from each district council plus additional funding from the County) was set aside for administration purposes. By far the largest sum, £200,000, was earmarked for Active Sports to cover the cost of the Active Sport Manager post and seven development officers responsible for equity and a range of sports including basketball, swimming, outdoor recreation and cricket. A series of grant-aided projects accounted for much of the remaining budget and included grants to support table tennis, an outdoor recreation coaching initiative and a facilities inventory. There is some additional income from the County, but it is limited: for example, covering part of the senior sports development officer's salary.

In the mid- to late 1990s there was, among the County's SDOs, not only a

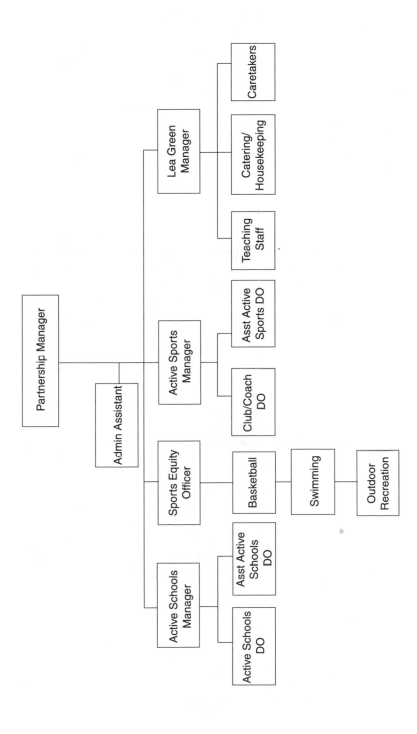

Figure 5.1 The structure of the Derbyshire County Council sports development unit

clear idea of what sports development was, but an equally strong view of what it was not. Anticipating the current emphasis on partnership, the dominant view in the authority was that sports development involved managing the 'progression pathway' through the sports development continuum, a task which could best be fulfilled through the establishment of close partnerships with a variety of clubs, governing bodies and other agencies. Good practice in sports development was not about direct delivery of programmes by County SDOs, but rather constructing and managing a delivery system. To that end, the County has made a major investment of SDO time and financial resources in developing the county-wide Derbyshire and Peak Park Sport and Recreation Strategy,[2] and a complex partnership of agencies as the primary vehicle for the achievement of Council sports development objectives.

The partnership, the Derbyshire and Peak Park Sports and Recreation Forum, is between the County, Derby City Council, the eight district councils, the two local Education Authorities for the area and the Peak National Park Authority. Only the ten local authority elected members and the one representative from the Peak District National Park Authority have voting rights on the forum, although the forum does contain a large number of observers, including those from the voluntary sector, Sport England, the two local education authorities, the Derbyshire Sports Development Officer Forum, as well as officers from the local authority partners. The forum is supported by a Steering Group comprising the senior leisure officers in each of the districts. Reporting to the forum is a series of sub-groups which reflect the primary objectives of the strategy, one each for Active Schools, facilities development, outdoor recreation, strategy and Active Sports and which mirror the organisational structure in the Derbyshire Sports Development Unit. The County Sports Development Officers Forum and the Facility Management Group also provide advice to the forum and its sub-groups.

The forum is both a vehicle for the delivery of the strategy and also a lobbying coalition which aims to 'promote and influence provision for sport and recreation in the county and Peak National Park and to encourage greater involvement in this process' (Derbyshire and Peak Park Sport and Recreation Forum 1998: 3). In such a large and diverse area the aim is not to apply a uniform set of policies to the population but rather to utilise the combined resources of the partnership so as to 'respond to local circumstances' more effectively (*ibid.*: 5). The perceived advantages are to achieve closer co-ordination of 'effort and expenditure on the development and delivery of sport and recreation'; to be better placed to make effective bids for external, particularly National Lottery, funding; to develop a more effective range of 'sport and recreation opportunities for young people and the population as a whole'; and finally, to avoid 'unnecessary duplication of sport and recreation facilities and their programming' (*ibid.*: 4). The County Council sports development strategy is one and the same with the forum strategy and, as such, reflects the clear view that, at county level, sports development should focus on enabling, influencing and supporting those bodies that control the bulk of resources, mainly the district councils.

The strategy took as its national policy reference points: first, the English Sports Council's 1997 strategy *England: The Sporting Nation* which focused on young people, lifelong participation, performance development and achieving excellence; second, the long-established sports development continuum and its fourfold distinction between foundation, participation, performance and excellence; and third, the more recent trio of Sport England corporate objectives of 'more people, more places and more medals'. The strategy also referred to the context set by the previous regional strategy for the East Midlands which had identified six underpinning priorities: namely, young people; increasing opportunities; filling gaps in provision; working towards equal opportunities; planning ahead for long-term development; working together. At the local level the Derbyshire and Peak Park Strategy had, as the title indicated, incorporated recreation 'due to its obvious implications for the Peak Park' (Derbyshire and Peak Park Sport and Recreation Forum 1998: 11).

The background research for the Derbyshire and Peak Park Strategy indicated that, in relation to participation objectives, the most elaborated and successful programme framework concerned young people through the National Junior Sports Programme, but that gender-specific sport and recreation opportunities were 'limited', as were the attempts to promote opportunities for target groups such as ethnic minorities, the elderly and the unemployed. The research also indicated that provision for disabled people was 'variable'. The facility base to support participation was also weak with the research noting a shortage of specialist facilities, only limited development of the dual use of school facilities and a variable standard of both indoor and outdoor facilities. The facility survey also noted interestingly that 'the dispersed nature of the County makes the influence and accessibility of facilities in areas outside Derbyshire and the Peak Park a significant issue for consideration'. This observation anticipated the increased emphasis on partnerships by the Department of the Environment, Transport and the Regions (DETR) and even those which cut across traditional county boundaries.

If the picture in relation to the goals of 'more people' and 'more places' was patchy in the county, it was no different in relation to the objective of 'more medals'. The research found that pathways linking schools to clubs were 'not well developed and orchestrated', there were fewer qualified coaches than could be expected in a county with the population of Derbyshire, the lack of a strategic overview for sport and recreation meant that 'the development of programmes and facilities in the County has been sporadic and uncoordinated', and finally that 'there were only limited opportunities for talented individuals to achieve the highest possible level of performance in their chosen sport within the County' (Derbyshire and Peak Park Sport and Recreation Forum 1998: 13).

The aim of the forum was to use the strategy to achieve 'beneficial change', which was defined as 'the generation and promotion of sustainable structures which enable people to take part, improve and (where desired and appropriate) excel' (*ibid.*: 16). All forum partners agreed a set of core principles which would be integrated into their own development activity. The core principles were generally expressed, but gave clear priority to young people, increasing overall levels of participation, improving performance development, and achieving excellence and facility development. Around these principles was elaborated a more detailed core programme which included talent identification, coach development, the prioritisation of specific sports, the development of pricing policies attractive to young people and providing competitive opportunities particularly for the young. Running through the strategy was a concern with the sustainability of programmes. The interconnection between the core programme and the two supplementary programmes in the areas of 'sport for all' and 'recreation for all' and with the underpinning strategy is indicated in Figure 5.2.

The series of recommendations made by the forum was strongly focused on young people and on sports outcomes (rather than primarily on social or community development outcomes). Consequently, the initial action plan of the forum linked its work to a number of existing programmes, for example TOPs and Active Sports. In addition, it also gave priority to the maximising of income from the National Lottery, which was seen as the primary source of finance for strategy delivery. The strategy also identified four focus sports (initially swimming, basketball, outdoor recreation and cricket) with the aim of raising sufficient funds to employ development staff for each sport. The concern was clearly to establish a sustainable infrastructure for sport across the county which would provide support for the rolling programme of focus sports. The strategy placed sports outcomes firmly at the heart of the work of sports development with the promotion of 'wider social, health and educational benefits of sport and recreation' referred to as one of a series of priorities in the supplementary programme. The assertion of policy independence from the emerging thematic policies of the 1997 Labour government, such as those of regeneration, lifelong learning and social inclusion, was emphatic, if also a little quixotic. Equally quixotic was the explicit statement of a willingness to continue 'involvement in English Sports Council programmes and initiatives', thus making it clear that the adoption of ESC programmes was a choice to be made by forum members rather than an obligation and adoption of English Sports Council programmes should not be taken for granted.

Given the complexity of the forum membership, it is not surprising that it took some time for momentum to be established and it was not until late 1999 that delivery activity started which was well over a year after the launch of the strategy and the formation of the forum. There have, nonetheless, been a

THE STRATEGIC VISION

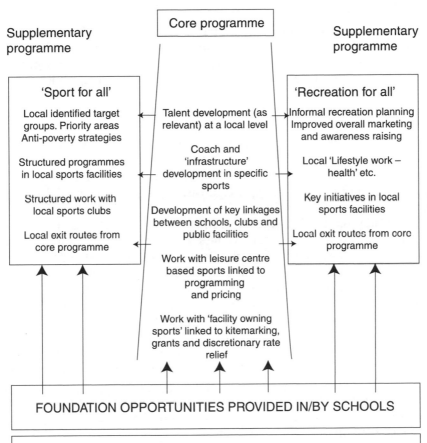

Figure 5.2 Derbyshire and Peak Park Sport and Recreation Strategy: the strategic vision

number of county-wide projects that reflect the objectives of the partnership, including the organisation of the Adventure Games in June 2001 held at Carsington Water. The event attracted 750 participants despite some disruption arising from the restrictions due to the outbreak of foot and mouth disease. The day was organised around a series of 'taster' sessions and competitive events. Sports offered included climbing, scrambling/abseiling, cycling, canoeing, bell boat racing, sailing and angling. Staffing was largely by volunteers from local clubs and the relevant national governing bodies, most of which had stalls offering publicity regarding local clubs. The event was clearly focused on encouraging participation in recognised sports and, as such, proved highly attractive to the range of governing bodies and local clubs involved. However, there was also a concern with broader sports development objectives, and the report of the event noted the relatively poor attendance of young people from ethnic minorities, as well as those with disabilities and from socially deprived areas, and stressed the need for more clearly targeted publicity in future.

A second project was the organisation of the Youth Games as part of the Millennium Festival. The Youth Games were partly funded through the National Lottery and partly from the County Council budget. Participation in the Millennium Youth Games in Southampton was judged to have been a success, especially as the Derbyshire team won the Daily Express Fair Play trophy. However, what caused concern was the subsequent suggestion from Sport England that Youth Games become a regular feature of county development activity. While the forum has agreed to organise a Derbyshire Youth Games in 2001, forum members have serious reservations about the appropriateness of the proposal over the long term. In part, the reservations arise from uncertainty over future funding from Sport England for the project, but more substantially from a concern that the Youth Games do not fit with the forum strategy and are therefore a drain on the scarce resources available for sports development within the county.

In September 2001 the forum conducted a 'mid-term' review to take stock of its progress in implementing the strategy, and also to reflect on the implications of recent shifts in government and County Council policy. The first issue that the forum had to address was the relatively slow pace of action since its establishment, particularly regarding the appointment of development staff. Part of the explanation lay simply in the number of organisations that needed to be co-ordinated, but part lay in the variable levels of commitment to the objectives of the forum and the relative importance of its activities to organisational priorities. For example, it is clear that the two local education authorities were unsure of their role within the forum and also how its objectives related to their core activities. Symptomatic of the attitude of the LEAs was the decision by the County to cease to fund its physical education advisory function. Only after considerable pressure, in part from the forum, did the county relent and agree to continue funding and to the transfer of the function to the County Sports Development Unit.

The second problem facing the forum arose from the sharp reorientation of national policy and the increasing prominence of cross-cutting or thematic objectives such as social inclusion, health and life-long learning. Although the forum has held back from explicitly embracing the government's social policy agenda, the Council plan prepared by the County clearly reflects the priorities of the Labour government insofar as it is organised around a series of themes that cut across traditional professional and departmental boundaries, including regeneration, community safety, learning community, social inclusion and environmental sustainability. The County had also integrated the government's concern with modernisation and Best Value. Although there is no explicit mention of sports development in the Council plan, many of the cross-cutting themes create opportunities for sports development activity. For example, the theme of regeneration refers to lifelong learning and the theme of community safety refers to the establishment of a multi-agency Youth Offending Service, a concern to reduce drug use and the provision of support for schools seeking to obtain the 'Health Promoting School Award'.

The third issue concerns the proliferation of partnerships. In addition to the forum, the County is also well advanced in developing partnerships which, depending on their particular priorities, might involve two or more district councils, the County Council and a variety of other bodies, such as the local health authority and local chambers of commerce. In addition to the Derbyshire and Peak Park Forum, successful partnerships include the Amber Valley Partnership which was established in 1996 and attracted funds totalling £5 million from the Single Regeneration Budget in its first three years to add to the £2.4 million allocated to the partnership by its partner organisations. The priorities of the Amber Valley Partnership include skills training, enhancement of the quality of life and community safety. The Meden Valley Partnership, launched in 2000, is similar and comprises a range of local authorities, health authorities, community groups and businesses and aims to tackle a broad range of issues, including those associated with housing, health, job creation, tourism, sport and recreation. The Partnership has already attracted £8 million from SRB 5 and has high hopes of receiving a substantial share of the £15.1 million SRB announced by the East Midlands Development Agency in 2000.

Both the Amber Valley and Meden Valley partnerships operate within the North Derbyshire and North Nottinghamshire Coalfields Alliance. The significance of the Alliance is derived not only from the fact that it crosses county boundaries, but also because it has attracted substantial funding from both the European Union and from national government, and that it is closely co-ordinated with the expanding role of the East Midlands Development Agency. The increasing significance of partnerships and of the regional development agencies and the declining significance of traditional local government service delivery mechanisms poses a substantial challenge for sports development. In an area where GDP per head and average earnings are respectively 74 per cent and 83 per cent of the national average and 78 per cent and 93 per cent of the regional average, it is not surprising that the priorities of the Alliance are focused on skills training, the development of enterprise and sub-regional marketing. However, there is also an emphasis on improving the quality of life, and it is in relation to this objective that sports development receives encouragement. In the section which deals with 'healthy communities', it is stated that 'Sport's impact on health, social inclusion and development of wider inter-personal skills leads on to a significant contribution to wider economic regeneration. This will be even more the case with the introduction of a Sport Action Zone' (North Derbyshire and North Nottinghamshire Coalfields Alliance 2000: 14).

The contrast is stark between the initial objectives of the Derbyshire and Peak Park Forum and those incorporated into the more recent Meden Valley and Coalfields Alliance partnerships. Far from defining the objectives or ends of the partnership, it is increasingly the case that sport now defines the means for the achievement of broader social and community ends. Those who work in sports development are used to the perception of sport as a convenient tool for solving non-sports problems, but the dismissal by the Coalfields Alliance of the possibility that sport might have its own objectives is clear. What is equally clear is that, if sport is to gain access to the additional funds generated by the partnerships, it would be on terms consistent with the strategic direction determined by the alliance rather than the result of a process of negotiation.

The Derbyshire and Peak Park Sport and Recreation Forum is an ambitious and extensive sports development partnership and as such demonstrates the potential of such arrangements, but also some of the challenges. As already mentioned the forum was slow to develop momentum which, in large part, was a consequence of the problems of managing large partnerships. Large complex partnerships clearly offer substantial benefits, but also incur equally substantial management costs in the time and energy spent maintaining the flow of communication and facilitating decision-making.

The forum was established at a time of considerable policy uncertainty. One of the key reference documents for the forum, the English Sports Council's *England: The Sporting Nation*, was soon overtaken by the more strongly articulated social agenda best reflected in the PAT 10 report to the Social Exclusion Unit. Although the refocusing of government policy on cross-cutting social issues poses the forum with a significant dilemma, it is only part of the extensive range of changes in policy emphasis with which it will have to cope. In addition to the publication of the PAT 10 report, the government has launched Best Value, issued a requirement for local authorities to produce Cultural Strategies, strengthened and quickened the move to regionalism, made substantial changes to the operation of the National Lottery, established more specialist sports colleges and introduced school sport co-ordinators. The forum cannot ignore these developments, though coping with such substantial change so early in its life while still not losing the momentum that it has gained will be a formidable challenge.

The most significant concern of a number of members of the forum is that, even if its partners were to incorporate the government's social agenda, so much of its effective delivery would depend on the existence of a firmly established sports development infrastructure. For example, the limited success of the 'Positive Futures' drugs education project piloted in Derby was partly due to the stimulation of demand for sport among vulnerable young people without there being a strong club structure with appropriate junior club sections for them to join. Having a strong sports development infrastructure in place is an essential prerequisite for the success of many of the government's sports-dependent social policy initiatives. This is especially important when the success of an initiative depends on the co-operation of voluntary clubs. While the involvement of clubs and sports governing bodies within the forum is strengthening, it is still much weaker than that of local authorities, and clubs and governing bodies provide a generally fragile, and also often sceptical, basis for the delivery of social policy objectives.

The role of Sport England and its regional offices remains a concern for the forum and its partners. While it is acknowledged that Sport England provides much useful advice on project implementation, there remains a deep ambiguity regarding its role. Among some members of the forum there is a clear view that the preferred role for the regional office of Sport England is one of protecting and promoting the interests of regional sport within forums such as the Regional Assembly, the government regional office and the Cultural Consortium in order to enable the effective delivery of local sports development strategies. However, it is considered that, rather than being an advocate for regional sport, the regional office is too frequently a vehicle for the implementation of national sport policy initiatives irrespective of the local context and the existing sports development objectives. For example, there is a view within Derbyshire that the regional youth games proposed by Sport England is a distraction from the objectives of the forum and a diversion of scarce resources from existing projects. Despite the fact that the original proposal for the regional games has been modified so that it is no longer a series of competitions and now includes a developmental focus, the view of some members of the forum is that the quality of developmental activity will be limited and the resources would be better used to augment existing forum projects. The regional office would no doubt argue that as part of Sport England it is obliged to help implement national policy and also that many local authorities have an exaggerated view of the effectiveness and appropriateness of their current sports development activity. In relation to the regional youth games, it could also be argued that they do provide a further opportunity to incorporate clubs and sports governing bodies more closely into the sports development infrastructure.

The final problem facing the forum is the emergence of economic regeneration partnerships which, whenever they take account of sport, tend to assume that sport is a tool at their disposal. The experience with the Sports Action Zone recently established within the Coalfields Alliance provides a good example. The initial proposal was to appoint an SAZ manager who, accessing Single Regeneration Budget funds, would manage the relationship between sports development activities and the variety of interested regional development agencies. Part of the problem lay in the creation of an additional independent agency, the SAZ and its manager, when the forum already existed and both Nottingham and Derbyshire already possessed large and experienced sports development teams. The two counties therefore suggested a modified management structure for the SAZ which would integrate the work of the SAZ into the forum strategy. When the proposal was rejected, the forum demonstrated its lobbying capacity by arranging a meeting between the chief executives of the two counties with the chief executive of Sport England, following which a compromise was reached that resulted in the activities of the SAZ manager being complementary to the objectives of the forum. However, the problem still remains of the existence of, at best, overlapping partnerships concerned with sports development and, at worst, a series of competing partnerships.

Despite the difficulties that the forum has encountered and the challenges it faces in adjusting to the changed policy priorities of the government and Sport England, it can point to some notable achievements and claim with some confidence to have anticipated a number of current trends. First, in terms of projects and new initiatives, the Youth Games and the Adventure Youth Games were both notable successes, and the implementation of Active Sports has undoubtedly led to closer working with sports governing bodies and some strengthening of the weak links between local authority and governing body sports development officers. Second, the forum has demonstrated a capacity to lobby effectively, both within the county – for example, in successfully preserving the role of physical education advisor – and externally – for example, in negotiating a compromise over the remit of the Sports Action Zone manager. Third, by taking steps to determine, publicise and gain commitment to a series of sports development objectives, the forum has been placed in a much stronger position for responding to the government cross-cutting agenda.

Overall, the Derbyshire and Peak Park Sport and Recreation Forum has been successful in establishing a clear framework for sports development across the county, although it would have benefited from having a further year or so to establish its momentum before the turbulence caused by recent policy debates. If, as seems likely, the government is going to increase the emphasis on the role of the region in policy delivery, the forum is well placed to take advantage of the move due to its clear profile within the region. Nevertheless, the experience of the forum shows, in about equal measure, both the attractions and problems of managing complex partnerships. The costs of partnership maintenance, in terms of staff time alone, are clear, as are the difficulties of ensuring that all partners are moving forward on policy at the same pace and in the same direction. However, these costs are outweighed by the benefits of combining resources for service delivery and the additional political influence that accrues.

Herefordshire Council

Herefordshire Council is a new unitary authority. Prior to April 1998 it was part of a larger authority with its neighbouring county of Worcestershire. Herefordshire is a large, sparsely populated authority of 218,000 hectares and 0.75 persons per hectare. Of the total population of approximately 167,000, just under one-third, 55,000, live in Hereford City with a further 30,000 or so living in the five towns of Ross-on-Wye, Leominster, Ledbury, Bromyard and Kington, each of which is roughly equidistant from Hereford with the exception of Kington which is a little further. The age profile is slightly older than for the rest of the West Midlands region with 19 per cent aged 65 years or over compared to 16 per cent for the region. Employment is concentrated in three sectors: manufacturing, 26 per cent; wholesale and retail trade, 20 per cent; and public services, 28 per cent; and while the level of unemployment is generally below the national average, so too is the average weekly wage. Indeed, the average weekly wage for the former county of Hereford and Worcester remained stubbornly below the national figure, increasing only marginally from 1987 when the figure was 86.7 per cent to 87.1 per cent in 1997.[3] The figure in 1999 for the county of Herefordshire alone is even bleaker at 80 per cent of the national average (Herefordshire Council and Herefordshire and Worcestershire Chamber of Commerce 2000: 38).

As most indicators of deprivation are defined in terms of urban areas, it is consequently difficult to present an accurate picture of a predominantly rural authority. For example, as noted in the County Economic Assessment, 'there is still no measure of access to services, an important issue in rural areas, and a source of social exclusion' (Herefordshire Council 1998: 25). While the county appears to be close to the national average on many indicators of social deprivation and has none of its wards ranked among the worst 10 per cent in England, a small proportion of its enumeration districts are among the worst 7 per cent in the country, suggesting that some small areas of severe deprivation exist. Much of Herefordshire is covered by a Rural Development Area and part of the area has European Social Fund Objective 5b status which is designed to promote structural economic and social adjustment in rural areas.

The overall assessment of the authority provided in the most recent economic assessment is not a simple catalogue of weaknesses. Unemployment is low at 2.4 per cent (June 2000) and compares favourably with the regional average of 4.1 per cent and the national figure of 3.7 per cent. A similarly positive element in the county's profile is the level of educational attainment, which shows that 52 per cent of young people leave school with five or more A*–C grades at GCSE compared to a figure of 45.1 per cent for England. However, the balance of the assessment lays greater stress on weaknesses, including low wages and the poor quality of employment opportunities, low levels of productivity, significant employment in economic sectors considered to be vulnerable, a high level of outward migration of young people and a skills shortage in potential growth sectors.

The sporting profile of the county is also mixed. While the county has over 340 local sports clubs, these vary considerably in size and are not evenly distributed across the county, tending to serve the urban population disproportionately. There is also only a limited range of opportunities to play top level professional or amateur sport. Hereford United Football Club of the Nationwide Conference, Herefordshire County Cricket Club of the Minor Counties League, Hereford Rugby Club (Midlands Division One) and Luctonians Rugby Club (Midlands Division One) represent examples of the highest level of competitive sport available in the county. However, the county does possess development groups or forums for hockey, rugby union, cricket, table tennis, swimming and football which help to ensure that for these sports there is a vibrant level of competition at the county level and pathways to elite level competition and coaching. In addition, the county has a number of individual sportsmen and women who compete at international level in a variety of sports, including kayak, rowing, triathlon, wheelchair tennis and bowls.

With regard to the delivery of sport and leisure services, the most significant features of the county are the low population density, the small number of pockets of severe deprivation, competition between the five towns outside the City of Hereford for resources, and problems of access to sport and leisure for the half of the population who live outside the six main urban areas. It is within these constraints that the Leisure Services section of the Culture, Leisure and Learning for Life Division operates. Within the Leisure Section there are three main areas of responsibility – namely, sports development, parks and countryside, and leisure development – and a total of twenty-seven full- and part-time non-clerical staff. The Principal Sports Development officer reports directly to the Leisure Services Manager and is responsible for a team of nine which comprises a mix of permanent, fixed-term and fractional posts (see Figure 5.3).

The fact that the authority was new gave it the opportunity to look afresh at policy objectives and the strategy for their delivery. In its Service Delivery Plan for 1999–2000, the County identified three policy themes of anti-poverty, community development and environment, all of which not only had substantial implications for sports development – although the first two are the most significant – but also aligned the authority with the emerging priorities of the Labour government. Further support for a thematic approach to the delivery of sports development came from the Herefordshire Plan (Herefordshire Partnership 2001), the development of which was led by the Council but involved a partnership including the

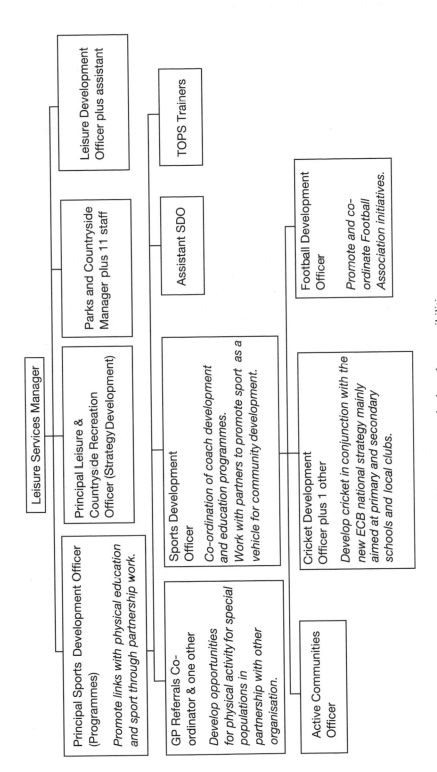

Figure 5.3 Herefordshire sports development staffing structure and selected responsibilities

Health Authority, the Regional Development Agency, voluntary bodies and the police. Among the guiding principles were building 'an equal and inclusive society' and 'realising the potential of people and communities'. The objective most relevant to sports development was to 'develop Herefordshire as an active, vibrant and enjoyable place to be', which was to be achieved, in part at least, through the construction of sustainable partnerships with voluntary and community organisations. This approach to implementation was reinforced with the publication of the Herefordshire Cultural Strategy, which echoed the objectives stated in the Herefordshire Plan and made clear that success in sports development would be measured in terms of its capacity to enhance the 'quality of life and economic activity of the County' (Herefordshire Cultural Consortium 2001). Perhaps the clearest indication of the relationship between sports development and non-sports objectives comes from the section's submission as part of the Quest quality improvement programme run by Sport England, where a list of objectives is provided, one of which is to 'receive the highest weighting in terms of their relevancy and overall contribution' to the Council vision (Quest 2000: 3). The list also includes references to health, crime, poverty, community empowerment and environment, although there is no direct reference to sport or sports-specific outcomes.

The particular objectives developed by the Leisure Services section were also close to the dominant themes of the new government and included the development of 'a community driven approach to the delivery of leisure services', the maintenance and enhancement of the Council's existing leisure facilities 'through the optimisation of both internal and external resourcing', and the development of 'a partnership approach' to the delivery of service objectives. Within the sports development section, the intertwining of sports development objectives and the broader social priorities of the County was not seen as problematic. Indeed, there was, and still is, a belief that the close integration of sports development work with, for example, the Youth Service, has given SDOs access to a wide range of services and has helped to sharpen sports development objectives. The more recent business/service plan for leisure services covering the period April 2001 to March 2002 confirmed the integration of sports development objectives with broader socio-economic priorities. The mission is expressed as '[balancing] social and economic development in order to make Herefordshire a better place to live and work' (Herefordshire Council 2001: 1). The mission is to be achieved through 'providing access to information; providing access to choice of leisure and cultural opportunities; improving the environment; [and] creating the conditions for economic prosperity and community well-being' (*ibid.*).

Not surprisingly there is no separate sports development strategy as the priority is to demonstrate the integral nature of sports development activity to the achievement of wider Council objectives, as reflected in the Herefordshire Plan and the Cultural Strategy. However, the Leisure Services section did produce a Delivery Plan which complemented many of the priorities of the government, such as community development and partnership, but also reflected the pressures under which many authorities now operate in the emphasis given to the need to attract external funding and also in the need to rely on partnerships for the achievement of council objectives. These last two elements offer the prospect of strengthening the council's capacity to achieve its objectives through the attraction of additional financial resources, such as from the National Lottery, and the human resources of partner organisations. However, there is also the possibility that council objectives become compromised and diluted as a result of the process of bidding and negotiating for resources.

In summary, sports development within the county is driven by the authority's objectives of community development and the need to tackle social exclusion, but is also shaped by a complex pattern of resourcing and service delivery arrangements. The social orientation of sports development was given substantial reinforcement by the social inclusion and modernisation agenda of the incoming Labour government. However, one of the problems that the authority faced on its creation was the need to integrate and reconcile the models of sports development that had been established in the former second-tier district councils that now constituted the new Herefordshire Council. The four constituent districts of the new unitary authority were of a very different character, with two relatively cash rich following the recent sale of council houses and two having much more limited resources.

The cash-rich districts, although in a strong position to provide significant capital-match funding for National Lottery projects in the early days of the fund's existence, failed to take into consideration and anticipate the revenue implications of such schemes that would be borne by the new County of Herefordshire. The facilities that the new authority had to develop through its revenue budget placed even greater pressure on sports development resources, which were at the time only a quarter of the combined resources of the districts on transfer.

At local government transfer in 1988, only Hereford City Council was able to identify a core sports development budget and, as a result, it was the city's contribution that provided the only funding to support the continuation of the function within the new council. Although no revenue support or mainstream posts came from Leominster District or South Herefordshire District, both authorities had managed their financial preparations prior to transfer with care and sensitivity to the obligations being passed on to the new unitary authority. This was not the case with regard to Malvern Hills District, where financial provision for sports development functions was poor and where the district council had incurred a number of incremental revenue obligations to clubs that were left unresolved prior to transfer. These obligations proved to be highly problematic and acrimonious to resolve and clouded the early months of the Herefordshire Council sports development service, and caused especial difficulty in integrating sports development in the Ledbury and Bromyard communities into an otherwise coherent county service. The district council's strategy was essentially one of short-term financial opportunism rather than a strategic approach to sports development. Despite the general reluctance to commit from mainstream budgets, the predominant attitude to service provision among the former district councils was one of direct delivery rather than enabling, which consequently made for severely restricted provision. The exception was the former City of Hereford Council which, though also allocating little from its mainstream budget, compensated by adopting a strategy to sports development that involved networking and partnerships. It was this model that was adopted by the new council, which focused around the work of the voluntary sector in the form of the Herefordshire Sports Council.

It was therefore the attitude of the more strategically oriented former districts that set the tone for the approach to sports development in the new Herefordshire Council. Only an extremely modest initial budget was allocated to sports development, some £12–14,000 per year, on the strategic assumption that there would be no involvement in direct service delivery and that the section's efforts would focus on networking and facilitating the efforts of other partners, such as the Physical Education Association, Herefordshire Football Association, Herefordshire County Cricket Board and the more progressive local clubs. Even though the budget was later raised to £113,000 in 2001–02, the assumption remains that these funds are for the management and facilitation of networks and partnerships rather than direct provision. Thus the decision to allocate a supplementary budget (a rare event for any service) to sports development to implement the community TOPS programme in 1999–2000 is an indication of the capacity of the sports development section to manage programmes effectively, and also the value placed on visibly successful projects and programmes such as TOPS. The adoption of a strategy of seeing sports development as reliant substantially on external funding and the resources of partners did not therefore imply a lack of support for sports development within the council, as the lack of direct funding was balanced by a very positive evaluation of the service by councillors. Activities related to sports development were valued because the service had been so successful in generating external income, and also because of the capacity of sports development to support the policy objectives of other services. In its first three years, sports and leisure services projects have raised £3.4 million in lottery income, which includes two supplementary awards. Success in generating external funding has also enabled sports development to obtain a disproportionate share of the Council's capital programme. In 1999–2000 the service gained just over £1 million in comparison to its pro rata allocation of a maximum of £100,000. This financial success gave officers responsible for sport and leisure services access to a broader range of policy debates than might have been expected, and has also allowed the Council to equalise, to some extent, facility distribution across the new authority. Thus, while the financial resources available for sports development activity are limited, the fact that they are discretionary has worked, so far, to the benefit of the service. However, the continuation of the success in leveraging internal capital funds depends, in the words of one sports development officer, on the continuation of the perception among elected members that sports development can 'make a difference'.

'Making a difference' requires considerable ingenuity given that so few resources are under the direct control of the sports development team. If financial resources are limited, so too are the number and range of physical resources. Only fifteen facilities are owned by the County, eleven of which are dual use and were therefore exempt from CCT, with the other four facilities being run by the County's Direct Service Organisation as the CCT contractor. Unlike other local authorities, where any expansion in dual-use facilities on school sites is often opposed by districts due to the possible impact on the income stream of their own leisure centres, this is not a problem in Herefordshire, partly because of the unitary status of the authority but also because most dual-use sites are in the rural areas well away from existing sports and leisure centres. There is, though, some apprehension regarding the possible impact of dual-use schemes that may be supported through the new funding scheme, 'Spaces for Sport and the Arts', as there may be development on the sites of urban schools without due regard to the sustainability of existing operations.

There is a significant and rising number of facilities, frequently dual use, that are operated by trusts often based on local clubs. The trust model is supported by the Council as it has proved to be highly successful in some very rural areas. Two trusts, Wigmore and Lady Hawkins Community Leisure, for example, receive only modest subsidy – approximately £20,000 each per year – yet manage to offer events and sports services seven days a week. Part of the achievement of the trusts has been their success in obtaining lottery funds and, more importantly, given the poverty of some areas, their success in raising matching funding of over £55,000.

The Wigmore Trust, which is responsible for the Mortimer Leisure Centre, is a good example of a successful trust in operation. Mortimer Leisure Centre is based on the site of Wigmore High School and is a dual-use facility run by a management committee that includes the head teacher, local county and parish councillors, and nominees of organisations that use the centre. In 1988, the new head teacher was acutely aware of the shortage of community recreational facilities in the area, with the nearest facilities being about twenty-three miles away. With the support of a small group of local residents, a management committee was established which initially opened the school hall for two evenings each week, with families as the target market. The range of activities gradually expanded and the management became more formal through the establishment of a Community Association. However, facilities were limited to a medium-size school hall and the challenge facing the association was to raise sufficient capital to build a sports hall and outdoor all-weather facilities. Capital was accumulated from a variety of sources, including the sale of some school land, a grant from the Foundation for Sport and the Arts and further grants from both the district and county councils. The first phase of building was completed in 1997, and the project was completed with the support of a National Lottery grant. The current range of facilities comprise: a four-court sports hall with a balcony area for spectating and pool and table football; a fitness suite; and an outdoor all-weather area with four tennis courts, which is also marked out for a range of other sports, including basketball, football and hockey. Surprisingly, for a scheme such as this, there is no revenue subsidy as the trust runs at a surplus even though it employs three part-time staff. This is largely achieved by letting facilities to clubs which then fulfil many of the routine functions associated with facility use, such as setting out equipment, and some of the more routine management responsibilities such as the collection of membership fees which are then passed on to the trust. Clubs exist for a range of sports, including badminton, football and cricket, although casual use is allowed for the fitness suite. Overall the trust fills a clear gap in the provision of opportunities for sport and recreation and has managed to do so in a manner that is self-sustaining.

The second example involves another school, John Masefield School, and the shared use of playing fields and buildings with the Ledbury Rugby Club. The authority offered to fund the construction of a community room on the site and encouraged the rugby club, whose members possess many of the necessary business skills, to lead the trust. The £728,000 project was completed in 2000 and is largely managed by the rugby club, which employs a full-time manager. The club has strong community links and hosts a netball club and a junior football club, in addition to a full range of rugby teams including teams for juniors and for women. The scale of school use has reduced following the laying of a synthetic pitch on the school site. The County is currently hoping to encourage at least two further sports clubs to establish trusts and seek lottery funding.

Other innovative schemes include a Treasury-funded Active Communities project in South Wye, which was selected as a rural pilot for the West Midlands region. South Wye is an area of significant deprivation and is also an Education Action Zone. The South Wye partnership involves a broad range of organisations, including the Council, police, health authority and local voluntary organisations. A partnership manager (Active Communities Development Officer) has been appointed and funding is in place for a five-year period. The focus of the partnership is young people, and initial activity has included the conduct of an audit, the formation of a young persons' forum, the construction of a skateboard park and discussions with an outdoor adventure centre with a view to developing a programme of activities for the youth of the area. The project is an interesting example of the ambiguity inherent in Active Communities where it is unclear what the balance is expected to be between sports outcomes and community development/empowerment outcomes. For, while the sports outcomes are modest (to date at least), there is evidence of capacity building within the community through the involvement of members of the community in wider activities that are only tangential to sport. However, the role of the council was simply to act as a facilitator for the project with no commitment of local authority resources beyond that of staff time.

A similar facilitating role was played by the sports development section in helping to establish a joint project between Hereford City Sports Club and the council's Education Department, which was required to establish a school for emotionally and behaviourally disturbed children. The club – which was based in a listed building that was in need of substantial refurbishment – and the Education Department had to find premises for the new school. Full funding for the school was available from the Department for Education and Employment and, with the sports development section acting as intermediaries, it was proposed to refurbish the club premises in return for using some of the space to locate the school, whose pupils (approximately fifty in total) would have use of the facilities during the school day.

Finally, a particularly novel scheme for extending the funds available for sports development is 'Ready, Steady, Win Ltd', a partnership between the Council, the Rotary Club of Ross-on-Wye and the Leadership Trust, which has been in existence for four years and which was reformed as a limited company in May 2001. Among the aims of the company are the following:

* to generate funds from donations from corporate bodies, individuals and fundraising events;
* to provide bursaries to qualifying young sports people in the age range 10 to 20 years irrespective of gender, race, creed or ethnic origin to help them achieve and maximise their own personal potential within a recognised sport;
* to provide grants to sporting coaches to enable them to gain higher coaching qualifications for the benefit of young sporting people.

(Memorandum and Articles of Association 2001)

Although the company is in its infancy, it has already had considerable success in generating external income, having raised about £100,000, mainly from private companies. The target for 2001–2 is to raise £200,000.

An important element in the resource infrastructure of the authority is an active and very effective local sports council. Herefordshire Sports Council (HSC) aims to provide a source of information about sport in the county, particularly for clubs, governing bodies and coaches, but also for the general public. The council also has a lobbying role as it aims to 'act as the collective voice for the local sporting community', and to seek to 'develop opportunities for improved access to sport' (Herefordshire Sports Council n.d.: 1). The council, which includes Herefordshire elected members, incorporates three forums covering youth sport, coaching and disability. Its work in relation to youth sport provides a good illustration of its activity and priorities. The Sports Council, through its sub-committee, the Herefordshire Youth Sport Action Group, produced the Herefordshire Youth Sport Plan in 1996, which has been twice updated and remains the key strategic document for youth sport. In part, activity has been directed at lobbying within Herefordshire Council on behalf of youth sport, but the Sports Council has also sought to work closely with schools and the Youth Service. The Action Group has been heavily involved in promoting physical education in primary schools, assisting with the organisation of the Millennium Youth Games and supporting youth coaching projects.

Two projects that further illustrate the contribution of the Sports Council to the development of sport in Herefordshire are the annual Herefordshire Primary School Sport Project and the publication of the guidance pack 'On the Right Track'. Held annually since 1993, the Herefordshire Primary School Sport Project aims to bring high quality coaching into primary schools and offers a series of six one-hour coaching sessions in a range of sports. The coaching is delivered to all children in the class and also involves the class teacher and takes place within normal curriculum time. Sports are selected only if there is an established opportunity at club level for children's participation. In 1999/2000 coaching sessions were arranged in five sports, gymnastics, netball, hockey, rugby union and tennis, with over 1,500 children taking part. Among the sports development outcomes were the formation of mini-leagues and the invitation to the more able children to join local clubs. In some schools, the project simply added a degree of diversity to the existing curriculum, but in others there was the clear impression that it represented a rare opportunity for children to participate and receive coaching in 'basic core sports and body management skills'. The Herefordshire Youth Sport Guidance Pack, 'On the Right Track', is designed to provide advice on the development of sports opportunities for young people, and, as such, it is aimed primarily at club officials, but also at parents and coaches. Guidance is provided on the establishment of school–club links, child protection, generating resources and development planning.

Overall the Herefordshire Sports Council makes a major contribution to the development work in the county, with the honorary secretary having a close working relationship with county sports development officers. The Sports Council provides strong support for the small County sports development team, partly through the provision of additional administrative and organisational resources, but also through the detailed local knowledge possessed by its members and its capacity to lobby Herefordshire Council and Sport England independently on behalf of sports development objectives. However, as the example of youth sport shows, the priority of the local Sports Council is to promote sport and there is an admitted unease with the perceived drift to projects such as Active Communities, which are seen as running the risk of subsuming sport within a social agenda.

The concern to establish trusts and strengthen partnerships with schools and local clubs is part of a broad strategy to maximise resources and to compensate for the continuing uncertainty regarding the authority's own budget. Because of this pressure, the authority is highly selective in the external Sport England programmes it supports. For example, it is concerned that, because of limited resources, it is unlikely to be able to contribute to the Active Sport programme, and that its involvement in Active Schools and TOPs is likely to be less extensive than it would prefer. However, as demonstrated above, the County Council has often, in conjunction with the Herefordshire Sports Council, taken action to stimulate youth sport activity within clubs in line with the priorities of the National Junior Sports Programme. In addition to the production of the Youth Sport Guidance Pack, the County, again working closely with the Herefordshire Sports Council, has developed its own rugby sports development programme – as part of the Herefordshire Primary School Sport Project mentioned above – aimed at introducing children to tag rugby as part of a six-week course, with coaching coming from local rugby clubs. The success of the rugby scheme encouraged its extension to include four further sports: tennis, gymnastics, hockey and cricket.

Overall, policy is driven within the authority by a set of broad national social objectives adapted to the circumstances of a sparsely populated rural area. Consequently, there is a closer fit between the priorities of the Leisure Services section and those associated with health, community development and the Youth Service than with Sport England priorities as reflected, for example, in the Active programmes and the sports development continuum. Indeed, there is a perception of Sport England as being more concerned to promote its service priorities than to support local innovation and attempts to address the specific features of local needs and resources. While Sport England claims to offer a range of programmes from which local authorities can select, it is considered in Herefordshire that Sport England uses its influence over funding to exert pressure to adopt new initiatives rather than to support those that are appropriate to local circumstances. One officer referred to Sport England as attempting to use the Active programmes and its influence over lottery funding 'to pull us back into line'. However, the changes to the principles governing the distribution of National Lottery funds and the introduction of the New Opportunities Fund (NOF) and Awards For All have proved to be to the significant advantage of the Council. Not only has the British Gymnastics Association obtained £57,000 from NOF to pay for an after-school gymnastics club, but, more importantly, the Council has found that Awards For All has suited the small-scale projects that tend to be generated in relatively sparsely populated rural areas. Herefordshire received the second highest number of awards per head of population in the region, after Birmingham, from the Awards For All fund. The awards have clearly met a substantial need for small amounts of money to help keep the infrastructure of clubs functioning and, in so doing, have, in the words of one officer, 'changed the face of sport in the county'.

The endorsement of a commitment to community development and overcoming social exclusion has affected the extent to which the authority supports activities across all elements of the sports development continuum. In the early 1990s there was a much greater willingness to work in partnership with some of the more affluent sports clubs in the City of Hereford, but the county is now much more selective and will work with clubs only if they have clear community objectives such as the previously mentioned Ledbury Rugby Club, which not only established development programmes for women and young people, but also agreed to provide funding for a club member to visit local primary schools as part of the rugby development project. However, while the authority will work with clubs to achieve participation and inclusion objectives, it is more constrained in contributing to programmes at the performance and excellence end of the continuum. Whereas in the past the districts were content to divert a proportion of their income from mass participation activities to support elite development, for example, through Champion Coaching, the current expectation is that this and similar performance and excellence programmes will be co-ordinated and resourced through clubs and county governing body associations. Local hockey clubs, for example, have already established links with a number of schools in order to provide development sessions and a pathway from school teams to club sides.

Herefordshire is a good illustration of the pressures facing the less affluent rural authorities and the necessity for innovation in service delivery if sports development is going to persist and thrive. The creative development of partnerships with schools, and especially with clubs, and the use of community-based trusts amply illustrates the increasing complexity of the infrastructure for the delivery of sports development. The fact that the infrastructure is maintained with an extremely modest contribution from the authority's mainstream budget is further evidence of the quality of the management. However, while Herefordshire's experience is a valuable example of what can be achieved through the effective development and management of partnerships, it also highlights some of the challenges facing future expansion and refinement of the service.

Three issues are of particular note. First, there are the implications of the marginal nature of sports development. On the one hand, sports development activity is well regarded because of its capacity to generate income and to contribute to the achievement of social objectives; on the other hand, sports development has suffered from a high degree of financial instability over recent years and, in times of budgetary austerity, is always vulnerable to disproportionate budget cuts because of the higher priority given to statutory services such as education and social welfare. In 1998, despite being able to demonstrate that sports development delivered value for money, the budget was cut by 7 per cent. However, within two years the sports development budget was restored to its pre-local government review levels substantially because of its demonstrable capacity to deliver across a range of the corporate priorities identified in the Herefordshire Plan. Nevertheless, sports development remains one of the few services that is constantly having to demonstrate its utility and, while this might appear to give sports development an advantage in the more critical environment of Best Value, the rewards for success are limited with the service having to work hard at advocacy to generate additional investment from the authority's core budget. Consequently, there remains the long-term problems of, first, reconciling the marginal position of sports development in terms of core funding with its politically valued contribution to the delivery of corporate objectives and, second, translating political recognition into long-term embedded support for the service. As is noted in the Leisure Services business plan, the service still has 'No clear political mandate – Herefordshire Council is not clear what its priorities are for the service' (Herefordshire Council 2001: 1). However, this issue is scheduled to be addressed by the proposed 2001/2 service review and Best Value inspection.

A second issue is the increasing separation between more sports-specific development activities and those with a greater potential to contribute to social objectives. Development activity concerned with the performance and excellence elements of the sports development continuum are being left increasingly to clubs and national governing bodies to lead and manage. The few sports-specific SDOs that still exist in the county, such as those for tennis, table tennis, football and cricket, are now funded and managed via national governing bodies and clubs. The SDOs that remain with the local authority have generally moved further away from direct provision of development activities and are expected to fulfil a more generic and strategic role and focus on projects where participation objectives can complement those associated with community development and social inclusion. However, while one might applaud the shift of staff time away from direct provision towards the provision of strategic advice and the facilitation of networking, it is easy to underestimate the resources required for this type of activity. One concern expressed in the Leisure Services business plan was that the 'service is only able to provide for management of critical issues' (Herefordshire Council 2001: 1). Later in the same document it was stated that 'higher level technical/professional support [is] continually being sought from the community – only time-limited advice can be afforded if maximum benefit is to be achieved', and the 'lack of resources to optimise access to funding regimes' was also noted (*ibid.*: 3). One of the difficulties of moving to an effective enabling role is that, while the eventual service output might be greater than under direct delivery, the output is less easily and readily associated with the contribution of sports development staff of the council. In Best Value terms it would be difficult for the general public, who under Best Value must be 'consulted', to have a sophisticated appreciation of the contribution of the sports development section to the outputs and outcomes they see in their community. It is much more likely that the trust, school or club will receive the credit for the provision of services that the sports development section has been instrumental in facilitating.

A third concern relates to the role of Sport England. While the authority has clearly benefited from success in bids to the Sport England Lottery Fund, this was largely before the 1998 National Lottery Act introduced a stronger strategic element into the award of grants. There is some concern that Sport England will use its greater influence to place pressure on authorities like Herefordshire to adopt centrally developed programmes rather than continue their successful practice of local programme development. However, there is a strongly held view within the authority that it can deliver effectively the sports development contribution to corporate objectives without recourse to Sport England programmes. For example, the Council has been successful in accessing money from the New Opportunities Fund of the National Lottery for sports development projects. In addition, there is ample evidence that governing bodies of sport are keen to work in partnership with the Council directly rather than through Sport England. Finally, there is the clear perception within the sports development section that had the Council operated within the Active Sports programme it would not have been as successful as it has been in attracting external funds.

Kent County Council

With a population of 1.57 million in mid-1998 Kent is England's most populous county. The economy of the county is generally buoyant with employment across a range of economic sectors such that the steady decline in manufacturing has been more than offset by growth in business services, construction, education and tourism. However, the county's economic performance in terms of per capita GDP, earnings and employment is weaker than that for the South-East region as a whole and has been so for some time. GDP per head in February 1999 was £9,837 (£11,455 for the South-East and £10,711 for the UK), average gross earnings per hour £8.93 (£10.00 SE; £9.54 UK), and the unemployment rate was 3.9 per cent (2.6 per cent SE; 4.6 per cent UK) (Kent County Council 1999: 1). Economically, the county is mixed with some centres of wealth – for example, around the towns of Tunbridge Wells and Sevenoaks – balanced by areas of relative deprivation such as Thanet, Dover and Shepway. Thanet, ranked by the DETR as the 64th most deprived district, has suffered particularly from the recent pattern of structural change in the economy with the cessation of mining leaving a 'relatively low-skilled workforce in a geographically isolated area' (*ibid.*: 13). Unemployment in Thanet at 6.7 per cent (9.1 per cent male unemployment) is four times that of Sevenoaks. However, three other areas, Dover, Swale and Shepway, were, along with Thanet, identified by the DETR as among the worst ten districts in terms of changing patterns of socio-economic deprivation between 1991 and 1996. In the South-East region Kent has the lowest proportion of its population with a higher degree, although the proportion of children who obtain five or more GCSEs at grades A*–C at 49.2 per cent (1998) is higher than the national average (46.3 per cent in England in 1998). In terms of ethnic diversity, Kent has a relatively small ethnic minority population, approximately 2 per cent, mainly in the north of the county, although 'research suggests that some ethnic minority communities encounter difficulties accessing the labour market' (*ibid.*: 14).

The county is eligible for a variety of economic and social grants. The north-east of the county has Objective 2 status while substantial parts of the county are designated as Rural Development Areas, Assisted Areas, and as such are eligible for Single Regeneration Budget programmes. Between April 1998 and November 1999 Kent (excluding the unitary authority of Medway) received £22m in European Union funding as well as £20m SRB funding in the 1998–9 financial year. Politically, the county is traditionally Conservative with the Party increasing its majority from eight in 1997 to twenty in the 2001 elections. Sport is significant in the county on a range of measures. 1.7 per cent of the county GDP comes from sport and supports over 12,500 jobs. Approximately two-thirds of the population take part in sport at least once per month, a figure which is higher than those in employment or in education.

The Sports Development Unit (SDU) is located within the Education and Libraries Directorate's Community Services Division. The mission statement of the Sports Development Unit is 'to enable the people of Kent to fulfil their sporting potential'. The three accompanying principles emphasise, first, the importance of partnership, 'concentrating on the development of facilities, strategy and planning, performance and excellence, coaching, disability sport and school sport', and, second, its ambition to be 'proactive, dynamic, highly professional … delivering … customer focused services in addition to providing general co-ordinating, networking and communication services'. The third principle not only emphasises the importance of developing 'sustainable sports opportunities', but also stresses the centrality of sports outcomes though it does acknowledge that the unit is 'conscious of the economic, social, educational and health benefits of sport' (Kent SDU n.d.). The primacy of sports-focused outcomes indicated in the mission statement is reinforced in the unit's business plan although it is noted that 'much of the Unit's work … will fit within the Division's priority themes of regeneration, lifelong learning, quality and external bidding' (Kent SDU 2001a: 1).

For the authority as a whole, a series of Strategic Statement Targets provide political direction. Two targets which directly affect sports development are to 'support leisure, sports, entertainment and cultural facilities' and to 'promote/develop sport in Kent, and encourage the dual use of the school and school sports fields by the community' (quoted in Kent SDU 2001a: 2). At directorate level, the Education and Libraries Directorate Plan identifies a series of themes to guide its work, one of which is to 'provide strategic leadership for the development of sport in Kent' (*ibid.*). Both the Strategic Statement and the Directorate Plan make clear reference to the role of the SDU in developing sport, although both documents also refer to the cross-service themes, such as lifelong learning, regeneration/economic development and health. The recent consultation exercise *Opportunities for Kent: The Vision* (KCC 2000) was also careful to avoid subsuming sports objectives under the emerging range of cross-cutting policy objectives. Thus, sport and recreation were to be promoted and developed, but their potential to contribute to non-sports goals associated with learning and health were also acknowledged. As a result there is a confidence within the unit that it has a brief to maintain a primary focus on *sports* development as long as this is complemented by an explicit contribution to broader County goals.

The attitude of staff in the unit towards some national and regional Sport England initiatives is similar to that found in Herefordshire – treating them with a degree of pragmatism and referring to the 'centralisation of Sport England funding away from regions, resulting in little flexibility for Sport England to fund priority issues determined locally' (Kent SDU 2001a: 3). Staff also emphasise that while some national schemes will be a priority for Kent, others will not, and that there should always be the flexibility to allow sports development funds to be spent to best effect on priorities determined locally, such as the funding of county school sports development officers not to deal solely with Active Sport. Kent, it is argued, is distinctive in the range of national and international factors that impinge on its activities. In addition to the government's modernisation agenda, the Unit points to the implications of its proximity to mainland Europe and the consequences for the county's elite athletes of the decision to locate the UK Sports Institute regional centres some distance away, in Hampshire and Bisham Abbey. In addition, there is some concern that many of Sport England's initiatives do not necessarily result in higher levels of participation. Although the products and services under the framework of Active Schools, such as Activemark, Sportsmark, TOPS and Coaching for Teachers, have been deemed to be extremely successful in Kent, it is believed that the national programme does little to support existing structures such as the Kent School Sports Council and the school sports associations which organise inter-school competitions and county squads. Active Schools provides new programmes which are superimposed on existing networks rather than providing enhancement of existing county priorities. The school sport work of the Unit in Kent is anticipated to move away from the fairly prescribed framework of Active Sport once Sport England funding ceases and the work will focus more on increasing competitive opportunities for young children. The mix of wariness of the Sport England political agenda and the distinctive features of the Kent county led the Sports Development Unit to state in its business plan that Kent should 'set its own agenda in sport in accordance with its needs, taking advantage of regional or national structures and programmes where appropriate' – a clear perception that Sport England is a resource for the county to use rather than the County being a vehicle for the implementation of national DCMS or Sport England policy.

The orientation of the Sports Development Unit is towards the provision of strategic planning of sport rather than the direct delivery of services. Its strategic role covers the provision of advice relating to facility development, developing school sport and disability sport, support for coach development and training, raising the level of sport performance and excellence, and the creation and maintenance of pathways that allow progression through performance to excellence (Kent SDU 2001b). The unit also sees itself as a resource for governing bodies, clubs and voluntary bodies to turn to for advice and strategic support. The unit has six fully funded core staff plus well over twenty further staff who are funded in part by the unit but also externally and are located within, and administratively supported by, the unit, including two partnership posts for the Active Schools and Communities project. The unit provides networking, administrative and secretarial support for twelve sports-specific development posts and nine further posts such as those related to the work of the unit in supporting disability sport (see Figure 5.4).

Funding for the unit's core costs is met by the County Council and amounted to £410,800 for 2001–2, although a further £285,000 of income is generated from external organisations for particular projects such as Champion Coaching, Kent Youth Games and Active Sports. Overall, the revenue budget for the Sports Development Unit is £1 million, which includes funds that it acts as banker for on behalf of county-wide partnerships. In addition, the unit has substantial influence over County Council spending on school sports and physical education facilities. The County has been very successful in securing funding from external organisations such as the Sport England Lottery Sports Fund and the National Lottery New Opportunities Fund. Organisations in Kent received just over £5 million in sports lottery awards in 1998–9 and received over £17 million between 1995 and 1999, giving an average cumulative per capita figure of £10.94 – three times the average for the arts. Kent also has a high National Lottery success rate, with 56 per cent of county bids to the lottery being successful compared with a national success rate of 28 per cent. The success rate is even higher at 80 per cent for those bids where the advice of the Sports Development Unit has been sought.

In summary, sports development in Kent is reasonably well resourced, not only because of the full-time staff of the County Sports Development Unit and its access to the council's mainstream budget, but also because of the extensive network of sports organisations and funding providers that the unit has been able to establish over the years. The SDU uses its resource control to influence service development and delivery across the sports development continuum while also fulfilling its supplementary role of

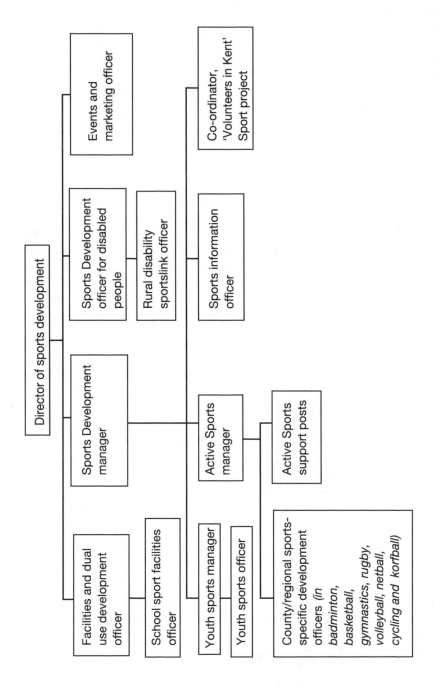

Figure 5.4 The structure of Kent County Council sports development unit

contributing to County cross-service targets in the areas of health, regeneration and lifelong learning. At the performance and excellence end of the sports development continuum, the SDU has taken a number of initiatives designed to ensure that within the county there are clear pathways along which talented sportspeople can proceed. Consequently, the SDU, in consultation with governing bodies, has produced criteria for designating a series of county Centres of Excellence which include both physical and human resource requirements. The unit has also been instrumental in establishing a Kent Institute of Sport, as a private company, to meet the needs of elite sports performers and reduce the need for them to travel to the regional institute at Southampton. A similar motive underpinned the 'FANS' scheme, which was established in 1998 as a partnership between the County and all the districts, including Medway unitary authority, and was designed to allow elite sports performers within the county to obtain free access at off-peak times to fifty leisure and sports facilities for their personal training. Eligibility was limited to sportspeople who were members of a national team or squad, ranked in the top ten of their age group, or had achieved success (top ten finish) in any national age group competition in the previous twelve months. By the end of 2000 the scheme had 250 national level performers registered.

More broadly, the unit provides extensive specialist advice to a wide range of sports organisations, including schools and clubs, on framing bids for lottery funds. In the six years from April 1995, the unit has helped to secure £43 million of external funding from the National Lottery and other external sources, with more Lottery grants than any other county in England and more than Greater London in 1999/2000. The unit provides advice through the publication of guidelines for the preparation of feasibility studies, sports development plans, business plans, etc., and also makes available the services of a specialist officer. The unit also undertakes regular research designed to identify gaps in facility provision as a resource for those organisations preparing funding bids. The most recent research covered twenty-nine individual sports and the deficiencies in multi-sport facilities, namely, artificial pitches, sports halls and swimming pools. The results of the research are distributed to all governing bodies and local authorities in the county, and to potential funding agencies, therefore fulfilling the dual function of identifying facility deficiencies and thus prompting bids for external funding and also providing supporting evidence of need when bids are being evaluated by potential funders such as the National Lottery Sports Board.

Two projects of particular note in the county are in the area of disability sport. Kent has had a specialist disability sports officer for eight years and was one of the first local authorities to make the area of disability sports development a priority; the unit gained funding from five different organisations in order to establish the post. The Gravesham Disability Sportslink Scheme was established in early 1995 as a partnership between the County

SDU, Gravesham Borough Council and Gravesham Social Services with the aim to

> work at foundation level to support disabled people to participate in a variety of sport, leisure and recreational activities in a formal or informal setting. The opportunity for choice is deemed as being vital so that disabled people are able to take part in what they want and where they want.
>
> (Hodgkins 2000: 1)

The scheme grew out of a realisation that few disabled people were using local leisure facilities; those who attended the occasional 'taster days' rarely became regular users; many disabled people needed one-to-one assistance to enable participation; many disabled people and their carers lacked information about what was available in the area; and, finally, many disabled people lacked the necessary skills and confidence to use leisure facilities. Overall, records showed that fewer than 100 disabled people were using the Gravesham facilities each year despite Gravesham having a good record of arranging sports events for people with disabilities and also having well-trained staff. The appointment of a Disability Project Co-ordinator was designed to fulfil a number of objectives, including the provision of encouragement and support for disabled people to take part in a variety of activities offered by the major leisure facilities, the development of links between leisure services and the welfare services in the borough, and the provision of advice and training to leisure centre staff to enable them to provide support to disabled users.

The sustained success of the project is supported by clear evidence. The initial round of publicity and visits to local groups resulted in a significant increase in the number of disabled users to the extent that a second officer was employed to cope with the volume of users, which was as high as 100 per week within six months. In the first year eight activities were offered, some of which were sports-specific, such as trampolining, swimming or squash, while others were more general, such as use of the health suite. Gradually the number of activities was extended until a range of fourteen activities were available each week. Running alongside the programmed activities were a series of special events, such as Gladiators and a Disability Sports Day, which fulfilled the dual function of bringing together existing service users and also publicising the project to potential new users but, perhaps more importantly, to local councillors and the regional office of Sport England. As the programmes became established and the special events became a regular feature of the calendar, the project began to develop a range of links with the community, some in the form of independent leagues or sports opportunities, such as the tenpin bowling league and the programme of regular football sessions, and others in the form of regular forums for the discussion of project development. In addition to the consolidation of the programme at the facility level, the establishment of the project has led to a greater concern to develop links with the schools for children with moderate learning difficulties and those for children with physical disabilities, both within the borough and in the neighbouring authorities.

The project has also provided a range of training opportunities for leisure centre staff and other support staff. Training has been offered for the Community Sports Leader Award, Assistant Teachers Award in Disability Swimming and also Deaf Awareness. However, one area where the project team admit that progress has been slower than they would have wished is in enabling disabled people to undertake training courses. Part of the explanation was 'the lack of flexibility involved in many of the National Governing Body Coaching courses i.e. no allowances for the person's impairment so people would fail the course due to an inability to physically perform some of the tasks' (Hodgkins 2000: 7). A further problem concerns the difficulty of arranging disability awareness courses for leisure centre staff due, in part, to the rapid turnover of staff. A third concern relates to the transfer of responsibility for the management of the two main leisure centres in Gravesham to GCL Limited, a private contractor. Although the aims of the project are clearly written into the contract specification, there is an anxiety regarding the 'priority of the Disability Sportslink Project in relation to other GCLL operations' (*ibid.*: 130). All three issues illustrate some of the problems of partnership working. On the one hand, partnerships create a greater pool of resources, but they also create a more complex set of dependency relations where one or two weak partners can undermine effectiveness.

Overall, the project has certainly fulfilled its original aim of providing opportunities for participation at foundation level. The most significant challenge facing the Kent Sports Development Unit is how to take the project forward. There is a clear awareness that unless pathways to other elements of the sports development continuum can be established the momentum behind the project may dissipate. The manager of the project makes a distinction between project management and sports development and suggests that while the project has been successful, unless it is integrated into a broader pattern of progression opportunities for participants, it will not contribute significantly to sports development objectives. Indeed, the very success of the project might have had the effect of reducing pressure on the borough council to create opportunities for participation by disabled people in the council's mainstream sports development programmes. As Hodgkins notes, there is a need for a sports development plan that establishes 'links between the Project, Gravesham Borough Council, county, regional and national networks ... if the project is to expand and develop' (Hodgkins 2000: 17). If such pathways are to be created, then a much greater commitment is required from the borough council, governing bodies and the network of local sports clubs.

Although the future expansion and development of the Gravesham Project is unclear, its initial success – and especially its identification as a model of good practice within the PAT 10 review – led to the establishment of a parallel project focused on participation by disabled people in sport in rural areas. The Kent Rural Disability Sportslink Scheme has similar objectives to the Gravesham Project, with the additional concerns to make existing facilities in rural areas more accessible to disabled people and to enable access for disabled people in rural areas to urban facilities. The Kent Rural Disability Sportslink Project was approved in January 2000 for a five-year period, with the project officer being appointed later in the same year, in September. The funding for the project came from Sport England's Active Communities Showcase fund and, as such, is considered to be a national pilot.

The early phase of the project involved observation and assessment of existing activity and consulting with those organisations already working in the area. A number of initial activities have been identified, including work with the Association for Rambling for Disabled People, the Kent Association for the Blind and district SDOs to produce a booklet, in a variety of formats, detailing all guided walks in Kent. A second project involves collating information about countryside parks that make provision for access by the disabled, and also discussing with district authorities the opportunities for improving access. A third project involves working with three privately owned outdoor activity centres on issues of timetabling and pricing. Part of the motivation to build partnerships with outdoor centres was the feedback coming from users of the Gravesham Project, which indicated that users would like to have the opportunity of participating in more exciting sports such as climbing and canoeing. As a result, one centre has agreed to halve its prices and increase the hours when specialist coaching will be available. Other projects are under way focused on riding, sailing, cycling and archery. Development work is also in progress in the sport of climbing focused on the Arethusa Venture Centre and provides a useful illustration of how a development infrastructure needs careful nurturing. The Arethusa Centre already had some experience of hosting disabled climbers during week-long or two-week residential activity holidays. The Centre therefore had some experience of working with disabled climbers, but the participation of disabled climbers was still unusual and exceptional rather than routine.

Discussions with the Arethusa Centre have led to a series of training events for existing climbing instructors to increase their capacity to work with disabled climbers and the purchase of specialist equipment for the centre. Recently, the Centre has established a specialist climbing club for people with a disability which meets fortnightly and has about eight members. New volunteer staff have been attracted to the Centre and the Centre staff have begun outreach work at local specialist schools to further expand and develop the club. One longer-term ambition for the club was to take part in the annual festival of climbing at Birmingham in December 2001. The Rural Project, like the Gravesham Project, illustrates the importance of establishing a network of committed partners as part of the development process in order to ensure that the initial marketing or focus event enables participants to identify pathways out of foundation and participation to performance and excellence.

In addition to projects that are largely local authority focused, the SDU has, as a priority, also worked closely with governing bodies to develop sports pathways. In gymnastics, for example, the unit worked with the county gymnastics association in the mid-1990s to identify four locations for gymnastics centres on club sites and then helped to raise finance from the Foundation for Sport and the Arts and the National Lottery for facility development and coach development. Kent now has a complete performance pathway in the sport, and the success of the programme is reflected by Kent developing a significant proportion of the top gymnasts in the South-East region. A similar successful programme was undertaken with rugby union. The county hosts three rugby youth development officers funded by the governing body who, during 2000, worked with 300 schools and organised twenty rugby festivals involving at least eight schools in each, and also organised ten rugby 'roadshows' which involved over 800 children. The work at participation and performance level is supported by a sophisticated computer-based talent identification and monitoring process which keeps records of the progress of young players and also of coaches. Currently, Kent has five members of the England under-18 squad who came through the county development process.

A final example relates to the emergence in the late 1990s of a growing concern within county sports governing bodies that they were witnessing a slow but steady decline in volunteers willing to fulfil important roles such as judges, scorers, umpires, treasurers and secretaries. The Sport England Volunteer Investment Programme was not a suitable response as it was aimed primarily at improving the skills of existing volunteers, not with volunteer recruitment. However, Sport England agreed to fund a part-time post designed to provide an analysis of the volunteer needs of county governing bodies and then try to meet those needs through contact with volunteer agencies, such as the Council for Voluntary Services and the Volunteer Bureaux, none of which had previously placed sport on their list of potential activities for volunteers.

Sports development within Kent is generally well funded, wide ranging and imaginative and has had a number of its projects identified as innovative and models of good practice. But even in a local authority where sports development is so strong there are a number of issues and problems that need to be addressed. First, there is the level of understanding and appreciation of the service by elected members. So much of the work of the Sports Development Unit is as project management agency, where the emphasis is on making links between existing providers, providing funding advice, offering expert advice, project monitoring and evaluation, that there is a concern that without the higher profile events member support might be more difficult to foster. The nature of the work of the Unit prompts a similar concern with regard to Best Value, where the public's understanding of the Unit's contribution to the schemes delivered by voluntary or other public sector providers might be limited. In addition, the growing emphasis on a thematic cross-service agenda on issues such as health, lifelong learning and inclusion, both at national level and within the local authority, is making it increasingly difficult for the Unit to sustain its current approach which emphasises the primacy of sports development outcomes. Despite the ample evidence that most of the SDU's projects make substantial contributions to the fulfilment of cross-service objectives, there is growing unease about being seen to be more obviously 'on message' and to foreground the social agenda. There is the clear perception within the Unit that its primary contribution to cross-cutting issues, such as lifelong learning, is through the promotion and development of coaching qualifications rather than in organising after-school literacy classes based at local football clubs. However, the wariness of shifting emphasis towards an overly close embrace of cross-cutting issues is also based on a concern for the impact on voluntary clubs and governing bodies whose infrastructure is fragile and relies heavily on support from the SDU. Where the Kent SDU has a clear advantage over many equivalent organisations is in having a lead officer at a sufficiently senior level to be able to promote and defend the work of the Unit among other senior officers and among elected members.

A second concern relates to the role of Sport England and a strong perception that Sport England is less concerned to support local innovation or the tailoring of programmes to suit the peculiarities of local areas than it is with the implementation of relatively uniform national programmes. Staff in Kent point to the gradual loss, over the last five years, of control over funding by the regional office of Sport England as money has been drawn back to the national office to help fund national initiatives. As a result, Kent lost five sports development posts which Sport England had been part-funding with the Unit.

A third concern relates to the increased emphasis on the regional level of government and the potential for an enhanced role for the Sport England regional office. There is a strong view in Kent that the appropriate level for co-ordination and strategic sports development activity covering all levels of the sports development continuum is the county rather than the region. Consequently, the SDU seeks to build partnerships with its districts, county governing bodies of sport and clubs to deliver on both participation and excellence and sees regional decisions, such as the location of the regional centre of the UK National Sports Institute in Southampton, as weakening the performance pathways established in the county. Given that Kent is the most populous county in the UK, its confidence in its ability to sustain a comprehensive sports development infrastructure is plausible.

The fourth concern is one that is not unique to Kent and relates to the problems of increasing the level of dual use of school facilities. The potential of dual use to contribute to the available facility base for participation has long been accepted, although progress has generally been slow in the past and often attributed to the reluctance of school head teachers to co-operate. However, in Kent, as in many other counties, there is a reluctance among some district councils to embrace dual use of schools which are county-owned facilities. The reluctance is due to the fear that dual-use sites will draw users, and consequently income, away from their own sports and leisure facilities. A preoccupation with income generation is a significant element of the legacy of the introduction of compulsory competitive tendering and one that Best Value may be unlikely to eradicate.

Coventry City Council

In the middle of the twentieth century, Coventry was part of the industrial heart of the British economy with highly successful businesses in the automotive, aerospace and electrical engineering industries. The rapid structural change in the British economy that took place in the last quarter of the century faced the city with severe problems. At present Coventry is still in the process of reorienting its economic base to take account of the rapid decline of its traditional industries. While successful engineering and manufacturing industries, such as Jaguar and Peugeot, remain prominent (accounting for 26 per cent of employment) there has been a shift in employment to service industries such as distribution, hotels and restaurants (19 per cent) and public administration, health service and education (28 per cent).

For the city as a whole GDP per head at £12,013 in 1998 compared well with the average for the West Midlands region (£12,548) and was higher than that for the UK (£11,455). However, the calculation of average figures for indicators of wealth masks the significant degree of variation within the city. While there are affluent areas to the south of the city centre, the city is characterised by middle- to low-income areas and some pockets of severe deprivation to the north-east of the city centre. Unemployment in the neighbourhood of Willenhall is 30 per cent compared with an average of 3.6 per cent for the city. The wards of Foleshill and St Michaels are among the 5 per cent most deprived wards in England. By contrast the Wainbody ward is among the least deprived 10 per cent of wards in England and has an unemployment rate of 1 per cent. The wards in the north-east are part of the Advantage West Midlands Coventry–Nuneaton Regeneration Zone while the Wood End–Henley Green area recently won major government funding under the New Deal for Communities programme. Of the seventeen wards within the city, nine are eligible for grant aid according to the criteria used by Sport England for the allocation of funding under the Priority Areas Initiative. Politically, Coventry is firmly under the control of the Labour Party. Despite losing nine seats in the 2001 local elections, the Labour Party was still solidly in control, holding 35 seats compared to the fifteen held by the Conservative Party, three by the Socialist Party and one held by the Liberal Democrats.

As regards the sporting profile of the city, at the high-performance level Coventry offers club competition in football, with Coventry City FC who are currently in the Nationwide Division One of the Football League, rugby union (Coventry Rugby Club who finished fifth in the 2000–01 season in National Clubs Division One), ice hockey (Coventry Blaze), athletics (Coventry Godiva Harriers which counts sprinter Marlon Devonish and long jumper Jo Wise among its members), and basketball (Coventry Crusaders of the National Basketball League Conference which reached the play-offs in the 2000–01 season). Many of these clubs have well-established junior sections, which make them an integral part of the sports development pathway for talented young athletes. Coventry Crusaders, for example, has an explicit commitment to 'bring basketball to all people regardless of ability, age, size, race or colour' and provides coaching sessions in local schools and during summer basketball camps. Coventry Blaze ice hockey club has recently established a junior section following the success of a taster session held early in 2000.

The broad range of opportunities to play high-level competitive sport owes much to the industrial sporting heritage of the city and the network of industrial sports clubs. Although industrial clubs remain important, the network was seriously weakened during the de-industrialisation of the 1980s despite the efforts of the City Council to provide financial assistance to management committees to buy the freehold and re-establish clubs as trusts. Recent years have witnessed a second wave of pressure on a number of the remaining industrial clubs, prompted less by the closure of businesses and more by a desire within companies to realise the asset value of the land used for sports fields and buildings, and a greater concern with issues of work-force fitness and health rather than the provision of opportunities for team sports. A further pressure on the industrial club structure is the ageing of club officers, many of whom became involved in the 1980s when the first trusts were established and are now close to retirement. The City Council acknowledges the importance of clubs and provides substantial support not least of which is a generous interpretation of its powers to grant exemption from the payment of rates.

The location of the sports development section within the Cultural Development Division of the City Development Directorate is an indication of the role that sports development is expected to play in achieving Council objectives. The Council's Best Value Performance Plan (City of Coventry 2000a) and Coventry Community Plan (City of Coventry 2000b) identified six priorities which were determined following a process of public consulta-tion, namely: the creation of more jobs for Coventry people; tackling crime and making communities safer; tackling poverty; investing in young people; creating a vibrant city centre; and meeting the needs and aspirations of older people. The mission of the City Development Directorate, derived from these priorities, is to 'inspire the successful regeneration of the City, as the heart of the sub-region, through investment in people, jobs, culture, entertainment and the environment' (City of Coventry 2001a: 1). The centrality of regeneration is also clear in the mission statement of the Cultural Development Division which is to 'inspire successful regeneration of the City through all aspects of cultural activity including the arts, sport, play heritage and parks' (*ibid.*). The strategic objectives for the Cultural Development Division strongly reinforce the cross-cutting objectives of the Council and of the government and include commitments to:

- support the regeneration of the city, city centre and priority neighbour-hoods;
- help create more jobs for Coventry people;
- support healthy lifestyles;
- support lifelong learning;
- develop the cultural life of the City;
- help tackle crime;
- help create a high quality living environment;
- help create equality of opportunity, social justice and social inclusion;
- help provide quality services and opportunities; and
- create opportunities for young people and older people.

Although the strategic objectives are clearly derived from the dominant social and economic policy themes of the current Labour government, there is significant scope for the pursuing of objectives more directly associated with sports development outcomes. The service objectives derived from the Division's strategic objectives are a mix of the service specific and the thematic and include those to:

- promote cultural sector jobs;
- help make the city centre vibrant;
- develop cultural industries;
- help create opportunities for lifelong participation in cultural activities by everyone in Coventry;
- help create pathways for everyone in Coventry to achieve their potential;
- celebrate cultural and ethnic diversity;
- celebrate achievement in cultural activities; and
- steer the continuous improvement of cultural and leisure services in the city.

It is these service objectives that are used to construct the individual work plans for members of the sports development team, thus enabling all staff to see how their day-to-day activities link to the broad corporate objectives of the Council.

Two years ago the former Leisure Services Department became a division of the City Development Directorate, which took responsibility for most services apart from social services and education. With the shift of administrative location came a reorientation of sports development priorities towards support for the broader cross-cutting issues such as regeneration, health and crime. However, the shift in emphasis was not dramatic as the earlier 1995 strategy, currently under review, already contained a mix of both sports and social objectives. The 1995 strategy clearly saw sports development as a process that involved the Council in developing opportunities at all levels of the sports development continuum. The aim, to 'develop opportunities for everybody to participate in sport and achieve their potential', was elaborated in terms of the sports development continuum and as such had a focus on sports-specific outcomes, but was linked to a statement of corporate objectives which located sports development activity within a strongly articulated set of social and economic priorities, including community and economic development, community safety and equal opportunities (City of Coventry 1995: 3).

The acknowledgement of the Council's corporate objectives notwithstanding, the overall emphasis of the strategy was on the development of programmes and activities designed to produce a series of sports-specific outcomes and benefits with the generation of broader social benefits a welcome, but not primary, concern. The five 'key elements' of the strategy reinforce the sports-specific focus referring to the need to maintain and improve facilities, improve access, ensure that sufficient numbers of coaches and other officers are available, and publicise the available sports opportunities. As was conventional for the time, the 'key elements' identify important target groups: namely, young people, those on low incomes, those with disabilities, women, older people and ethnic minorities. The difference between sports development policy now by comparison to a few years ago is that, whereas in the mid-1990s projects and programmes were evaluated primarily, and sometimes exclusively, in terms of criteria related to sports outcomes, much greater emphasis is now placed on social and economic criteria which generally take priority over more narrowly focused sports-specific outcomes. Whereas the 1995 sports development strategy referred, for example, to the ensuring that sports opportunities were made available to people on low incomes and older people, the more recent Community Plan identifies 'tackling poverty' as the priority, within which it refers to support for 'coherent measures to alleviate poverty including the provision of accessible leisure and recreation services' (City of Coventry 2000b: 6) and to meeting the needs of older people within which it identifies the sub-objective of promoting the independence of older people through the provision of a 'wide range of social and leisure services' (*ibid.*: 9).

The current sports development section has eight full-time development officers each of which has a series of overlapping responsibilities for a geographical area, for one or more specific sports and for a particular target group. The overall budget for the section was about £185,000 in 2001/2. Given the small staff in the section and the limited budget, it is not surprising that, as in the other local authorities examined in this chapter, the emphasis in the section is on establishing and managing a network of delivery partnerships rather than the direct delivery of sports development activities.

In this regard Coventry is fortunate insofar as it has a long history of working with trusts. In the mid-1980s David Moorcroft set up the Coventry and Warwickshire Awards Trust as a project designed to promote sport for children in deprived areas. With financial support from the urban programme fund the Awards Trust built a sports centre in 1987 which, in addition to a broad range of generic sports facilities, contained a number of specialist athletics facilities. Over the intervening years the centre reduced the emphasis on its athletics specialism and is now a broad-based community sports facility, 'Centre AT7', which, in 2000, received a National Lottery grant for refurbishment and expansion. Centre AT7 offers a wide range of indoor and outdoor facilities similar to those found in a conventional local authority sports/leisure centre, including a six-court sports hall, fitness suite, martial arts studio, climbing tower, synthetic and grass pitches and netball courts. The centre is also managed in a manner similar to publicly owned facilities insofar as there is no membership requirement and a variety of concessionary cards are accepted. Another early example of a sports-related trust was the Midland Sports Centre for the Disabled located to the south of the city centre, which merged with Centre AT7 to form the Coventry Sports Foundation and enabled the foundation to offer an increasingly wide range of specialist sports development activities and services. In addition to its activities aimed at the disabled, the Foundation also runs a number of projects directed towards schools. One such project is PEPS (Physical Education for Primary Schools) which was established in the early 1990s and was designed to address the identified lack of opportunities for PE and sport for children in many of the city's inner area schools. Currently, twenty-nine primary schools are involved (about 1,200 children) each week in a series of programmes that aim to introduce young children to a range of sports and sports skills and as such has much in common with the TOPs programmes.

Other outreach programmes organised by the Foundation include a range of outdoor projects which grew out of the Foundation's involvement in the Duke of Edinburgh's Award Scheme. With the aid of a lottery grant the Foundation bought equipment for use at the centre and also has water-based equipment located at Lake Bosworth in Leicestershire. At present the centre is a major provider of outdoor activities in the area licensed under the Adventure Activities Licensing Act 1996 and regularly organises activities for a range of groups such as the scouts, schools, and the probation service, as well as special needs groups such as the RNIB and the city's special schools. Complementing the outdoor activities, the Foundation also runs a

Mobile Youth Scheme (MOBYS) based at the Midland Sports Centre, which involves taking both instructors and equipment into the local community where a range of street sports and recreational activities are organised. Finally, the Foundation has its own sports development unit which provides coaching and also organises sports and recreational events, a youth development unit which runs after-school activity clubs and a series of youth nights on weekdays, and, most recently, a healthy lifestyles promotion unit which offers health and fitness screening from a mobile trailer unit that tours the local communities.

Given the range of activities organised by the Foundation, the Grant Aid Agreement between it and the City Council reflects the confidence that the city has in the Foundation and states that the Council 'sees their partnership with Coventry Sports Foundation developing on a long term basis' (City of Coventry 2000c: 2) and forming an important and integral part of the contribution of sport to the objectives of the Coventry Community Plan. 'The Foundation will be expected to consider how their services can help achieve the priorities in the Coventry Community Plan and will be involved in the consultation process for developing and implementing future plans' (*ibid.*: 4). However, it is clear that such an expectation is simply reinforcing existing practice within the Foundation as the agreement notes that 'the Foundation already has excellent links with the Area Co-ordination teams in the North-east and the Council recognises the success of outreach work that has taken place' (*ibid.*: 5). As should be evident, the Foundation has always had a strong orientation towards social issues and consequently found the increasing emphasis on cross-cutting issues an endorsement of its primary concerns and work practices rather than a challenge.

Such had been the success of the Coventry Sports Foundation that in 1999 the City decided to establish the Coventry Sports Trust to take over responsibility for the management of all the City's sports facilities, thus creating a situation where the City now has no facilities under its direct management. The trust is managed by a board comprising mainly of people from business and from local community groups. Its work is underpinned by a formal agreement with the City Council on funding and a set of agreed service priorities formulated initially by the council. Regular liaison meetings provide a key mechanism for ensuring a continuing working relationship with the council. However, it should be stressed that the relationship is close and there are no signs that the trust is keen to interpret its responsibilities in a way that is markedly different from the view of the Council. Indeed, officers in the sports development section were at pains to emphasise the degree to which the working relationship between the Council and the trust is an improvement on the previous relationship between the Council and the CCT contractor even though the personnel is largely the same. The shift away from CCT and the tensions between sports development objectives and income generation has produced a genuinely smoother working relationship. At present the trust acts as a major resource for the

City's sports development activities and is closely involved in many of the major projects of the sports development unit, including its 'inclusive fitness' programme where the trust provides vouchers for reduced entrance to fitness suites, the formulation of a joint bid to the New Opportunities Fund to establish a 'healthy living centre', and involvement with the City Council's outreach work in local schools where the trust provides staff.

The trust is also likely to be heavily involved in the recently established Greater Warwickshire Active Sports partnership for which Coventry is the host authority. As with the other forty-four Active Sports partnerships, the Warwickshire area was identified initially as a potential location for a partnership by Sport England. After Sport England gained the agreement of the local authorities in the proposed partnership area, it was readily agreed that Coventry Council would be the obvious organisation to act as host authority given its share of the population and the range of its existing sports development activities. The key responsibility of Coventry, as the host authority, is to provide a base for the Active Sports manager and to act as his employer on behalf of the partnership. Direction is given to the work of the manager and to the partnership as a whole by a steering committee which comprises all local authority partners plus representatives from Sport England's regional office. Sports development officers are not represented directly on the steering group but do have their own forum which is linked to the steering group. Other satellite groups include a club development group and a coach development group, both of which are co-ordinated by the Active Sports manager.

As with all Active Sports partnerships, the work programme of the manager is determined mainly by the outcome of the required audit of current provision and the identification of gaps and areas of weakness in relation to the priority sports identified by Sport England on the basis of their popularity among the young.[4] The Greater Warwickshire partnership added dance to the list of selected sports and is currently focusing on tennis, swimming and cricket, although the intention is to gradually expand the work programme to include all target sports. On the basis of the audit, the manager has devised a work programme which has been agreed by the steering group. Part of the remit of the manager is to prepare a development programme for each sport which will hopefully receive the endorsement of the relevant governing body.

The manager has only been in post a matter of months and is still at the early stages of planning his work programme, but agreement has already been reached on the location of a new tennis club in one of the poorer parts of north-eastern Coventry recently designated a 'New Deal for Communities' area. The location of the club reflects Coventry's concern that the projects flowing from the Active Sports Partnerships should neither duplicate existing sports development work nor create programmes or facilities that do not complement existing strategies. For example, while the new tennis club provides access to the sport in an area where a demonstrable gap in provision existed, it is not yet clear how, and to what extent, the club will be integrated into the governing body's development pathway as the Lawn Tennis Association has an extensive but highly structured talent identification and development process. At national level, the LTA is committed to Active Sports, but how that national level commitment in principle is translated into implementation in practice has yet to become clear.

In general, Coventry has a very close and positive association with the clubs in the city. The sports development section has a 'Charter for Sports Clubs in Coventry' which all clubs are invited to sign. The Charter reflects some of the core values and priorities of the Council, including equal opportunities expressed as a desire 'to encourage participation by everyone in Coventry regardless of age, race, gender or disability', and the promotion of fair play, in regard to which the Council states that 'We will seek to encourage good sporting conduct and fair play by everyone associated with the club in all its activities' (City of Coventry n.d.). The Charter also includes commitments by the club to support its coaches and officers and to encourage the provision of opportunities for young people of all abilities to participate. Part of the incentive to commit to the Charter is undoubtedly the prospect of support from the sports development section for applications from clubs for exemption from rates, the local tax on property. However, an equally strong incentive is the wide range of services offered by the sports development section which, over the years, has led to the development of a close and normally co-operative working relationship.

A generally well-attended presentation evening is held each year, used partly to celebrate sporting achievements in the city and partly as an opportunity to update club officers on current and forthcoming programmes from both the city and Sport England. At the presentation evening in 2001 sessions covered: partnership working, which used a local junior football club as an example of what could be achieved; Sport England's 'Volunteer Investment Programme' and the 'Running Sport' training programme; the new guidance from Sport England on bidding for lottery funding and how the sports development section could help; and progress on the establishment of the Active Sports Partnership. In addition to this annual event, the sports development section runs training/awareness courses, not only in the standard areas of first aid, bidding for lottery funding and managing volunteers, but also in a range of more controversial areas of increasing concern to clubs. This latter category includes training/awareness sessions on coaching and the law, child protection and injury prevention and management. Recently the sports development section received very positive support from clubs when it asked them whether they would prefer the City Council to co-ordinate the new procedure for gaining clearance from the Criminal Records Bureau for those seeking to work with young athletes.

Although sports development benefits from a series of partnerships with external bodies, all those discussed so far are with organisations such as the Coventry Sports Foundation, Coventry Sports Trust and sports clubs, whose

primary rationale is sport. Many of the more recently established partnerships are less service specific and reflect attempts to develop integrated
responses to social and economic issues, with the consequence that the
sports development agenda is less obvious and has to be promoted more
vigorously. However, while the contribution of sport has to be established
rather than taken for granted, the new partnerships offer the opportunity to
access substantial new resources both directly and also indirectly through
co-operation with other city council services.

One of the most significant new cross-cutting partnerships to be established in recent years is the New Deal for Communities partnership in the
north-east of the city. The delivery plan draws on the work of the government's Social Exclusion Unit and its recommendations on neighbourhood
renewal. The 'vision statement' for the partnership is to create a 'normal
community', and two of the ten key elements of that normality are the
desire to 'have positive things to do' and to be 'fit and well and [not to] die
on average ten years younger than in other areas of Coventry' (City of
Coventry 2001b: 7), both of which offer opportunities for sports development to make a contribution. Preliminary consultation indicated that there
was considerable dissatisfaction with existing opportunities for leisure in the
area: 46 per cent of those surveyed indicated that they were very dissatisfied
with the council's leisure services and 55 per cent wanted more local sports
and leisure centres. The Leisure Task Group, established to co-ordinate the
formulation of proposals in response to the consultation, made a number of
suggestions that have been incorporated into the delivery plan, including a
proposal to build a new leisure facility in the area. Other proposals include
an application for funding from the Football Foundation to develop, in
consultation with Coventry City FC, the infrastructure for football in the
locality – to 'ensure co-ordination of programmes and to make sure that
young people with talent have access into the football clubs and academies'
(*ibid.*: 52). A similar link has been developed with Coventry Crusaders to
develop a basketball project which also provides an exit route for those
involved who show talent for the game. Interestingly, while these projects
strongly support the community renewal objectives, they also can claim to
be contributing to the development of sport as well as the development of
the community.

The sports development team are heavily involved in the partnership and
were able to contribute a number of existing projects funded through the
government's 'Quick Wins' programme. One such proposal involves funding
an Active Communities post to co-ordinate a series of projects including the
football development programme and the introduction of Coventry Sports
Foundation's MOBYS (Mobile Youth Scheme). Although it is early in the
development of the partnership, the football development scheme had, by
June 2001, run a number of successful Saturday training sessions which
attracted between fifteen and twenty young people each week and also led to
the identification of two local people who could be trained as coaches to

continue the project. Similarly, the MOBYS has been delivered at three locations in the area by staff from the Coventry Sports Foundation, attracting over 100 young people.

Not all partnerships give sports outcomes such prominence. In contrast to the New Deal partnership bid, the recent SRB 5 Challenge Fund bid titled 'Valuing young people', while clearly recognising the important role that sport and leisure could play in promoting positive lifestyles for young people who may otherwise be tempted into crime, could be seen as granting sports development a merely supporting role. The seven-year, £19.56 million project was aimed at socially excluded young people aged between 14 and 24 and involved a wide range of partners, including the health authority, the careers service, police, further education colleges and a number of voluntary bodies. The aims of the project are to promote social inclusion and active citizenship among young people and develop their social and work-related skills and capabilities. Sport features among the list of practical steps, but only as a 'diversionary opportunity' and as a chance for coaches and sports leaders to provide information on employment and training opportunities.

In conclusion, the City of Coventry sports development section has undergone a substantial reorientation of its work over the last two to three years and, in many ways, typifies the extent to which the social agenda of the Labour government has permeated local government. Fortunately for Coventry, the gap between its policy and administrative practices in the mid-1990s and the current Labour priorities was not wide. The existing neighbourhood-based administrative structure, the long-standing priority given to economic regeneration and the commitment to social policy all made the transition relatively smooth. For the sports development section, the criteria by which it had to justify its projects and programmes altered significantly with sports-specific outcomes alone rarely being sufficient. However, the extent to which day-to-day sports development practice has changed should not be exaggerated. In the example of the sports development section's involvement in the New Deal for Communities partnership, there were clear sports-specific outcomes illustrated by the pathways for those participating in the football and basketball projects. To a large extent, the increased emphasis on cross-cutting issues simply requires sports development teams to make more explicit the contribution that many of their existing projects already make to a wide range of social objectives. However, this should not disguise the fact that there has been a loss of discretion in deciding which projects to undertake, as it would now be much more difficult to embark on a project which had few demonstrable social benefits but marked sports development benefits, thus making support for some sports and sport in some areas of the city less likely. Furthermore it is also more difficult to justify projects where the sole, or primary, criterion is sporting deprivation/disadvantage: sporting deprivation must be supported by, or subsumed within, an analysis of broadly defined social deprivation.

Perhaps because of the longer-established orientation towards social- and area-based issues, Coventry appears to work closely with its regional Sport England office and sees it, not as a constraint, but more positively as a valuable resource. The regional office is seen as providing support and expertise, particularly regarding access to new National Lottery funding initiatives such as the New Opportunities Fund. The relationship is clearly helped by the organisation of regular lottery briefing meetings by the regional office. In general, rather than seeing the regional office as imposing its objectives on the authority, the sports development team see the region as offering opportunities to attract funding and broaden its range of activities.

The sports development section has also managed the reorientation of its activities without losing the co-operation of local clubs. With a few exceptions, the clubs remain important partners in the delivery of sports development objectives. The close relationship has been achieved in part through the provision of valued services by the council and in part through the incentive of rate relief. While the relationship may quite properly be seen as mutually beneficial, there were one or two clubs that considered that they were in a dependent relationship which gave them little scope for negotiating with the council over objectives. However, given the financial and managerial fragility of some of the clubs in the city, the alternative to Council patronage is probably closure. Within the sports development section, there is a strong concern that the club infrastructure is weak and that too many clubs operate on a very thin resource base and consequently see the sports development section, in particular, and the Council, in general, as providing professional support services that help to secure club viability. With this concern in mind, the city made a bid to Sport England for funding for a post of Sports Club Development Officer, but was unsuccessful.

Overall, while the reorientation of sports development activity was not without its difficulties, there is a strong perception within the sports development section that the dominance of cross-cutting issues provides an important opportunity to make a stronger case for sports development within the Council given the capacity of the service to contribute across a range of objectives. However, there is a concern that that contribution is not as readily acknowledged as it might be. Consequently, the current emphasis is on ensuring not only that sports development is integrated into cross-cutting partnerships, but also that the section systematically collects evidence which can demonstrate its contribution.

Conclusion

In the introduction to this chapter, attention was drawn to the change in fortunes experienced by local government in relation to sports development since 1995, having been brought in from the margins of policy to be given a central role in delivering central government policy of sport for all. Equally important as the reversal in the fortunes of local government was the long overdue recognition of the role that sports development officers have to play in fulfilling the government's ambitions. With recognition has also come additional funding, albeit funds that had to be bid for and often bid for in fulfilment of the funding agency's objectives rather than those of the local authority. The combination of more generous funding and political recognition in the form of the DCMS strategy offered the prospect of a period of service consolidation and expansion for sports development. While the four case studies provide many examples of successful service development and innovation, they also raise a number of issues regarding the direction of sports development.

First, and most important, is the emerging tension between sports-related objectives and those which are directed towards contributing to the cross-cutting issues identified by the government. Herefordshire and Coventry had wholeheartedly embraced the social and economic agenda even if, as in the case of Coventry, it had meant a fairly rapid reorientation. In both authorities it was argued that not only did sports development have an obligation to support the achievement of cross-cutting objectives, but that the enthusiastic involvement in projects associated with health improvement, community development and lifelong learning produced substantial benefits for sports development particularly because of the access that it afforded to additional funding. Moreover, it was argued that it was politically important to demonstrate the value of sport to colleagues in services such as education, welfare and health who were often ignorant or deeply sceptical of the capacity of sport to deliver benefits beyond those narrowly focused on sports-specific outcomes.

The vulnerability of sports development within local government should not be underestimated. It still remains a precariously balanced service, tolerated rather than deeply embedded within the range of obligations of local government, and consequently a strategy of enthusiastic involvement in the cross-cutting agenda might be a wise move. Kent and Derbyshire retained an approach to sports development which gave priority to the identification of sporting deprivation/need and to sports-specific outcomes, notwithstanding the fact that both sports development units had projects in place which clearly contributed to broader social goals. The emphasis on projects concerned with disability sport in Kent and young people in Derbyshire would not have been out of place in a social-inclusion and capacity-building strategy. Furthermore, SDOs in both Kent and Derbyshire also argued that in order for sport to make a contribution to cross-cutting issues there needed to be a well-established sports development infrastructure in place. The consequences of sports development being incorporated into a social policy agenda and then failing to produce the expected outcomes runs the risk of significantly harming the long-term position of sports development at the local government level. However, SDOs in both Kent and Derbyshire were acutely aware of the risk of being perceived as ignoring or rejecting the priority given to cross-cutting issues and acknowledged that a closer accommodation was inevitable given that the political momentum behind the government's agenda was so strong. While the embrace of cross-cutting issues might be both inevitable and produce tangible longer-term benefits for sports development, one highly likely unavoidable cost will be a narrowing of the focus of development activity. The experience from Herefordshire and Derbyshire, in particular, but also that of Coventry, suggests that it is becoming increasingly difficult to be active across all elements of the sports development continuum and that a concentration at the participation and, to a lesser extent, the foundation levels is difficult to avoid. This was best illustrated by the general decline in the number of local authority-funded sports-specific development posts. While many local authorities continue to host sports-specific SDOs, they were usually employed and funded through the national governing bodies. Kent was the only authority to retain an explicit emphasis at the performance and excellence level, although whether it can be sustained over the longer term is open to question.

In the discussion of the positioning of sports development in relation to the government's cross-cutting agenda, one important qualification regarding the selection of case studies must be borne in mind. One notable respect in which all four authorities differ from most others is in the seniority of the lead officers and their level of political experience. All four lead officers were unusual in sports development units in being relatively senior and thus having access both to other senior officers within their respective authorities and, possibly more importantly, to elected members. Furthermore, all four were active in the wider policy community for sports development, such as members of their regional sports board or Sport England working groups, and, as such, possessed political skills and had the opportunity to deploy them. In this respect they were in a better position than most officers responsible for sports development.

One of the defining characteristics of sports development over the last five years has been the almost irresistible expectation that development activity should be based on a network of partnerships, with the sports development unit acting as the orchestrator and manager of the pattern of relationships. All four authorities showed the substantial benefits that follow from successful partnerships, and particularly the capacity of partnerships to enable local authorities to leverage additional resources for their area. Herefordshire's network of trusts, some of which were financially self-sufficient, showed vividly how opportunities for sports participation could be enhanced even in areas that suffer the double handicap of low income and low population density. Coventry, where all facilities are now in the hands of trusts, showed how an authority can use its limited resources to generate additional sports resources and still retain a focus on participation objectives. Clearly, well-managed trusts and partnerships focused on sport are capable of providing substantial additional opportunities, and also adding to the social capital of a community, thus contributing to the achievement of broader social policy goals.

However, partnerships were not without their problems, the most significant of which was the cost of management. Trusts generally impose the lowest management costs on the local authority – at least, once the initial design and construction has been concluded – but continuing partnerships need careful, and often intensive, nurturing. The Derbyshire and Peak Park Sport and Recreation Forum, one of the more complex partnerships, demonstrated the energy needed to sustain the initial momentum and to keep partners for whom sport is a secondary concern, such as the local education authorities, committed to the partnership objectives. A further problem, again illustrated by Derbyshire's experience, was the management of overlapping partnerships, particularly when overlap involved not just geography but also policy objectives and primary sponsors. While it might be argued that the adoption of sports objectives by the Meden Valley Partnership, part of the Coalfields Alliance, provided additional resources for the partners in the Derbyshire forum, it is more likely that the overlap will confuse and dissipate scarce sports development expertise, especially that of senior staff.

In three out of the four case studies, the role of Sport England has been controversial. Sports development staff in Derbyshire, Kent and Herefordshire argued that the balance between a supportive and facilitative role, on the one hand, and an overly regulatory and interfering role, on the other, often swung too far towards the latter end of the spectrum. However, caution should be exercised in generalising from a small sample of admittedly atypical local authorities. Coventry clearly perceived no such tension and referred to the relationship with Sport England as both positive and supportive. A possible explanation for the tensions felt by the other local authorities is that Sport England is more used to dealing with authorities that have small and junior sports development teams and which probably rely more heavily on Sport England for advice and guidance than do those authorities with larger and more experienced teams. There is evidence that in recent years, following the long period of neglect by successive Conservative governments, at least until that led by John Major, Sport England found it difficult to define its role, especially in relation to local authorities. The election of the Labour government and the central role of Sport England in the distribution of National Lottery funding has given the organisation a clearer policy focus and a responsibility for the effective use of a substantial amount of quasi-public (National Lottery) finance, and consequently resulted in a more assertive and interventionist stance towards local authorities after a long period of relative quiescence. However, just at a time when it appeared that Sport England was defining its role more clearly, even if this was not to the liking of all its local authority partners, the organisation entered another period of uncertainty prompted by the appointment of a new Minister for Sport, the third in four years, and the premature departure of Derek Casey, the vastly experienced chief executive officer. As a result, local authority sports development sections enter a further period of uncertainty regarding the role and style of their most significant partner.

Overall, the case studies paint a picture of energetic service development and innovation and suggest that sports development is capable of adapting very successfully to the much more dynamic, and indeed turbulent, policy environment established in the late 1990s. However, it is likely that the capacity to manage effectively will be further tested as there are a number of changes in the organisational and policy environment of sports development already under way or on the horizon. The impact of local authority and regional cultural strategies is only just beginning to filter through to the day-to-day work of sports development. The regional cultural consortiums and the regional assemblies are still in their infancy and have yet to exert their full impact on sports services. More generally, the potential implications of the government's ambitions for a much more prominent role for regional institutions focused on strengthened regional government offices are only slowly being acknowledged at local government level. These plans will provide further tests of the adaptability of sports development and will be explored more fully in chapter 7.

6 Sports development and four national governing bodies of sport

Introduction

Many governing bodies of sport were established as voluntary organisations in the nineteenth century in order to regulate and administer their sport. They were primarily concerned with drawing up the rules of their sport, organising domestic competitions and selecting national teams to play against other countries. As sport has developed, the role and remit of governing bodies has changed. Some are now concerned with managing major facilities and championships, and all have become aware of the need to develop their sport from grass roots to international level. Whereas in the early days government policy had minimal influence on governing body activity, in the twenty-first century there are few governing bodies that can afford to ignore it. The government now sees sport as part of culture, and the performance of national teams in international competitions as a matter of national pride. Public funding is available to governing bodies to help them run and develop their sport, but it comes with strings attached.

The government has little direct relationship with governing bodies (the Football Task Force was an exception) but works through the Sports Councils who have the unenviable task of adjudicating funding levels among the demands of a wide range of sports. The basis of funding has, over the last ten years or so, come closer to a rational model of forward planning typically based on four-year development plans that used the sports development continuum as a framework. When the National Lottery was introduced in 1996, some governing bodies received a substantial financial boost through World Class Performance funding, but this was accompanied by performance targets and demands for a step change in their approach to performance planning. Since the late 1990s there has been an emphasis on improved corporate governance and financial management as governing bodies have been encouraged to modernise. In addition, governing bodies are required to have equal opportunities and child protection policies in place, and demonstrate that they are implementing them.

It is not surprising that, given the voluntary tradition and ethos of autonomy that existed in governing bodies, there is something of an uneasy and ambivalent relationship between some governing bodies and the Sports Councils. Governing bodies, no less than local authorities, resent being told what to do by the Sports Councils and feel that they know what is best for their sports.

In *A Sporting Future For All* the government was unequivocal about the importance of governing bodies to the achievement of sporting success for Britain, and particularly the key role to be played by coaches. The government also recognised the pressures under which the governing bodies operated, especially those of the less commercial sports, and consequently offered a 'modernising partnership' according to which

> The public sector will continue to support sport as it has done in the past – and give sports greater say over how these funds are spent – but on two conditions: that commercially successful sports also contribute to the same pot and invest in grassroots facilities; and that all governing bodies agree to work to a number of clear and agreed targets for the development of their sport.
>
> (DCMS 2000a: 19)

For the commercial sports the expectation was that they would contribute a proportion, between 5 and 10 per cent, of their income from broadcasting to the development of grassroots sport, for example, in school and club facilities and in coaching development. For all governing bodies the requirement was modernisation and professionalisation. In particular, the government would only devolve greater responsibility for the use of public funds if 'governing bodies have a clear strategy for participation and excellence; and commit themselves to putting fairness and social inclusion at the heart of everything they do' (DCMS 2000a: 20).

The incentive of greater control over public funds depended on the adopion of a more professional approach to management and a clear commitment to the government's social policy objectives. More specifically governing bodies would be expected to meet the following targets:

- developing sport in schools and the community, especially in areas of deprivation;
- providing appropriately trained coaches to support teachers in primary and secondary schools;
- improving the opportunities for ethnic minorities, people with disabilities and for girls and women to participate, lead, coach and officiate;
- having strong talent development plans to enable those with the wish and ability to reach the top levels of competition to do so; and
- having robust management, planning and monitoring of all their activities.

> (*ibid.*: 20)

In *The Government's Plan for Sport* published in 2001, the expectations that governing bodies would contribute to the equity and inclusion agenda were re-emphasised:

> From April 2001, Sport England will make the development and promotion of equity and inclusion action plans a prerequisite for the delegation of powers and funding to NGBs [and] ... a requirement to monitor and evaluate impact on inclusion and equity must be built in to all funded projects,
>
> (DCMS 2001: 27)

The section on governing bodies and World Class Performance in *The Government's Plan for Sport* addresses some of the sources of tension between governing bodies and the Sports Councils. It deals with grass roots investment and schools sports associations, devolved powers, and World Class and the United Kingdom Sports Institute. However, compared with the earlier sections of the document that dealt with sport in schools and sport in the community, the section on governing bodies is very thin. It comprises only three pages of somewhat disjointed ideas, whereas the schools section, six pages, and the local authorities section, eleven pages, are far more comprehensive and coherent (DCMS 2001).

The government has three objectives for governing bodies and their clubs: the first is that they should take greater account of the social priority of social inclusion; second, that they should seek to improve the quality of their management and use the tools of modern business practices, such as strategic planning, target-setting and monitoring and evaluation, especially when planning the identification and development of talented young people; and third, that the quality of coaching should be improved. Fulfilling the first of these objectives will require governing bodies, but particularly clubs, to work much more closely with local authorities and with schools in order to ensure that ethnic minorities, people with disabilities, women and other under-represented groups are made more welcome. The second objective will require, on the one hand, a much more rigorous and systematic approach to talent identification and development, and, on the other, a more professional management of resources and the consideration of mergers to form multi-sport clubs similar to those found in mainland Europe.

Engineering greater social inclusion and more systematic talent identification and development are not necessarily incompatible, but there is a tension between the two objectives. Many sports are experimenting with, or seeking to develop, talent identification systems which should allow them to replace the standard and much more haphazard 'percolation' principle, according to which wide participation was encouraged on the assumption that the wider the pool of players the greater the chances of an adequate core of talented players being identified. Wide participation is not a prerequisite if an effective talent identification system is in place. Indeed, the most ambitious talent identification systems aim to identify potential and therefore do not depend on young people already playing the sport.

The third objective is closely linked to the second for, as the government notes, 'Talent identification and coaching development go hand in hand with club development, and these are the keys to future sporting success ... The Government recognises that coaching is central to the development of sport at every level' (DCMS 2001: 29, 31). Among the government's proposals regarding coaching was the establishment of a Coaching Task Force to undertake a review of coach education and consider the feasibility of the creation of 3,000 full-time paid coaches by 2005, the introduction of a licensing system for coaches and a review of the future role of the Sports Coach UK (formerly the National Coaching Foundation).

The need to ensure that coaching resources were adequate to meet the greater emphasis on elite sports success had already been identified in the late 1990s by UK Sport, which initiated a review of coaching along with the other Sports Councils, the British Olympic Association, the National Coaching Foundation and the National Training Organisation for Sport, Recreation and Allied Occupations. The strategy that resulted from the review anticipated many of the suggestions in the DCMS documents. The core element of the strategy, *The UK Vision for Coaching*, was the desire for professional status for coaching. 'By 2012 the practice of coaching in the UK will be elevated to a profession acknowledged as central to the development of sport and the fulfilment of individual potential' (UK Sport 1999: 5). Professional status will provide coaching with a 'common code of ethics and conduct'. The strategy also suggested a licensing system and more systematic and rigorous training and professional development programme benchmarked against national standards.

The extensive consultation exercise and subsequent publication of *The UK Vision for Sport* made a limited impression on the preparation of *A Sporting Future for All* and *The Government's Plan for Sport*, but the latter two documents raised more questions about the future organisation of coaching than they answered. On the one hand, the general concern expressed in *The UK Vision for Sport* for better training and professional development of coaches was endorsed; on the other hand, *The Government's Plan for Sport* was clearly equivocal about the future role of Sports Coach UK. Part of the government's concern is in relation to the development and support for high performance coaches and, particularly, the appropriate relationship between Sports Coach UK and the network of UK Sports Institute regional centres. Given that over 70 per cent of Sports Coach UK income comes from Sport England and UK Sport, there must be some concern that there will be a risk of duplication of funding once the UKSI centres are operational. However, while there is clearly some uncertainty about the future role of Sports Coach UK, there is little doubt that the government has acknowledged the central importance of coaching to the achievement of its aspirations for UK international sporting success. As a result of the emphasis on high-quality coaching, there is increased pressure on national governing bodies to have in place robust arrangements for the development and delivery of high-quality coaching within their individual sports.

For many years governments had displayed a surprising level of deference towards governing bodies of sport, often being prepared to distribute public money with little control over how it was spent. While a level of residual deference still remains, the Sports Councils are generally more confident in setting expectations and conditions for the use of grant aid.

The case studies that follow explore the ways that the governing bodies of four different sports – rowing, rugby union, hockey and tennis – have approached sports development work over the last thirty years. In particular, they trace the different priorities and initiatives the governing bodies have taken, and the factors that have influenced them. The case studies are based on a review of governing body documents, some of which are in the public domain and some of which are not, and a series of interviews with key development personnel as a way of achieving an insider perspective on their sports development and policy making. Because of the breadth of sports development activity, the cases are in part selective in their focus, although how they have responded to equity and inclusion policies is a common theme. Each case draws attention to one or more issues of relevance to current sports development activity. The case of rowing provides an opportunity to examine in some detail the way in which Britain's most consistently successful Olympic sport has addressed the issue of social inclusion. The study of rugby union provides an opportunity to examine the work of one of the pioneers of youth sports development among governing bodies, and to explore the impact of the emergence of women's rugby on the Rugby Football Union and the extent to which development activities, especially of the RFU, were co-ordinated with and supportive of those of the women's game. The case study of rugby provides an interesting contrast with hockey where the men's and women's governing bodies recently merged to form the English Hockey Association. The case study of hockey examines the construction of the sport's elite development strategy, and also focuses on the extent to which governing bodies are supportive of community-based initiatives such as Active Sports. Finally, the case of tennis complements that of hockey insofar as it also focuses on the strategy adopted by the governing body to secure the production of high performance achievement.

Rowing

Introduction

Competitive rowing dates back to the middle ages when rowing was a widespread means of transport on the Thames and other waterways. The Amateur Rowing Association (ARA), founded in 1882, is the governing body for men's and women's rowing in Great Britain and England. It is split into two sections, one that deals with international rowing for Great Britain, and one that deals with the organisation and development of the sport in England. Rowing is arguably Great Britain's most successful Olympic sport. Rowers have featured among the medal winners in every Olympic Games since 1976, and have won gold in every games since 1984. This success comes from a sport which has traditionally had a fairly narrow participation base, with boys' independent schools and the universities providing most of the facilities, coaching and time necessary to nurture talent. The consistency in elite achievement in rowing was one reason for its selection as a case study; the other was the series of initiatives to promote sports equity and widen access to rowing.

Participation

The *Rowing Facilities Strategy* estimates the number of committed rowers, coaches, officials and supporters at 30,000 (ARA 1999b). About half of these are registered members of the ARA, and of these members, two-thirds are male and one-third are under 18. Membership is rising by 3 to 5 per cent per annum, and development programmes are predicting an increase of young participants of 35 per cent by 2002. Not surprisingly, there is an uneven geographical distribution of members with 44 per cent of the membership based in the Thames region. In 1999 there were 254 open rowing clubs, 105 affiliated schools and 154 affiliated universities and colleges. Approximately 90 per cent of the affiliated schools were in the independent sector. Coaching is a well-established part of the sport and there were 1,132 qualified registered coaches in 1999.

The governing body

The ARA is a medium-size governing body with an annual turnover of £3.1 million and 37 paid staff. Its most recent 'Forward Plan for 2001–2005' gives a good indication of its work and priorities. In moving forwards to 2005 the plan states: 'We need to consolidate and sustain development for the two major new programmes, World Class Performance and Young People, that are the hub of our future development' (ARA 2001: 4). The plan then goes on to identify aims and targets in nine areas: corporate governance, equal opportunities, high performance rowing, young people, coach education and training, club and volunteer support and development, competition, members and participants, and communications. Unlike the RFU's plan, one-third of which was a substantial section on business, the ARA's plan shows a greater emphasis on sports development, with corporate governance and equal opportunities as essential underpinning for the development work.

Evolution of sports development work

Sports development in rowing came from a basis in coaching. The ARA appointed its first national coach in 1965 as a Director of Training, and seven years later brought over Bob Janasek, a well-respected coach from Czechoslovakia, to set up the coach education scheme and take responsibility for men's rowing. Although the import of foreign coaches has recently become a widespread phenomenon in British sport, the ARA were one of the first governing bodies to do this and their action was justified by the results achieved. At the same time as Janasek was working with the national squads, a series of national coaches were based in the regions with a remit to improve standards of performance, and in 1973 Penny Chuter was appointed as the first national coach with responsibility for women's rowing.

Chuter (a former schoolteacher and European silver medallist) went on to become men's chief coach from 1979 to 1982, then Director of Coaching from 1982 to 1986, and Director of International Rowing from 1986 to 1990. She was exceptional in holding senior positions in coaching in Britain at a time when there were very few women in such positions (White *et al.* 1989). It is reasonable to assume that her presence contributed significantly to the substantial development of both rowing in general and women's rowing in particular that occurred in the 1980s.

However, she was not the only influential woman in rowing. During the late 1970s and early 1980s all but two of the single-sex women's clubs amalgamated with men's clubs and women who joined them became the founder members of women's sections within a wide geographical spread of clubs. The ARA's Women's Rowing Commission had representatives from all regions and appointed Rosie Mayglothling as national coach with responsibility for women's rowing in the early 1980s, who provided huge support for the inclusion of women's events in regattas. Henley Women's Regatta was one of Mayglothling's most successful projects, providing a prestige event for overseas competitors as well as opportunities for college and university crews to participate in a mainstream rowing event.

The development of women's rowing in the 1980s and 1990s is illustrated by changes in participation in the annual Head of the River race. In 1980 only 25 women's crews participated, but by 1988 there were 128, and by 1996 there were 252. Much of the interest in women's rowing was stimulated by university clubs opening their doors to women, so giving women at university a chance to try a new sport. Several of the Oxford and Cambridge colleges became co-educational at this time and many clubs that were formerly sex segregated became mixed. Women's rowing benefited from the general move towards co-education and integration and it seems the women leaders of rowing supported that approach.

The ARA depended on Sports Council funding more than sports such as tennis and rugby union and so introduced individual registration in 1987. This was encouraged by the Sports Council as a way for the governing body to connect more directly with its membership and to raise revenue.

Rosemary Napp, who had previously worked for canoeing, was appointed to the ARA to manage this process, and she became, and remains, another senior woman administrator and influential figure in the ARA.

In the mid-nineties the Sports Council introduced the system of prioritising certain sports for funding, based on whether or not they achieved international success and/or provided participation opportunities for young people (see chapter 3). Rowing was categorised as a sport which did well internationally, but which did not have significant junior participation. The Sports Council indicated its intention to continue to invest in the performance and excellence aspects of rowing and advised rowing that it needed to develop its young people's programmes. However, because of the relatively small participation base among young people, and the fact that very few state schools offered rowing as a sport inside or outside the curriculum, rowing did not feature in the National Junior Sports Programme (NJSP). Though not included in the NJSP, the ARA developed its own National Junior Rowing Programme (NJRP) modelled on the NJSP and developed a 'Young People and Coaching Business Plan' in 1997 based on research conducted by Southampton University and funded by Sport England. Again, coaching was the cornerstone of sports development in rowing.

The NJRP's vision statement is interesting as it puts 'equal opportunity for young people from whatever background to experience the sport of rowing' as its first objective (ARA 2001). This is followed by an objective about the development of skills and enjoyment in club, school and community environments, with a third objective about the provision of facilities, equipment and coaching. Sports equity policies were in place by this time, and the ARA clearly embraced them in the thinking and philosophy of the NJRP.

One key element of the NJRP is Project Oarsome, an initiative to identify a limited number of clubs with the desire and capacity to link with state schools and provide participation and coaching opportunities for their pupils. There are four stages to the programme: first, roving ambassadors from the club visit year 7 classes in identified local schools; second, coaches from the club introduce dry rowing to those youngsters who are interested; third, there is an assessment of how many children can make the transition to wet rowing based on water safety considerations and club capacity; and finally, youngsters are introduced to wet rowing in the club environment. Coaching and skills tests are an important part of the process. Starting with a pilot of three clubs in 1999, there were 18 clubs in the programme by September 2000. Thirty-five state schools new to rowing had set up indoor rowing clubs, giving up to 5,000 11 year olds the chance to try the sport (*Regatta* 2000). The project is financed from a mix of sources, with 65 per cent coming from the National Lottery Sports Fund, and the clubs and Henley Stewards contributing the remaining 25 per cent and 10 per cent of costs respectively. Clubs apply to the ARA's Facilities Panel to join Project Oarsome and decision-making at this level is effectively devolved from Sport

England to the ARA. Sport England puts some parameters on decision-making by insisting that the selection of clubs is in line with the recommendations of the Facilities Strategy. In year 1 the clubs were selected on the basis of capacity to deliver, but in the second year Sport England encouraged the ARA to favour clubs located in areas of deprivation in line with social exclusion policy.

Sports equity

Reference has already been made to the development of women's rowing in the 1980s and 1990s, the sports equity principles underpinning the NJRP and their mainstreaming through the delivery of Project Oarsome. The ARA have recognised the need to open up their sport to people from different backgrounds and have responded more positively than many governing bodies to the Sports Council's encouragement to do so. It accessed special funding from the English Sports Council in the late 1990s and some of the resulting projects are cited as good practice in Sport England's *Equity Guidelines for Governing Bodies* (Sport England 2000b). One of these is Oxford Adaptive Rowing (OAR) set up by students at both Oxford universities to promote rowing for people with physical and learning difficulties and teach them to row, coach and reach a high level of proficiency. The ARA published a report on this initiative (ARA 1998) to act as a template for other groups wishing to promote rowing for the disabled. This report analyses the successes and failures of past efforts to set up rowing for the disabled and explains how OAR was established.

Other equity projects have been designed to recruit and train more women umpires and coaches. A project led by the West Midlands and WAGs Umpires Commission made the recruitment of women a major objective (ARA 1999a). As part of the first stage of the programme a questionnaire was distributed to all women members of the ARA in the region to establish why more women did not become umpires. Analysis of the returns caused the Commission to conclude 'that by adopting changes in our perceptions of umpires and the way in which we promote our activity we could increase the participation of women in this area' (*ibid.*: 5) and went on to identify five changes it would make in its approach. These included presenting a change of image by recruiting younger women and encouraging regatta organisers to accommodate the desire of some women to compete as well as umpire. The methods used in the project are interesting as they demonstrate the preparedness of the Commission to change the sport to accommodate women, rather than expecting women to change to fit into the sport.

The overall approach of the ARA is to mainstream equity into all its programmes. The measures being taken through schemes such as Project Oarsome should make rowing more accessible, particularly as equity is part of the club accreditation scheme and is included in all monitoring reports.

The association also encourages proactive initiatives such as the OAR and Umpires Recruitment programmes cited above. Other proactive measures include talent identification camps for women and courses for international women rowers to recruit them into coaching, where there is currently a dearth of women at the higher levels.

While there is evidence that the ARA has taken sports equity seriously, it is more difficult to assess how successful they have been in making rowing more inclusive. There is no doubt that as regards gender equality, significant strides have been made to open up the sport to women both as participants and competitors, though in common with most sports there are few women coaches at top level. The ARA is unusual among mixed governing bodies in having a number of strong women leaders, such as Penny Chuter, Rosemary Napp and Rosie Mayglothling, who have influenced its work over the past twenty years. Moreover, its chairman, Di Ellis, is a highly respected leader, not only of the ARA but also more widely in the sports world. The equity section of the ARA's 2001–2005 Forward Plan states that they have no information about participation levels by ethnic minority groups or disabled athletes and propose collecting such information in future through membership forms. Despite the commitment to sports equity and some innovative projects, anecdotal evidence suggests that so far only limited progress has been made in opening up rowing to people with disabilities, and little progress in attracting people from black and ethnic minorities to the sport.

The impact of the National Lottery

When National Lottery money became available for sport in 1996, the priorities were support to international performers and development of community facilities. The Sports Council allocated World Class Performance funding to selected sports on the basis of the likelihood of them winning medals for Britain. With its reputation for international success, rowing was an obvious choice for Sports Council investment. Over £9 million was invested between 1997 and 2000 in high-quality coaches, scientists, and administrative and medical staff. Subsistence grants to individual athletes allowing them to focus full time on their preparation were also introduced. The investment paid off handsomely, with Olympic gold medals for the Men's Eight and Coxless Four, and a first-ever medal for women, a silver in the Quadruple Sculls in the Sydney Olympics. As the ARA Forward Plan acknowledges, 'The sport has received unprecedented coverage and exposure, particularly through the achievements of 5 times gold medal winner, Steve Redgrave, and 3 times gold medal winner Matthew Pinsent' (ARA 2001: 2). Rowing clubs also benefited from the capital development programme with £17.8 million of lottery money going to 62 projects from the inception of the National Lottery to July 2001.

Project Oarsome is also financed by the National Lottery, and although it is early days for this programme, it should broaden the recruitment base and provide pathways to excellence for talented rowers. The existence of this programme caters for young people's development in a similar way to that provided to other sports through the Active Sports programme. Active Sports is county based and rowing is not seeking inclusion in the programme as Project Oarsome is custom-designed for rowing and based around clubs with water to row on. However, the ARA will buy into 'partnership services' provided by Active Sports. Similarly, the Active Schools programme has little to offer rowing, though partnerships are being formed with some specialist sports colleges.

Summary and conclusions

Rowing is Britain's most successful Olympic sport because the ARA has always concentrated on international success and placed a strong emphasis on coaching. The early appointment of coaches with responsibility for coach education and training, and the development of sports science support and doping control, put rowing ahead of other British sports. The key has been the ARA's support to a limited number of top-level rowers who have tended to come through a relatively small number of independent schools, universities and clubs.

Project Oarsome is a good example of an innovatory sports development initiative geared to the unique characteristics of the sport while drawing on generic sports development ideas and practice. The introduction of this programme has balanced the ARA's emphasis on excellence, though it could be argued that performance development pathways are not yet in place to link the junior and excellence programmes. The ARA's new Forward Plan focuses more on the 15–18 age group through club development and a review of competitive structures, and this should help bridge the gap.

It seems that it has been generally beneficial to the development of women's rowing to be governed by a mixed NGB. Although rowing is still male dominated, the ARA has paid attention to women's rowing over the last twenty years and the presence of women in senior positions in the organisation has had a significant influence.

Rowing has been relatively unaffected by wider sport policy until recently, although it has always had good relationships with the Sports Council. It received a relatively high level of funding from the Sports Council prior to the introduction of the National Lottery and welcomed the focus on excellence and young people as expressed in *Sport: Raising the Game* (ARA 2001: 2). It has shown greater commitment than most other NGBs to the principle of sports equity, developing some innovatory projects, and is now ready to take what opportunities exist to develop rowing in deprived areas and contribute to the regeneration agenda.

Rugby union

Introduction

Rugby football originated at Rugby school in the first half of the nineteenth century. The Rugby Football Union (RFU) was founded in 1871, and the Rugby League was established in 1895 when a number of clubs in the north of England broke away from the RFU in a conflict over amateurism. The evolution of the different forms of the game, and the historical class–cultural differences between the codes, have kept the two games distinct. Rugby has traditionally been seen as a male preserve (Dunning and Sheard 1979), though women have played the game since the late 1970s and the Rugby Football Union for Women was established in 1983. This chapter is concerned with sports development in men's and women's rugby union in England. Rugby union was chosen as a case study because of its traditional base in boys' public schools, the fact that the women's game developed much later than the men's game and has retained a separate governing body, and the evidence which suggests that the RFU was one of the first governing bodies in Britain seriously to address youth development and establish a network of Youth Development Officers.

Participation

The RFU have recently adopted a new Strategic Plan for 2001–2007/8 (RFU 2001). It contains an analysis of the market places within which it operates. Comparative data from the top ten rugby playing nations in the world show England as the largest rugby playing nation by a considerable margin (*ibid.*: 14–44). Participants are estimated at 634,000, accounting for 37 per cent of participants in the top ten countries (South Africa has 21 per cent and France 13 per cent, with all other countries having less than 10 per cent). Fifty-eight per cent of these participants fall in the junior/mini category, well above that of other major countries. England also has by far the largest number of coaches among the top ten countries with 47 per cent, though it has fewer referees per player than all other countries except Scotland. Although there are more affiliated clubs and schools in England than any other country, the RFU estimate an overall decline of 15 per cent in participant numbers over the last five years. Approximately 3,000 secondary schools, 9,000 primary/junior schools, and all the universities in England are affiliated to the RFU.

The Rugby Football Union for Women (RFUW), which governs the game for women in England, has 193 affiliated clubs, 5,130 registered players, a further estimated 1,300 unregistered players, 1,400 juniors and 1,280 coaches (RFUW 2000). Student rugby comprises a significant part of the women's game and in 1995 this was estimated at 40 per cent (RFUW 1995). There has been substantial growth in the junior game in the last five years, and since a ruling in 1996 to stop under-16s competing in senior games, there has been an increase in junior clubs to around 100 (RFUW 2000).

Excellence

Since the introduction of international rugby for women, three world championships have been held. England came second in 1991, first in 1994 and third in 1998. In comparison, the England men were also second in 1991, but came fourth in 1995 and lost in the quarter finals in 1999. Based on analysis of the Rugby World Cup and results of internationals between England and top-rugby playing nations, the RFU's World Class Plan estimates England Men's world ranking as fourth or fifth (RFU 2000).

The governing body

The RFU is a large governing body with 164 paid staff. It owns its own ground and offices at Twickenham and in 1999/2000 reported a pre-tax profit of £14.5 million (RFU 2000). Does it see itself as a business or a sports administration and development agency? The answer is probably 'both'. Its recently published strategy (2001) identifies three distinct activity areas – elite rugby, community rugby and business activities – each having very different characteristics. Reflecting this, the RFU has adopted an overarching mission statement supported by three separate statements, one for each area. The overarching mission statement is: 'To promote and govern rugby union in England through maintaining stable structures for the game that enable its successful development at all levels for the benefit of all its participants', and those for the three component areas are:

> To be world leaders through excellence in every aspect of the elite game; to promote and develop the game within the community so as to encourage optimum participation and enjoyment at every level; to be commercially and financially the strongest Union in the world to provide the investment resource necessary to achieve our aspirations for the game.
>
> (RFU 2001: 5)

The strategic plan has a separate strategy for each of the three areas, each with its own set of objectives. The elite area includes domestic and international competition structures and the bringing together of international and elite club interests, drawing closer to elite rugby league, implementing the World Class Performance Plan, the Club England policies for England teams and the new management structure for England teams. The community area is wide ranging and includes a refocusing of the youth and university development resources, improving competition structures and rationalising regulations to halt the decline in participation, increasing the number of referees, developing the game in rugby league areas, promoting 'casual' forms of rugby and implementing the facilities strategy. The business area has the most substantial strategy and includes negotiation of television rights, development of e-commerce, effective licensing, sponsorship and commercial enterprises, implementation of a marketing plan, development of the Twickenham Stadium and associated traffic infrastructure plan, and securing support for a World Cup bid in 2007.

In contrast to the RFU, the Rugby Football Union for Women is a relatively small governing body with just 10 paid staff. It does not own any facilities and is heavily dependent on the patronage of clubs prepared to share their facilities and coaches and develop women's sections and teams. The RFUW's second four-year development plan, 2000–2004, has the subtitle 'To create a level playing field' (RFUW 2000). Its mission statement is 'to provide opportunities for all girls and women who wish to participate to achieve their full potential in all aspects of the game' (*ibid.*: 3). Taking a player-centred perspective, it is based on a survey conducted in 1999 of all registered members. The plan recognises the significant opportunities that exist with the continued expansion of the game at junior levels and inclusion in Sport England programmes such as World Class and Active Sports. These opportunities will stretch the existing infrastructure and the RFUW realises it has to face this challenge. Being so heavily dependent on the men's game, the development of men's professional rugby also affects the women's game. Clubs are struggling to support women's teams and coaches, who can now expect payment and are less likely to work with women's teams. Considering these challenges, the plan identifies five aims: raising playing standards, success in international competition, development of under-16 rugby, effective management and raising the profile of the game. The plan projects an annual expenditure of between £350,000 and £450,000 per annum.

The relationship between the men's and women's game and how they have affected sports development

With the very limited resources available to the RFUW, the focus of the organisation during the 1980s was to formalise competitive structures in terms of leagues and establish international competition. A five-year development plan was produced by the then voluntary 'Coaching and Development Officer' in 1988 and starter packs were given to students leaving university to help them set up women's sides. It took five years for any funding for the women's governing body to be forthcoming from the Sports Council, partly because the Council were reluctant to recognise and fund new governing bodies where the sport already had an established governing body. It would have preferred there to be one governing body for men's and women's rugby. Meanwhile the development of women's rugby was pushed forward by a group of young women graduates who had played rugby at university and wanted to continue playing when they left. Several were located in London and they persuaded some established men's clubs, such as Richmond, Wasps and Saracens, to set up women's teams and provide facilities and coaching. Four women members from Richmond ran the first Women's World Cup in 1991 with some funding from the Welsh Sports Council. Significant debts were incurred, largely due to the Russian team turning up without any money, and the RFU was magnanimous enough to help pay some of these off. However, during the early development of the women's game there was no suggestion from either side that women's rugby should come under the auspices of the RFU. The leaders of women's rugby at the time informed the RFU about their activities, but wanted to make their own decisions (Isherwood 2001, personal interview). There was also the belief that the women were more likely to be able to access public funding if they were separate from the RFU. This proved to be the case when the Sports Council agreed to fund the RFUW's development plan in 1995 and a full-time national Development Officer was appointed. The Sports Council's decision to fund the RFUW at this time was probably influenced by the 1993 Policy on Women and Sport (see chapter 3) that recognised the legitimacy of separate development of women's governing bodies in some sports.

The position of the RFU was, and is, to confine its responsibilities to the men's game, though the RFUW were granted associate membership of the RFU in 1994. It is interesting that in the RFU's latest strategic plan, the women's game barely gets a mention whereas relationships with Rugby League (which is also a separate game with its own governing body) gets several mentions. In contrast, the RFUW's latest plan devotes a whole section in its Introduction to 'Relationship with the RFU' (RFUW 2000: 6). This section charts growing support from the RFU from junior development through to joint projects on child protection, the Active Sports framework and the National Facilities Strategy. The latter three initiatives have all had support from Sport England who, recognising the potential of the women's game and the vast differential in resources and capacity between the men's and women's governing bodies, have encouraged closer working relationships. The RFUW's plan states that 'Sport England ... accepts that amalgamation of the two bodies is not a realistic prospect at the current time' (*ibid.*: 7), which rather suggests a feeling that a forced amalgamation in which they will lose their independence and autonomy is still on the agenda.

At club level the rationale for some traditional rugby clubs including the women's game is debatable. Was it an enlightened policy based on a commitment to sports equity, was it a way of involving girlfriends and wives in the club to help retain male membership, or did they think the presence of women would have a civilising effect on club culture?

The evolution of youth development work in rugby

At the same time as the RFUW was becoming established, the RFU had the capacity to develop the schools and junior side of the game, and did so. Moreover, although the RFU did not have responsibility for women's and girls' rugby, it included girls in its junior development programmes. This was done with the agreement of the RFUW but was not formalised in any way. It was informally agreed between development personnel from the RFU (who came from an education background) and officers of the RFUW. The informal arrangement demonstrates how individuals can influence and make policy in the absence of a policy position or even in opposition to the officially stated position.

Looking at the evolution of sports development work by the RFU over the last three decades, the approach has been to build from the bottom up by introducing modified versions of the full game to young boys and, to a lesser extent, to girls. Mini rugby, a nine-a-side version of the game, was introduced in the mid-1970s, but the more significant development was the introduction of New Image rugby in 1985. Officers of the RFU drew on New Image from New Zealand and Tag rugby from North America to design an English version of New Image. This non-contact game for young people of all abilities resulted in an unprecedented growth of the sport in primary, junior and middle schools, and an upsurge in interest in rugby among girls. According to Shaw (2001, personal interview), rugby was fighting for survival at school level in the early 1980s. Teachers' industrial action curtailed extra-curricular sport and rugby was competing with other sports that were easier to organise, such as soccer and individual sports. The approach of the RFU in the mid-1980s was for 'Divisional Technical Administrators' to support schools and clubs in offering playing opportunities to young people. Coaching was neither established nor accepted in rugby circles, and the first development officers were not put in place until the latter part of the decade.

The introduction of Youth Development Officers (YDOs) from 1988 was a landmark in rugby sports development. A briefing paper published by the RFU in 1988 provided the rationale and set the blueprint for the development of the YDO network (RFU 1988). This paper identifies a situation where clubs could no longer rely on schools to provide them with young players who had already learned to play rugby. The physical education curriculum was perceived to be at a crossroads with greater emphasis on health-related fitness and the decline of traditional team games. Other sports were competing for young people in the same market place and a 'demographic time bomb' was forecast with changes in the birth rate suggesting a fall of 25–35 per cent of school leavers by the early 1990s (*ibid.*). A pilot scheme was set up with a budget of just £18,000 from the RFU, augmented by funds from a variety of other sources including the Sports Council, local authorities and commercial sponsors. The essence of the YDOs' role was to assist clubs in setting up junior sections and recruiting young people from local schools. Although there was a national blueprint for the network, and a clear definition of the aims and specific tasks of the YDOs, their work was driven by local targets and overseen by a local management group chaired by a voluntary officer from the county association. Some important principles of sport development work were established, especially local delivery to a national blueprint and co-operative working relationships between RFU paid staff and volunteers at county and local level. The RFU entered into a variety of partnership arrangements in order to finance and employ the YDOs. These partnerships included direct employment by local authorities, through 'research posts' at universities and through local trusts. A few worked independently as self-employed 'consultants'. Although these partnerships were formed for practical rather than ideological reasons, they paved the way for effective partnership work in sports development in the future and, where the YDOs were employed by local authorities, they benefited from interaction with other sports development professionals.

By the mid-1990s the county network was well established. Thanks to the work of the YDOs, nearly all clubs that could sustain junior activity were running mini sections catering for the under-13 boys and significant numbers of coaches had been qualified. The need for a change of emphasis was identified (RFU 1995b), particularly directed towards providing performance pathways for the 13–18 age group where there were insufficient development pathways in place. In 1996, two reports were published: the Horner Report from the RFU Working Party on Youth Rugby, and a policy statement from the RFUW on the development of junior rugby for girls (RFU 1996; RFUW 1996). The Horner Report set youth development as a responsibility of all clubs, recommending that all should play to one continuum and player drop-out at 12–13 should be addressed. Clubs were assisted in qualifying coaches to more advanced levels, and performance courses gave boys from non-rugby-playing schools the opportunity to enter the representative structure at under-16 level. It also considered the development of the girls' and women's game, recommending that 'girls are guided into Women's Junior Sections', and that 'clubs should support the RFUW's plans for expansion' (RFU 1996). The RFUW policy was produced in response to the growing popularity of the game for girls, and the lack of performance pathways for girls over 12 when they could no longer play mixed rugby safely. It sought the establishment of junior teams for girls, 'working through a "Partnership for Progress" with the Referees Societies and the RFU' (RFUW 1996: 3).

By the late 1990s, emphasis had moved up another age group in the men's game, and the RFU was providing structured playing and coaching opportunities at universities and other institutions of higher education through the work of part-time Rugby Union Student Liaison Officers (RUSLOs). The RFU is one of the few governing bodies to promote and support sports development in higher education in a systematic way and to see higher education as providing an important step in the player development pathway. Within the women's game, universities have traditionally provided an introduction to rugby for many young women who had little opportunity to play at school.

The success of the RFU's youth development initiative during the 1980s and 1990s can be attributed to three main factors. First, there was clarity of vision and purpose following early recognition of the changes in schools and the physical education curriculum and the challenges the sport was facing in recruiting young people and teaching them the basics of the game. The governing body stepped in where schools were failing, and the clubs rose to the challenge. Secondly, there was sustained and determined leadership over a period of time by professional educators turned sports developers. They applied the principles of sound educational practice to their work. A third reason for the success was the flexibility and innovation with which the initiative was developed and delivered. Sports development roles were defined and then continually developed and changed as the initiative grew, priorities changed, opportunities to form different partnerships were taken, and new management processes and structures were introduced to support the network.

The impact of the National Lottery

Since the inception of the National Lottery Sports Fund to July 2001, rugby clubs have benefited from a £25 million contribution to capital development. Though the awards were accompanied by conditions which required clubs to develop both the junior and women's game, the main beneficiaries have been adult male club players. However, a major boost to women's rugby came in 1998 with the award of £135,000 from the World Class Performance Fund for preparation and participation in the 1998 World Cup. This was followed up with a four-year award, the appointment of a female Performance Director, and plans to extend the programme to include World Class Potential and Start. Women's rugby was able to access public money from Sport England at this stage whereas the men's game was not able to demonstrate financial need; had they been part of the RFU, it is unlikely the award would have been made. After protracted negotiation, the RFU did succeed in obtaining a lottery award of £8 million for World Class Potential and Start in 2001, and by July 2001 the RFUW had received £2.8 million for its World Class Performance, Potential and Start programmes.

The availability of lottery funding for sport also provided new opportunities for rugby through the Active Sports programme. Whereas previously the RFU had developed its programmes with little reference to the Sports Council (indeed the RFU's youth development scheme served as a model that was used by the Sports Council to develop the National Junior Sports Programme), the more prescriptive approach to Active Sports lottery funding required greater compliance from the rugby governing bodies. In an internal RFU paper entitled 'The Evolving Roles of YDO Team Leader and YDO' (RFU 1999a), the need for 'a planning culture' was acknowledged along with the need to 'move to take advantage of the improved strategic environment'. A revision of YDO roles with new job titles and structures was proposed to enable rugby to take full advantage of the funding available from Active Sports. Cognisance was also taken of local authority changes and the impact of Best Value and mention was made of the RFU's commitment to social inclusion.

Sports equity

Gender issues in rugby have already been discussed in the context of the gender relations between the RFU and the RFUW and their personnel. The very different histories of the men's and women's games and the big differences in participation, wealth, human resources, media exposure and capital assets produce a very unbalanced relationship. In other sports where there has been a similar imbalance between a long-established and high-profile men's game and a much smaller women's game, such as cricket and soccer, the men's governing body has assumed responsibility for the women's game. The pursuit of separate development in rugby (but with areas of assistance from the RFU and clubs to the development of the women's game) has allowed the women's game to grow, become established and be controlled and led by women for women.

As regards disability sport, wheelchair rugby, played mainly in sports halls, has developed in a similar way to women's rugby, with its own governing body, the Great Britain Wheelchair Rugby Association, granted associate membership of the RFU at its July 2001 council meeting. New Image is well suited to players with learning, physical and sensory disabilities and the RFU has published 'Guidance for Coaches and Proficiency Awards for Players with Disabilities' developed in conjunction with Leeds Sports Development (RFU 1995b).

In common with most governing bodies, and encouraged by Sport England, the RFU has an Equal Opportunities Policy, and a joint RFU–RFUW Child/Young Player Protection Policy, both published in 1999. In 2001 the RFU was one of the first governing bodies to sign up to the Racial Equality Charter promoted by the Commission for Racial Equality and Sport England, and is now developing an extensive 'social inclusion' programme, including programmes focused on inner cities.

Summary and conclusions

Rugby union has been at the forefront of youth development in sport in England, and the RFU's initiatives have provided a blueprint for other sports. Though not overtly influenced by government policy, its officers were acutely aware of changes in education and sport during the 1980s and 1990s and the challenges these presented to the future of rugby. Their concern was the development of the sport of rugby, not development through sport, though their programmes were underpinned by a strong educational philosophy. Good sports development practice was established through partnership working between schools, local authorities and clubs. The volunteer workforce was developed and mobilised, and sensitive leadership enabled local development within a national framework. Through their network of YDOs with their changing roles and remit, the RFU helped to define sports development, and their bottom-up approach was clearly tied to the idea of progression through the sports development continuum. With the advent of National Lottery funding tied to the New Labour government's policies of development through sport and addressing social exclusion, rugby has been ready to respond. However, the extent to which it succeeds in widening its playing base remains to be seen.

The development of women's rugby alongside the men's game over the last twenty years is interesting as an example of governing bodies deliberately adopting a policy of separate development. Some clubs and the development arm of the RFU have been very supportive to the development of the women's game while respecting the autonomy of the RFUW. Despite the impressive progress, there is still an enormous imbalance in comparison with the men's game and women's rugby development is hampered by lack of human, financial and facility resources. Unless, and until, clubs and the RFU are prepared to share these resources with women, the women's game will remain the poor relation to the men's. Although there has been resistance to amalgamation in the past, it may be that the interests of both games in the future could be better served by an integrated approach where there is a commitment to redress the current imbalance in resources.

Hockey

Introduction

While the origins of hockey are obscure there is agreement that they are both varied and distant. The modern version of the game has its roots, like so many English sports, in the public schools where it emerged as a particularly violent pastime of the country's future leaders. During the nineteenth century, hockey established itself as a winter alternative to cricket, with a similar social profile of middle-class participants who proceeded to codify and establish an organisational structure for the sport. The Hockey Association (HA) was founded in 1886 and the All England Women's Hockey Association (AEWHA) in 1896. Until the late 1970s, the national governing bodies of both men's and women's hockey administered with modest ambitions and were broadly content to sustain a club structure which remained close to the public and grammar school roots of the game, a pattern of domestic competition focused on county and regional championships, and a pattern of international competition based on Home Nation, European, World and Olympic Championships. The success of the men's hockey team at the Seoul Olympic Games, where they won a gold medal, both reflected and gave greater impetus to the reform of coaching and national team development that had been quietly under way for the preceding ten years. The gold medal coincided with the establishment of a successful national league for men and stimulated a further rise in interest in the sport, which led the Hockey Association to comment in 1989 that 'Our international programmes; competitions and leagues; various sponsorships; our coaching and development activities and almost every single facet of the game are at a new high. Nevertheless, there is still much to do and achieve if we are to exploit our success and yet maintain the integrity of the game' (Hockey Association 1989). Hockey has been selected as a case study, in part, because it is a major team game for girls, it has received a high level of lottery investment (£22 million for World Class programmes and £55 million for community capital projects – mainly artificial turf pitches – between 1995 and 2001), and because of the recent merger between the men's and women's associations. However, hockey was also selected because of its involvement in the early phase of the Active Sports programme and because of its ambitions for international success.

Organisation and governance

The English Hockey Association (EHA) was formed in 1997 with the merger of the men's Hockey Association, the All England Women's Hockey Association and the England Mixed Hockey Association. The staffing structure comprises two major sections that reflect the twin priorities of international success and club and youth development, the first led by the Performance Director and the second led by the Development Services Director. The Performance Director is directly responsible for the activities of the men's national coach, the high performance manager and the women's national coach. The responsibilities of the Development Services Director include the ten regional development managers, the youth services development manager and the umpiring development manager. As Figure 6.1 shows these parallel responsibilities intersect most clearly at the regional level. The Performance section is 90 per cent funded by the National Lottery through the World Class Performance programme of Sport England and the Development Services section receives funding directly from Sport England.

The key unit of organisation of the EHA is the club. Clubs affiliate directly to the EHA and they are also normally affiliated to their county organisation, which are in turn affiliated to the regional association. Until recently the county/territory was the focus for competitive play either within county leagues or in inter-county/territory competition.[1] However, the recent move to a structure of national leagues has reduced the significance of county teams and made the club much more significant at the participation and

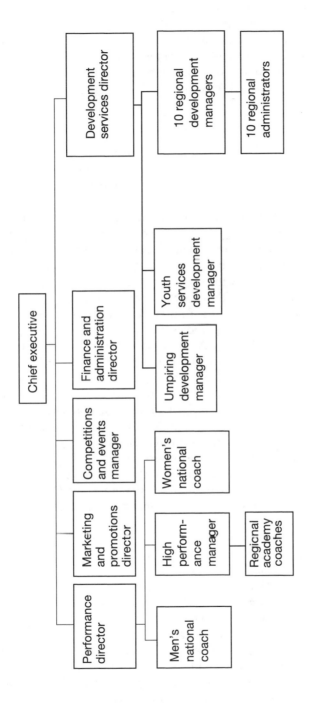

Figure 6.1   The organisation of the English Hockey Association

performance levels. From the 1998/9 season, elite hockey for both men and women comprised a three-division structure (Premier, Division 1 and Division 2) with the intention of improving the quality of top-class hockey and 'to put players under the kind of pressure they will face in international tournaments' (PMP Consultancy 1999: 14). Coaching was also reorganised in the 1990s with qualifications based on examinations and integrated with the structure of National Vocational Awards.

Strategic plan

In 1996 the All England Women's Hockey Association and the Hockey Association launched their joint strategy 'Tackling the Future' (AEWHA/HA 1996). The joint document was important, not just as a strategy for the development of hockey, but also because it provided the basis for co-operation between the soon-to-be-merged associations. The development plan of the strategy had four key objectives: first, to make hockey accessible to all; second, to provide effective leadership and support to develop the game; third, to achieve consistent international success; and fourth, to manage interaction with other sporting agencies and to secure English hockey a proper place within the world of hockey and other sports. One initial important step towards the fulfilment of these objectives was the merger of the separate governing bodies for men's, women's and mixed hockey to form the English Hockey Association. While over the years there had been intermittent discussions about the possibility of merger, it was only the realisation of the high cost of meeting the technical specifications for synthetic pitches for top-class hockey that prompted serious negotiations. The two major associations, the AEWHA and the HA, were encouraged by the Sports Council to consider merger as it would provide the strongest foundation for making bids for National Lottery funding.

'Tackling the Future' reflected the priorities set out in the government's strategy, *Sport: Raising the Game,* and focused on the twin objectives of achievement at international, particularly Commonwealth Games and Olympic, level and the development of youth hockey. The analysis that underpinned the hockey strategy is summarised in Table 6.1.

The strategy identified a number of key areas for development within the sport, including young people, where one aim was 'the recruitment of young people ... and the provision of a comprehensive training and competition infrastructure' (AEWHA/HA 1996: 8). The strategy also aimed to put clubs at the heart of the game, promote the game more effectively and increase the opportunities to play on artificial pitches.

One of the key proposals was the establishment of a network of ten regional hockey academies each of which now has a Regional Academy Coach, a proposal which was also an integral part of the sport's World Class Performance Plan. The regional coaches work with potential international players and, under the direction of the national coaches, men and women

Table 6.1   Hockey: a SWOT analysis

Strengths	*Weaknesses*
• health benefits, • the fact that it can be played competitively well into middle age, • it can be played by boys and girls in mixed teams, • it is played by many of Britain's ethnic minorities, and • its status as an Olympic sport.	• the high cost of equipment, especially for schools, • the lack of a clear vision for the future of the sport, • insufficient international success and media coverage, and • the cost of developing or hiring good quality pitches.
Opportunities	*Threats*
• hockey is a social game, • easy for schools to offer as can be played as a mixed sport as well as single sex, • new funding available, and • large number of professional people involved in the sport.	• increased competition from other sports, • too few clubs with artificial pitches threatens social basis of the sport, • too few clubs cater for young players, • increase in the number of people working at weekends, and • dealing with short-term initiatives from government agencies makes long-term planning difficult.

Source: Adapted from AEWHA/HA (1996)

who are already part of the national squads. The regional academies also have a Regional Development Manager responsible for co-ordinating and supporting the development of the sport (playing, coaching, volunteer activity and umpiring) below elite level and focusing mainly on clubs, schools and counties. The regional structure of the association is also connected to the UK Sports Institute regional network with some of the academies, for example, those at Loughborough University and at Bisham Abbey, being located on the same site as the regional institute. Where the geography of an area or player density suggests that one regional academy might be insufficient, the strategy allowed for the designation of a satellite. In addition, a further eight clubs have been identified as 'Premier Competitive Centres'. Taken together, the academies, satellites and premier centres provide an ambitious and comprehensive coaching and development infrastructure for English hockey. The regional structure was designed to support national level objectives for higher levels of international achievement and, as such, saw the proposal included in *Sport: Raising the Game* for a single centre British Academy of Sport as an important complement to regional performance and excellence activities.

However, the elaboration of a network of development centres with suitably qualified staff needed to be complemented by access to appropriate facilities, which in hockey have been subject to rapid change in recent years. The speed with which top-level hockey moved from grass surfaces to sand-filled synthetic turf and, more recently, to water-based synthetic surfaces has been rapid, but has also imposed severe problems for a sport that has only limited commercial sponsorship potential. At the 1976 Olympic Games, hockey was played on a synthetic surface and by the mid-1980s synthetic surfaces were rapidly becoming the norm for top-class competition due to the perception that the game was both more exciting and faster when played on a synthetic surface and also due to pressure from elite players to play on a 'true' surface. Between 1975 and 1990 over 300 synthetic surfaces were laid, with 255 being laid in the five years between 1985 and 1990. However, by the early 1990s the technology had moved on again with water-based surfaces emerging as the new elite level standard. The establishment of water-based surfaces as the standard for international competition posed an expensive problem for the EHA, which needed to integrate a facility strategy focused on water-based surfaces with its talent identification and development strategy. In *Tackling the Future* the objective was set for all English Hockey League Premier Division matches to be played on water-based pitches. However, by early 1999 only six clubs (three men's and three women's) had water-based surfaces.

In addition to the network of regional coaches, it was also proposed to appoint a parallel network of Regional Development Managers (RDMs) whose primary responsibilities were to 'support and develop hockey throughout the region' (AEWHA/HA 1996: 13) with a particular focus on young people and supporting the club and county/territory infrastructure. Young people were to be supported, in part, through the involvement of the Regional Development Manager in the National Junior Sports Programme and in the building of school–club links. Support for clubs was based on an acknowledgement that 'the ethos of the traditional hockey club appears to be threatened by the increased use of local authority and school artificial turf pitches' and a recognition that 'the future of the game depends on the future of clubs, supported by strong school links and based around good facilities' (*ibid.*: 15). The RDM would be expected to provide advice to clubs on business planning and funding opportunities as well as help clubs build partnerships with key organisations such as the Youth Sport Trust and the (then) National Coaching Foundation.

Tackling the Future was intended to establish a vision and development framework for hockey for the following ten years and, while much has happened since its publication, the EHA still consider the basic vision to be sound. The two major changes since 1996 have been the abandonment by the Labour government of the proposal to have a single high performance academy in favour of a series of regional centres and the revival of Sport For All as a policy objective. As will be shown below, neither shift in policy blurred the essential vision incorporated in the strategy and, indeed, current government policy is probably more supportive of the aims of 'Tackling the Future' than that expressed in *Sport: Raising the Game.*

Relationship of sports development work to the sports development continuum

Performance and excellence

One of the first challenges facing the new governing body was to review the existing talent identification and development strategies of the previous associations and produce a coherent strategy at the performance and excellence level of the continuum which would improve the performance of the national teams and also attract funding from the National Lottery under the World Class Performance programmes. Although there was some variation in the process of talent identification and development between men's and women's hockey, they both displayed broadly similar features, the most significant of which was the existence of three parallel structures based around education, clubs and age-based representative participation. Within education, a strong competitive structure existed at the level of school sport, although it is much stronger in the private school sector than in the state sector, and also within the higher education sector where competition was organised by BUSA relatively independently of the national governing bodies. Young players and adults might also be part of the second structure based on the progression from local club leagues to regional and possibly national club league and cup competitions. Finally, players might also be involved in 'representative' structures organised by age group at county, regional and national levels. While the existence of multiple structures reflected the roots of the sport and provided a wide variety of opportunities for competition, it was not clear what route the development pathway took through the various structures. Moreover, there was a growing awareness that competition between sports for the limited pool of talented young sportsmen and women made it essential that the new association had an efficient and effective system for identifying potential top players and also demonstrating to them that the sport had systems in place to make the most of their talent. Women's hockey, in particular, was faced with much greater competition for talented sportswomen. Ten years ago hockey and netball were the only significant winter team sports for women, but the recent growth in the popularity of soccer and rugby among young sportswomen, particularly at university, has required the association to compete more effectively.

In a recent review of the process of talent identification and development, the EHA identified four main weaknesses with the existing structures (EHA 2000). The first weakness was the confusion at youth level regarding the team, school, local club or county that a talented player should play for. Second, there was confusion over the performance pathway for talented

19–25 year olds. It was not clear what role university hockey should play in the talent pathway nor what role was played by the regional leagues and the under-21 regional tournaments, neither of which appeared to be tightly integrated into a process of talent identification. Third, there was a concern that there were too many competitions for talented young players which were restricting the time available for coaching. There needed to be a clearer distinction between competitions that were designed as part of the development pathway and those that were purely for participation. Finally, at the youth level, it was considered that there was too much reliance on knock-out cup competitions which meant that too many players had only one chance to play, improve their skills in competition and also impress the talent assessors.

The solution proposed by the EHA was to establish a clear development pathway through the existing pattern of competitions and leagues which would be integrated with and supported by the Active Sports and World Class Performance programmes and which would also focus on the needs of the individual player. Thus, for example, at the World Class Start level there would be a programme of assessment at under-15, -16, -17 and -18 ages, after which players would be invited to attend national assessment camps followed by blocked training periods at the regional academies throughout the year. Support for this programme would come from a series of age-specific tournaments, the BUSA inter-divisional tournament and the Regional Premier League fixtures. Other competitions would be outside the development pathway and, while players could still take part, in BUSA domestic tournaments, for example, assessors would not be present and the availability of talented players would be determined by the Regional Academy Coach. The intention of the specification of the development pathway was to prevent the over-commitment of talented players and also of skilled assessors. Once players reached the top level they then became eligible for nomination by the EHA for World Class Performance funding which currently supports forty-eight elite-level players (twenty-four men and twenty-four women) with £15,000 per year and a further forty-eight players with a smaller amount of £2–3,000 per year.

The talent development strategy is still in the early stages of implementation and will clearly take time to settle in and for the impact to be felt at the level of the national squads. However, the process of developing the strategy has highlighted a number of related issues that the association is currently addressing. One issue concerns the pace at which water-based pitches can be installed. In late 2001 the EHA considered that it was still about 12 to 18 months away from having the required number of water-based pitches, some of which were delayed by the slow pace of decision-making by the government over the structure and location of the UK Sports Institute. One consequence of the shortage is that regional training squads have to travel from the academy and, because of the travel time involved, fewer training sessions can be organised in a day, thus resulting in the organisation of parallel sessions requiring more pitches and also more coaches, some of whom may not be of the standard preferred for the development programme.

A second tension to emerge is that between the priorities of clubs and those of the national squad, and is similar to the tensions that have already surfaced in cricket and rugby union over recent years. Since the advent of World Class Performance funding of top class athletes, members of the national squads have had a much clearer contractual relationship with the EHA than with their clubs. The tension manifests itself not just in the withdrawal of players for international duty but also in the concern of the national coach to manage the broader playing lifestyle of players. For example, when the men's national squad returned from the Sydney Olympics, players were given six weeks' rest, much to the annoyance of clubs who needed their top players for the new league season. A related source of tension is the sense of disappointment felt within some clubs that the regional academy is not providing direct benefits for clubs – for example, by running development sessions for club coaches.

A third set of problems is associated with coaching structures and practices. The association has a strong development programme for coaches linked to the NVQ structure, with the justification that such a linkage emphasises that coaching comprises a set of skills that need to be taken seriously, adequately demonstrated and regularly developed. However, while level 1 qualification has not drawn criticism, those considering entering for level 2 argue that the requirements are too rigorous and are a deterrent. Although there is a concern that some potential coaches might be lost, there is a conviction that maintaining the NVQ link will help to raise and consolidate the status and quality of coaching.

A further problem associated with coaching concerns the likelihood that a young player with potential will encounter a number of different coaches during his or her formative years of training. A talented twenty-year-old player, for example, might have as many as four coaches, one each at university, regional academy, England and Great Britain levels. While a range of coaches is arguably of benefit to a player at a young age, it is considered to be less helpful to the development of top-class players.

Finally, for hockey, as for many other sports, coaching can be divided between the technical development of a player and/or team and the management of individual top-class players. At the highest level of performance top-class players need individual coaching support and development in order to fulfil their potential. For this to be achieved coaches need a range of sophisticated, complex and subtle skills which can generally only be developed through a similar process of individual mentoring such as that which is commonly used in the development of senior business managers. While Sportscoach UK is considered to provide valuable coach development training at the equivalent of NVQ levels 1, 2 and 3, it is seen as less effective at developing the skills needed for coaches seeking qualification equivalent to levels 4 and 5 which are essentially 'workplace-based' and difficult for Sportscoach UK to deliver cost effectively. In contrast, the British Olympic Association is seen as offering some valuable training for all elite level coaches in Olympic sports, but even these programmes are insufficiently tailored to the specific needs of hockey and those of the individual coach.

A fourth problem concerns the role of the regional academies. In 1997 the EHA took a conscious decision to develop its national squads through a series of academies rather than by bringing the squads together at one central location, as is the case in an increasing number of countries including Korea, Australia and the Netherlands. The basis for the decision was a concern that many existing and future top-class players would be lost because of a reluctance to relocate. However, the consequence is that the whole squad is together far less than is the case among England's main rivals and that, while the level of fitness of the English squad is comparable, this is not the case with regard to the quality and sophistication of 'core technical skills'. The disappointing performance of the British teams at the Sydney Olympics has reopened the issue. While it is not clear whether the current debate will result in a change of policy, it may well be the case that some modification of the existing structure is forced on the Association because of the limited overlap between the distribution of EHA academies and the network of UK Sports Institute regional centres, only some of which will have facilities for supporting hockey. Where a hockey regional academy and a UKSI centre are located close to each other or are on the same site, it is likely that they will emerge as stronger magnets for top-class players. However, even if there is some rationalisation of elite training within England, the problem of training a Great Britain team for the Olympic Games will still remain.

The fifth issue is the future relationship with universities which offer a potential third development route. At present the regional academy structure caters for young players up to the age of twenty-one, thus overlapping substantially with the university age group. There is currently no separate development route through universities and a number of elite players move into the regional academy while at university and compete within the university–BUSA (British Universities Sports Association) structure as well as the regional structure. The EHA acknowledges that universities are more important than previously, given the very high proportion of the sports talented players that proceed to higher education. While Loughborough University has men's and women's teams in the national leagues, most university competition is organised through BUSA. As mentioned above, the talent development strategy does incorporate part of the BUSA schedule of competition into the development structure. However, the association accepts that the university-level game could make a more substantial contribution. There is currently a proposal under discussion to organise an autumn competition between the top six universities in order to ensure their integration into the performance pathway.

Participation

In 1990 it was estimated that there were 90,000 regular adult (over sixteen years of age) players of whom 35,000 were women. Participation levels have risen steadily with, for example, women's participation more than doubling between 1977 and 1990. Most opportunities to play hockey are through the network of clubs and, somewhat worryingly, there has been a steady decline in the number of clubs and teams. In 1990 there were 821 men's clubs (with 2,771 teams) and 941 women's clubs (1,707 teams), but by 1998 the number had fallen to 721 (2,232 teams) and 881 (1,603 teams) for men and women respectively (PMP Consultancy 1999: 8).

At the junior level the number of young people playing hockey at least once in the previous twelve months in 1994 was 49 per cent, with 22 per cent considered to have played frequently (at least 10 times in the twelve-month period). Within schools in 1994 hockey was the sixth most popular sport with 20 per cent playing more than ten times in a year. However, by 1999 the figures for school participation showed a significant decline over the previous five years from 20 per cent to 17 per cent, with the decline being most marked at the secondary school level where it dropped from 32 per cent to 27 per cent. Overall the popularity of hockey declined from sixth to eighth place, and from second to fourth in secondary schools. On a more positive note, the proportion of children who participated in hockey as a club member increased from 1 per cent in 1994 to 2 per cent in 1999.

While there is no serious problem facing hockey in terms of participation, the data suggest that there is little scope for complacency and that hockey will have to market itself effectively in the increasingly severe competition for young players. As was stated in 'Tackling the Future', the EHA sees clubs as the key to ensuring the attraction of hockey as a participation sport and looks to the newly appointed Regional Development Managers to help fulfil the association's participation objectives. Not surprisingly, given the emphasis on schools within the government's strategy *Sport: Raising the Game*, the EHA looked to its clubs to build links with schools both as a way of supporting teachers in their delivery of the National Curriculum for Physical Education and as a means of attracting junior members. Local authorities were also identified as important partners, partly because of their control over playing facilities and partly because of their leading role in Active Sports partnerships where hockey is one of the priority sports. In this respect, the hockey development strategy 'Tackling the Future' reinforces the criteria outlined by the National Lottery Sport Fund in stating that the EHA will only endorse proposals for lottery funding which, inter alia, demonstrate clear links with the development strategy of the local authority, provide equal access for men's and women's teams and which demonstrate formal partnerships with local schools. Similarly, the EHA will only encourage and endorse the development of synthetic turf pitches on school sites where a community use agreement is in place and where there is a sports development plan in place. The same development objectives also appear in the criteria for the selection of satellite and premier competitive centres. In particular, prospective centres must possess a club structure that supports men's and women's competitive hockey and be able to demonstrate a clear commitment to junior development.

The promotion of the Active Sports programme in the late 1990s came at an ideal time for the EHA, who were in the process of appointing their Regional Development Managers, as it provided not only a broadly complementary focus to that of the EHA, but because it promised a ready-made network for implementation and also additional resources. Active Sports is aimed at young people with a primary focus on supporting governing bodies to provide a club and coaching infrastructure that will allow young people to participate more extensively in sport and also to progress. Active Sports also reinforces the government social inclusion agenda by emphasising the importance of equity and access. Given this remit, Active Sports is seen as filling the gap between 'foundation' level activities, such as TOP Sport and the National Curriculum for Physical Education and the county level of representative performance. 'Active Sports is therefore best summarised as an "Into Performance" programme, assisting young people to move from recreational play to a more serious participation in organised sport' (Sport England 1999b: 10). The four-stage model of Active Sports will enable young people to benefit from organised coaching, integrate them into a strong club structure and enable the more talented to progress to representative sport.

For the EHA the benefits were clear: 'Active Sports will enable English Hockey to put in place, for the first time, a nationally led, quality programme that will bring about consistent standards across the country for: the establishment of links between clubs and schools; the development of club youth hockey; the assessment and development of young players; [and] the recruitment, training and development of volunteers' (EHA/Sport England 1999: 11). An important additional benefit for the new EHA was that it provided clubs and regional associations with a further incentive to rationalise their structures and create merged organisations at the county and regional levels. In some counties, for example, there are still four or five separate associations (for men's, women's, boys' and girls' hockey, and sometimes for mixed hockey). The promise of Active Sports resources has acted as a catalyst for formal merger with the hope that practical co-operation will follow.

The role of the Regional Development Manager has been to: establish hockey action groups in each partnership area in order to prepare the hockey development plan for subsequent approval by Sport England; identify members on the group who will take the lead on key issues such as coaching and umpiring; and, more importantly, ensure that clubs are linked and committed to the partnership. Unfortunately, this is not always easy because, while 'Tackling the Future' put clubs at the heart of hockey, they tend to have a very narrow focus and many are essentially self-centred organisations suspicious of collaboration with other clubs which they often perceive as rivals rather than partners. Both clubs and counties tend to have relatively parochial attitudes towards the needs of the sport and sports development.

While Active Sports has many benefits to offer hockey, it is considered to be weakened by the narrowness of the age range that it covers insofar as it precludes projects that link or overlap with the entry routes from the foundation level and exit routes to adult competition. There is consequently a concern within the EHA to ensure that the programmes of the Active Sports partnerships are firmly located within a broader development strategy. These concerns notwithstanding, Active Sports lies at the centre of the participation strategy of hockey. While Regional Development Managers readily acknowledge that ideally they should have closer links with individual clubs and schools, with as many as 200 clubs in a region and many more schools such contact is clearly unrealistic. The Active Sports Partnership is therefore seen as the most efficient vehicle for reaching a large number of clubs and schools and furthering the development objectives of 'Tackling the Future'.

If educating and cajoling clubs to accept their role within the Active Sports Partnerships is at times difficult, then there is a similar problem with regard to counties who need to see their role more as supporters of the club infrastructure rather than the more prestigious role of being a structure for organising competitions and a stepping stone to national squad selection. One responsibility of the Regional Development Manager is to encourage counties to see club development as their primary responsibility and deal with the need for greater professionalism in club management and the need for a sharper awareness of such issues as equity, child protection and youth development.

Given the very early stage in the development of both the Active Sports Partnerships and the role of the EHA Regional Development Managers, it is difficult to draw firm conclusions about the success of sports development work at the participation/early performance levels but there are some promising signs. First, hockey is certainly well placed to take full advantage of the Active Sports Partnerships. Most regions are well under way in producing their hockey development plans, many of which have already been approved by Sport England. In addition, hockey, unlike many other sports, has a tradition of youth development (albeit largely through schools) to build upon. Second, the EHA should be able to meet its commitments for the inclusion of ethnic minorities because hockey is a sport that has reasonably strong roots within the Asian community, although it should be noted that leagues tend to have Asian teams/clubs rather than Asians being members of long-established and traditionally white clubs. Third, there are experiments with a form of hockey adapted to the requirements of disabled players, Zone Hockey, that is slowly gaining a wider audience. Zone Hockey has already been included in the Birmingham 2001 Youth Games and was a demonstration sport at the BAe Girls Hockey competition at the National Hockey Stadium at Milton Keynes in 2001. It is hoped that lottery funding will be made available to promote Zone Hockey more extensively.

Summary and conclusions

Despite the substantial progress that hockey has made over the last five years, some difficult sports development issues remain. The first of these is the increasing division between the processes and structures supporting talent identification and development, on the one hand, and those processes and structures supporting participation and non-elite level competition, on the other. The second issue follows directly from the first and concerns the challenge of encouraging counties, and to a lesser extent clubs, to accept a redefinition of their role and especially a less central position in talent identification and development. Third, there is the continuing need to rationalise the club structure. Despite the steady decline in the number of clubs, frequently through merger, Regional Development Managers are acutely aware that there are still too many clubs which function on the edge of viability, but are reluctant to consider merger or simply dissolving and joining a different club because of the depth of loyalty to their existing club. Fourth, and perhaps the most serious potential issue, is the future financial commitments that are being rapidly accumulated through the programme of pitch development. It is undoubtedly the case that, if English hockey wishes to compete for major international titles, it must have an adequate infrastructure of synthetic pitches and particularly water-based pitches, but the existing programme of pitch development relies almost totally on lottery funding, which is acknowledged as being in decline. The question therefore arises of where the money will come for pitch maintenance in the years to come and, more significantly, for refurbishment when it is needed in about ten to fifteen years' time. Finally, there is some concern that on the issue of gender equity the EHA is experiencing an erosion of the position of women in decision-making positions. Apart from those activities where gender equity is specified in the EHA constitution, for example, on some key committees and in the distribution of World Class Performance bursaries, there is evidence, though largely anecdotal, that at the county and regional levels women are not maintaining their number of elected positions which their share of the overall membership would suggest is appropriate.

Tennis

Introduction

Lawn tennis, a derivative of older racket sports, dates back to the middle ages. It became popular in the UK during the second half of the nineteenth century and the Lawn Tennis Association (LTA) was formed in 1888. The Wimbledon Championships, run annually by the All England Lawn Tennis Club, are recognised as one of the best tournaments in the world, attracting wide public interest in the UK and abroad. The profits from this tournament, which amount to some £30 million per annum, are reinvested in developing tennis in Britain. Despite this level of investment, the poor performance and standing of British players in international competition continues to give cause for concern and every Wimbledon fortnight sees a spate of articles in the national press analysing the reasons for Britain's lack of top-class players. Tennis has been selected as a case study in order to examine why a relatively rich and high-profile sport appears to have been so unsuccessful on the world stage and is also facing a decline in participation.

Participation

The LTA estimates that 4 million people currently play tennis, of whom 1 million people play at least once every two weeks (LTA 2001a). Among these players there is a fairly even split between the sexes (54 per cent male and 46 per cent female) with 57 per cent under the age of 24 and 70 per cent under 35 (LTA 1999). Park courts are the most popular venues for playing the game, though more committed participants join clubs. There were 2,360 clubs affiliated to the LTA and 3,398 schools affiliated to the British Schools Tennis Association in 1999 (*ibid.*). Unlike most governing bodies, the LTA directly invests in tennis facilities and there has been a massive input over the last ten years, resulting in the number of indoor courts increasing from 67 in 1987 to 910 in 1999 (*ibid.*). Despite this increase, access to indoor facilities (considered absolutely essential to the development of the game) is still uneven and limited, with just one indoor court for every 58,000 people in Britain compared with one for every 7,500 in Sweden (LTA 2001a). However, despite the significant investment in facilities, participation in tennis has declined significantly: it is now only 65 per cent of the 1994 level (J. Crowther in an interview in the *Daily Telegraph*, 30 June 2001).

Excellence

Taking the ranking of Britain's top five players over the last ten years as a measure of excellence, the picture is not good. British men have moved up from fifteenth to fourteenth place, largely due to the success of Tim Henman and Greg Rusedski (who is a product of the Canadian tennis system). British women have dropped from tenth to twenty-third place. In the words of John Crowther, Chief Executive of the LTA, 'If we were any other Grand Slam nation our results would be considered absolutely pathetic. We have allowed this to become the norm' (Crowther 2001). He goes on to describe the LTA as a well-intentioned organisation that has failed to deliver and says, 'We don't just need a change. We need a dramatic change' (*ibid.*).

The governing body

The LTA is one of the larger governing bodies in the UK with an annual turnover of £45.8 million and 220 paid staff. In 1999 it published *British Tennis and You: A Strategy for the New Millennium* and took as its mission statement 'The LTA exists to ensure the well-being and growth of British Tennis as a dynamic, healthy, year-round, competitive and enjoyable lifetime sport for all' (LTA 1999). One wonders if the phrase 'sport for all' would have appeared in the mission statement had New Labour not recently come to power. The strategy is prefaced by a statement from Tony Blair, the Prime Minister, who points out that tennis can be enjoyed regardless of age, ability or social background and applauds the LTA's determination to welcome more people into the sport, sustain their interest and maximise their full potential (*ibid.*). The strategy identifies seven principles it is applying to meet its objectives:

1   create a welcoming environment;
2   increase participation levels;
3   enhance standards of play;
4   have the most effective talent identification system;
5   raise our international standing;
6   improve the infrastructure; and
7   work in partnership to expand the sport.

Action agendas are included for clubs, coaches, the competitive structure and county associations, and quotes from volunteers, players, coaches and Board members illustrate the contribution that each can make. Overall the strategy document is much stronger on presentation than content. It was not until a year after its publication when Patrice Hagelauer, the new Performance Director, produced the National Tennis Performance Plan (LTA 2000) and Roger Draper, the new Director of Development, produced the Club Strategy (*ibid.*) that clear strategies for making changes were identified.

Evolution of sports development work

There appear to be four strands in the evolution of sports development work in tennis during the 1980s and early 1990s. The first was the introduction of 'short tennis' in 1980. This was based on the Swedish model that had been in existence since the 1970s and was designed to introduce young children to a modified version of the game. By the end of the 1980s short tennis had become a sport in itself with national championships, rather than an introduction to the adult game, and concerns were raised that it was not fulfilling its development function. Other variations of short tennis such as transition tennis and starter tennis were introduced later, but all have now been replaced by 'Mini tennis' as the official introduction to the game in 400 targeted clubs (Draper 2001, personal interview).

The second strand of development was the National Tennis School established at Bisham Abbey (one of the Sports Council's national centres) in 1982 with sponsorship from Rover. There were some initial successes from this scheme but the idea of removing children from their home environment to live at a national centre is now considered unwise. The Regional Tennis Centres that are being set up around the country will fulfil the same function as Bisham Abbey without requiring young people to be residential. The third strand of development activity was based on talent identification and coaching at county level through a network of County Development and Coaching Officers established in 1988. Although the word 'development' was included in the title of these people, they were tennis coaches employed by the County Associations to seek out and coach talented players. In contrast to the network of development officers put in place by the RFU at the same time, they did not relate to local authority or school structures and did not work to any overall national development plan (Draper 2001, personal interview). The fourth strand was facility development with the LTA providing grants and loans to clubs for the development of facilities, and the Indoor Tennis Initiative (ITI) established in 1990 with partnership funding from the Sports Council and the All England Lawn Tennis Club.

It was not until October 1995 that the LTA produced a four-year strategy for the development of tennis (LTA 1995). The 1995 strategy marked an approach that was far more outward looking than tennis had been until that time. It was based on extensive consultation with those who had responsibility for developing the sport at all levels as well as the Sports Council, the National Coaching Foundation, the Youth Sport Trust, the Central Council for Physical Recreation and 2,500 schools around the country (*ibid.*). The introduction to the strategy also states that account was taken of the recently published government policy *Sport: Raising the Game*. The document claimed that the resulting development strategy and the changes proposed constituted the most far-reaching review of British tennis ever undertaken (*ibid.*: 5). Its nine objectives covered the creation of a new club environment, employment of development staff, decentralisation to the counties, supporting the voluntary sector, coach development, maximising facilities, competitive opportunities, attracting more school children and juniors, and changing the tennis culture. Working in partnership was a key theme and development agenda for the LTA and counties, clubs, schools, further education and higher education, and local authorities were identified. Strategy implementation was to be driven by the Community Tennis Programme bringing together schools, clubs and local authorities.

The 1995 development strategy undoubtedly represented new thinking in the LTA, influenced by some experienced sports development personnel recruited from the Sports Council and sports development posts in other sports. It was a well-thought-out and thorough strategy, but was not easy to implement, partly because of resistance to change by tennis counties and clubs who had little understanding of sports development, and partly because the LTA itself did not take a holistic approach to development work. In particular, Performance and Facilities Directorates existed alongside the

Development Directorate, each with their own strategic priorities that were not drawn together in one overall plan.

Before the 1996–2001 development strategy had begun to take effect, further senior personnel changes occurred at the LTA with the appointment of a new chief executive, performance director and director of development. *A Strategy for the New Millennium* was published in 1999 (see above) that was then followed up with a National Performance Plan and Club Vision.

The National Performance Plan identifies a four-stage structure: tennis schools and clubs for 8–10 year olds; county training programmes for 11–13 year olds; regional centres for 14–16 year olds; and a national centre for 15/16–20/21-year-old intermediates and seniors (LTA 2000: 7). The programme is designed to help promising players make the transition into tennis champions. It has been devised by Patrice Hagelauer, the LTA's Performance Director who was recruited from France where he had been the national director of men's tennis. In an interview published in the *Daily Telegraph*, he attributed the lack of success among British players to the culture of British tennis clubs: 'Tennis in this country is a culture of leisure, not a culture of competition. So many of our clubs are no more than factories to lose weight. There's no way things are going to change without a new culture in the clubs … Clubs are not like this in other countries. In Belgium, in Switzerland, they have great junior programmes in the clubs. In Argentina, in Spain, the adults want to watch the juniors play, they are proud of them. It's a huge difference from here' (*Daily Telegraph*, 30 June 2001: S5).

Club Vision, a strategy for the regeneration of clubs, is designed to bring about the cultural change in clubs that Hagelauer and his colleagues want to see. Roger Draper, LTA Director of Development, recognising the fundamental weakness of club tennis in Britain, proposed a four-strand strategy: identifying development needs of clubs; streamlining LTA communication with clubs; prioritising LTA investment in clubs; and developing products and services to support club development (Draper 2000, personal interview). The 'Year One Interim Report' (LTA 2001b) suggested that Club Vision was being well received by clubs with 81 per cent of those surveyed rating it as a good programme. An innovatory aspect of Club Vision is the completion of a Club Assessment Form for all clubs, large and small. Just under 1,000 forms had been processed by June 2001 and some interesting findings have begun to emerge. Lack of competitive opportunities were identified as a major weakness, one-third of clubs employed unlicensed coaches, 60 per cent of clubs did not have child protection policies in place, and 30 per cent did not operate short/mini tennis programmes. The implementation of Club Vision is led by the network of County Development Officers whose role is very different from that of the first group. They are now multi-skilled and advise clubs on facilities and business planning as well as more traditional aspects of sports development.

In order to make tennis more accessible to people living in large cities the LTA launched City Tennis Clubs as part of Club Vision in June 2001. They have appointed Funke Awoderu as their Inner City Development Officer and enlisted the support of Ian Wright, former Arsenal and England footballer, to promote the initiative. Recognising that tennis is still widely seen as the preserve of white middle-class suburban people, Wright explains what the City Tennis Clubs programme is intended to do: 'It's about getting kids onto courts that aren't bumpy and messed up, in park areas that are safe to be around and not too far away from home. Then they need to have coaching on site that involves just a nominal amount for parents to pay' (LTA 2001c). There are five cities in the initial programme which is set to expand to twenty or more in the next five years. Over fifty expressions of interest had been registered by city councils and local authorities around the country by July 2001 (LTA 2001b).

Summarising the evolution of sports development in tennis, it initially tended to be somewhat insular and inward looking in its approach. The LTA was relatively slow to recognise the need to broaden the appeal of the game and make it more accessible, and to work in partnership with schools and local authorities. Development initiatives were fragmented rather than being part of a strategic vision for the development of the game. Club tennis revolved around the interests of members rather than the development of the game through the encouragement, coaching and nurturing of juniors. A comprehensive strategy for development was formulated in 1995 but was not followed through, although many elements of it have been repackaged and are now being driven forward by newly appointed personnel. There is now a public acknowledgement of the need for radical change in the way the game is run, and the need for traditional club culture to change. The Club Vision Programme is addressing the issue of club development in an innovatory and systematic way, and it will be interesting to see how clubs respond. It is also interesting that tennis has identified broadening the base as the key to greater success at top level when other sports (such as rowing) are successful with a much narrower participation base.

Sports equity

To what extent has tennis embraced the idea of sports equity given what has already been said about club culture and the need for tennis to be more accessible? In the field of disability sport, tennis has been one of the leaders with the development of wheelchair tennis. The game is well established in Britain and all the ITI centres have wheelchair access and support wheelchair squads. Lottery funding to clubs has also resulted in the upgrading of facilities to cater for wheelchair users. Wheelchair tennis is well developed with increasing numbers of local opportunities to introduce more people to the game through demonstrations and clinics, and ongoing coaching and court time provided. Weekend camps for beginners, juniors and women only are arranged, and, for the best players, there is a full competitive tournament programme at national and international level.

Unlike some other sports, players are graded by their ability rather than classified by their disability. Through the work of a full-time disability co-ordinator, the British Tennis Foundation also promotes tennis for people with learning disabilities and deaf people. Although not as well developed as wheelchair tennis, substantial progress is being made in these areas.

The City Tennis Clubs programme is a prime example of the LTA trying to make tennis more accessible to inner city children from poorer back-grounds. By enlisting the support of Ian Wright to promote the initiative, they are sending a clear message about the inclusion of people from black and ethnic minorities. In common with several other sports, the LTA signed up to the Racial Equality Charter for Sport promoted by Sporting Equals in 2001. Although there are specific initiatives, such as the ones outlined above, the LTA's main approach to equity is one of mainstreaming. To support this approach, the LTA have an equity group with representatives from within the LTA and outside, and have made a public commitment to pursuing a policy of equal opportunities in the areas of race, sex and disability.

Impact of the National Lottery

When the National Lottery Sports Fund was established in 1996, tennis clubs were well placed to bid for funding to support capital facility develop-ment. Unlike most governing bodies, the LTA already had a Facilities team to advise on investment, and was able to offer clubs interest-free loans for partnership-funding purposes, giving tennis a distinct advantage over other sports whose governing bodies could not provide such financial support. Consequently tennis clubs have received £71 million of lottery funding for capital development of over 500 projects since the inception of the National Lottery. The other strand of National Lottery funding, World Class, was not available to tennis as the LTA was not considered to meet the criterion of 'financial need'.

Influence of government and the Sports Council

In policy terms, it seems that central government has had little impact on tennis until recently. Although *Sport: Raising the Game* was referenced in the Introduction of the 1996–2000 Development Strategy, and a message from the Prime Minister, Tony Blair, is featured in the 2000 Strategy, the LTA has largely gone its own way. The rationale for recruiting more players from diverse backgrounds is more to do with reviving the health of the British game than an ideological commitment to promoting social inclusion.

The LTA has also been in the rare position of not being dependent on financial support from the Sports Council, which has meant that it has not had to take heed of sports development policy emanating from the Council in the way that other sports have. Where there has been Sports Council influ-ence it has been through the appointment of former Sports Council employees to the LTA, rather than through conditions attached to grant aid. However, the LTA has bought into Sports Council programmes such as the Volunteer Investment Programme and the National Junior Sports Programme where it thought they would help its work.

There was some irritation on the LTA's part that they were unable to access World Class funding, and a feeling that Sport England was being too prescriptive in its approach with governing bodies, so the government's proposals for granting devolved powers to governing bodies outlined in *The Government's Plan for Sport* (DCMS 2001: 38) were warmly welcomed. The LTA were one of the first governing bodies to put forward a submission to Sport England's National Lottery Panel seeking delegated authority for managing applications and funding to schemes within its national strategy in February 2001. At the time of writing the outcome of this application is not known.

Summary and conclusions

At the beginning of this section the relative lack of success of British tennis players in international competition was identified as a key question to address. The opinion of senior officers in the LTA is that the lack of success is due to the culture of tennis clubs and the lack of coaching and competitive opportunities for young people. While this might be a partial explanation, the lack of success might also be due to the lack of a systematic approach to sports development in tennis over the years and fragmentation between the various components of sports development, which failed to work together to provide a clear performance pathway from foundation through to excellence. Sports development ideas were not introduced in any systematic way to the LTA until the mid-1990s. The LTA developed facilities, but not the infrastructure of people to make links between clubs and schools and work with local authorities. Most clubs and county associations were inward looking and unconcerned with the overall development of the game.

There is clear recognition by senior employees at the LTA of the need for radical change and early signs are that Club Vision is being well received by clubs. However, cultural change is a slow process and it will take a long time for changes at club level to have an effect further up the performance ladder.

Conclusions

The case studies show how four national governing bodies have responded to the rapid changes in sport over the last thirty years. From a starting point where they were primarily concerned with domestic and international competition, they are all now working with schools to recruit young people to their sport in a competitive market, and trying to improve the quality of teaching and availability of coaching. The development of school–club links as the first step on the performance ladder is also a priority, with rugby union well ahead of the game in establishing its network of YDOs in the 1980s and 1990s.

Club development and the culture of sports clubs is another major issue for sports development in governing bodies. Although most clubs affiliate to the governing body of their sport, relationships are often fragile, if not overtly problematic. Clubs operate as autonomous organisations with their prime responsibility to the interests of their existing members, and most do not see themselves as part of the bigger picture of their sport's development. The inward-looking culture of many tennis clubs is perceived by senior managers in the LTA as a major barrier to the development of tennis, and hockey is also concerned about its club structure and capacity to play a full part in the development process. Rugby appears to have more success in persuading clubs of the need to cater for junior players, and, to a limited extent, women.

Excellence has always been seen as a prime responsibility of governing bodies, and the availability of World Class Funding from the National Lottery to some governing bodies in the later 1990s enabled them to put ambitious programmes in place to support their international competitors. Rowing's success was immediate with their outstanding performance at the Sydney Olympics, and the women's rugby team defeated the All Blacks for the first time in the summer of 2001, but hockey has been less successful despite enormous investment in the sport. The substantial injection of resources into the World Class Programme after years of underinvestment has brought its challenges. Governing bodies have been required to rethink and meticulously plan their performance strategies, as well as take on experts from overseas. This rapid development happened in the context of continuing uncertainty over the nature of the United Kingdom Sports Institute and the support it would provide, and the pressure to win medals in order to retain World Class funding. In some cases, the availability of World Class funding skewed the balance of the governing bodies' overall development strategy, leaving other elements underresourced.

For the governing bodies, there has not been the tension between the policy objectives of 'development *of* sport' and 'development *through* sport' with which many local authorities have had to grapple. Development *of* their sport is their raison d'être, and any development *through* sport is a by-product. Neither have governing bodies had to compete for resources in the same way as local authorities as their financial basis is entirely different. Indeed, governing bodies and high performance sport have been the primary beneficiaries of National Lottery funding. While much National Lottery funding has gone to local authorities, it has generally only compensated for the cuts in public expenditure that many authorities have suffered. In order for national governing bodies to access public funding they have had to acknowledge the wider policy objectives of the Sports Councils and government even though these were not always congruent with serving the needs of their existing members and affiliated clubs. However, the agenda set out in

Sport: Raising the Game, and the Sports Council's dual emphasis on excellence and young people in the early 1990s, was broadly congruent with the governing bodies' agenda. Those sports which previously had not engaged in much youth development, such as rowing, were happy to develop this work. Hockey, tennis and rugby all had a strong base in schools and they welcomed the government's endorsement of the centrality of traditional (team) games in the National Curriculum. The Sports Council's development of the National Junior Sport Programme gave added impetus to their work whether or not they were one of the core sports. Rowing, for example, though not included, developed its own National Junior Rowing Programme.

Commitment to sports equity in the mid-nineties, and social inclusion at the turn of the century, was less congruent with governing bodies' agendas. Sports equity was promoted by the Sports Council in the mid-1990s without government backing and without the financial incentive of substantial funding. While fairness and social justice are generally perceived to be underpinning values in sport, many governing bodies argued that they did not have the capacity to tackle equity issues and did little more than give lip service to the principle through an equity statement. Also, their constituents and stakeholders were club members who were generally unconcerned with such issues. The formation of the Wheelchair Tennis Association and the Rugby Football Union for Women are good examples of interest groups setting up their own organisational structures to enable previously excluded groups to play their sport. General progress towards a more equitable sports culture and the embedding of equity and inclusion was slow, though some sports like rowing did take several innovative initiatives. With the Labour government's commitment to social inclusion and its clear directive in the *Government's Plan for Sport* that Sport England will make equity and inclusion plans a prerequisite for funding to governing bodies, they are now being forced to take the social inclusion agenda seriously if they want to access public funding. It remains to be seen how effective they will be in embracing and delivering this agenda which is a long way removed from what the majority perceive as their core business.

7 Development of sport and/or development through sport?

Introduction

The picture of sports development in the early twenty-first century to emerge from the review of the selected local authorities and national governing bodies of sport in the two previous chapters is one of examples of generally successful innovation and service development, but often in an environment of policy instability and uncertainty. The four local authorities had all accepted the need for the development of partnerships as an opportunity for service enhancement though for some it was also a defensive measure but they had all, to varying degrees, demonstrated that partnerships can be effective in broadening and deepening sports development activity. Similarly, the four governing bodies demonstrated the extent to which the development of individual sports has become a much more professional, planned and effectively resourced activity. Taken together the case studies illustrate, first, the extent to which sports development activity has become a more accepted, if not yet an integral, element in the repertoire of policy instruments available to government and, second, the degree to which the refinement of the concept of sports development over the last thirty years or so has led to a differentiation and tailoring of the concept according to the priorities of particular sports and welfare interests.

Table 7.1 summarises the evolution of sports development as described in the earlier chapters of the book and indicates not only the faltering emergence of the service, but also the extent of its vulnerability to the whim and caprice of governments or indeed individual ministers. Moreover, the table indicates the difficulty of translating the conceptual unity given to sports development through the formulation of the model of the sports development continuum into co-ordinated and complementary projects and programmes. The model, while acknowledged throughout much of the sport policy area, did not appear to have generated much understanding or commitment in contiguous policy areas, such as education and health, or even within the DCMS and its predecessor, the Department of National Heritage. Even among sports organisations there was a tendency to treat elements of the model in isolation rather than emphasise, and seek to reinforce, the

Table 7.1   The evolution of sports development (SD) from the mid-1960s

Period	Mid-1960s to mid-1970s	Mid-1970s to early 1990s	Early 1990s to late 1990s	Late 1990s to present
Dominant description	Unity by common cause.	Unity by neglect.	Increasing compartmentalisation of SD activity and interests.	Fragmentation and demarcation.
Conceptualisation of SD	SD as facility development.	SD as an intermittent welfare instrument.	SD as a number of increasingly differentiated activities.	SD as (at least) two distinct sets of activities.
	Perceived common interest and mutual benefit between local authorities, clubs and governing bodies of sport in need for facility development.	Refinement of SD (e.g. through the formulation of the SD continuum) but largely an internal debate within SC or, at least, within sport, i.e. not engaging with important external/non-sport policy interests in government.	Increasing bifurcation of SD between young people/schools and talent identification and development.	Bifurcation and increasing distance between SD as youth and community development and SD as talent identification and development.
Pattern of interests	Local authorities as the engine of SD/facility building. Other interests (PE teachers, sports clubs, BOA, NGBs) grateful for public largesse, but wary. Sports Council finding its feet.	Administrative muddle and weakness. NGBs on the defensive (especially football) as were the Sports Councils and local authorities (CCT). Professional bodies such as ILAM and IBRM (later ISRM) weak.	Interests increasingly clearly defined by debates over the NCPE, general perceived decline in international sporting success and the proposed remedies, and commercialisation. Increasing differentiation of interests.	Differentiated interests and clusters of interests around young people/school sport, community sport/recreation, and high performance sport.
Political salience of, and attitude towards, SD	Low salience. Cautious and benign attitude towards sport.	Variable salience. Attitude oscillated between neglect and clumsy intervention.	High salience. Positive attitude towards SD and sport policy more generally, though only modest integration of SD with other aspects of welfare policy.	Moderate salience. High level of support for SD but based on a strongly instrumental attitude towards the service.

complementary and integrative aspects. The latent tensions within the broad field of sports development soon surfaced once the initial phase of facility development had been completed and the Thatcher period of neglect and disdain towards sport was nearing its end. Once there were resources to be divided, whether they were time within the national curriculum for physical education or funds from the National Lottery, rival conceptualisations of sports development rapidly emerged. Sports development for high performance sport focusing on talent identification and development soon surfaced as an influential conceptualisation to sit alongside conceptualisations of sports development which emphasised either a focus on young people and the school setting or sport as a contributor to broader community development.

The refinement of sports development is described deliberately in the table as 'fragmentation' rather than as 'specialisation', with the latter's more positive connotations. It would indeed be possible to argue that as a service concept such as sports development (or primary health care, life-long learning, or preventative medicine) matures it will be refined and redefined to suit the range of particular contexts within which it is applied. In this sense, the elaboration of a service concept produces, ideally, a series of complementary applications, each with its own group of bespoke programmes, micro-level specialist skills and knowledge and tailored resources, but which nonetheless subscribe to a common set of values and, again ideally, have a predisposition to share resources and the burden of resource reduction. According to this ideal type, specialisation may be considered a virtue and one that adds to the overall capacity of the service to generate, what Mark Moore refers to as, 'public value' (Moore 1998).[1]

Unfortunately, as the policy area of sports development has matured, the differentiation of activities that has taken place has led to the emergence of competing rather than complementary interpretations of sports development and exacerbated a number of latent tensions, the most significant of which is that between development of sport and community development through sport. The refinement and compartmentalisation of sports development practices has, in part, been engineered by increasingly distinct clusters of interests within the sport policy area, and has certainly reinforced their identity as discrete advocacy coalitions more ready to view other sports organisations as rivals for scarce resources rather than partners in a common enterprise.

The current context of sports development

It has already been pointed out that there is much evidence of good practice and innovation in both the local authority and governing body sectors despite claims of growing fragmentation within sports development. In order to assess the prospects for sports development over the coming years it is important to appreciate the current context of the service and to identify probable shifts in the policy environment. The analytical framework used in the first three chapters to summarise the pattern of change in sports development will be used here in order to explore both the current policy environment and also the emergent trends (see Table 7.2).

Deep structural changes

Changes to the structure of values and beliefs in a society, and the power relations on which they are based, take place slowly and great caution is needed in identifying and interpreting indicators of change at this level. What might at first appear to be signs of shifts in deeply entrenched values can often prove illusory and superficial. However, it is suggested that there are four trends at the level of deep structure that have affected and, should they persist, will continue to affect sports development policy and practice. The first is the greater acknowledgement and impact of equity issues. There is evidence of change in values and beliefs in a number of areas, most notably in relation to gender and disability, but less evidence in relation to ethnicity, class and age. As regards gender, it is important to accept the distinction between the increased presence of women in sport and sports development and a substantive shift in power in what remains an overwhelmingly male-dominated policy area. With that caveat in mind, it would be difficult to deny that gender equity issues have had an impact on sports development, whether measured by the range and number of programmes and projects that are targeted at women and girls or by the high proportion of women working in sports development. Much the same may be said in relation to disability sport which now has a public profile mainly due to the success of recent Paralympic Games and the particular success of British paralympic athletes. Many of the long-established disability sports bodies appear to have, at last, moved away from a medicalised definition of disability and a therapeutic view of disability sport and begun to lobby more effectively for a share of sports development resources. The greater acknowledgement of equity issues, particularly among traditionally male-dominated governing bodies of sport such as rugby union, is in large part due to the efforts of the Sports Councils and the linking of funding to the incorporation of equity issues in project proposals. The advocacy around equity issues undertaken by the Sports Councils was reinforced by local authorities, who generally had more experience of developing equity-based policies and who were such key policy actors in the promotion of sports development activity in relation to sports participation. The progress in sports development focused around disability in Kent and in tennis, and the progress in terms of the development of women's rugby union, are all indicators of changes in some deeply entrenched attitudes and values. However, this needs to be counter-balanced by the gradual marginalisation of the representation of women in the English Hockey Association following the merger, despite a constitution that strongly protects the interests of the former AEWHA members. At this stage in the evolution of sport policy it is

Table 7.2 Changes in the environment of sports development policy, 1997 to the present

	Variables	Changes from the early 1990s to 1997	Changes from 1997 to the present
Shallow and more vulnerable to change	Administrative arrangements	Establishment of the Department of National Heritage (1992) gave sport a voice in the Cabinet, but removed the Sports Council from its link with the DoE; establishment of English Sports Council and UK Sports Council (1997). Both changes increased complexity in the sport policy area.	DCMS replaces DNH, but with little significant impact; more important is the increasing prominence of the regional level of administration through bodies such as the Regional Cultural Consortia, Regional Development Agencies and Regional Assemblies; devolution to Scotland and Wales.
	Pattern of inter-organisational resources dependencies	Sports Council–CCPR relationship less abrasive. Introduction of the National Lottery and establishment of Foundation for Sport and the Arts increased funding influence of government at the expense of Sports Councils and local government. Local government expenditure under increasing pressure.	Increasing dependency of national governing bodies and local authority sports development units on National Lottery funding; bidding culture remains; sports development increasingly integrated with and, at times, reliant on the sponsorship of services more central to the delivery of the governments cross-cutting agenda.
More stable with change over the medium term	Interaction between structural interest groups:	Period dominated by the introduction of the National Lottery, the debate over the National Curriculum for PE, and competition for resources.	Greater clarity of definition of roles of the various structural interest groups, but more importantly emergence of clusters of interests which cut across structural interest groups, focused especially around elite sport and school/youth sport.
	demand groups (consumers of service outputs)	Still of marginal importance with the exception of some elite athletes who have influence through players' unions and bodies such as the BOA Athletes Commission.	Still generally weak although elite athletes have an additional organisation, UK Competitors, to represent their interests and some signs of elite demand group influence.

Variables	Changes from the early 1990s to 1997	Changes from 1997 to the present
provider groups (facility/club managers, sports development officers, PE teachers and leisure services managers)	*Sport: Raising the Game* did little to encourage local government interest in and lobbying on behalf of sports development work. SDOs getting more organised via an annual conference and regional meetings, but still a limited influence on policy.	*A Sporting Future For All* and the reform of the National Lottery gave local authority SDOs a higher profile, but not necessarily more influence over policy. National Association for Sports Development formed.
direct support groups (e.g. national governing bodies and schools)	Intensive lobbying around the content of the NCPE from NGBs and CCPR. NGBs and BOA influential regarding the content of *Sport: Raising the Game*.	Increasingly linked to aspects of sports development through specific programmes such as the Active programmes which give some influence, but also increases the resource dependency on government.
indirect support groups (related local authority services, e.g. land use planning, community development and non-Sports Council sources of funding)	Sport more marginal due to cuts in local government public expenditure. The exception was the issue of the sale and development of school playing fields.	Dominance of cross-cutting issues within local authorities tends to keep sports development on the margin of policies such as those supporting community renewal partnerships. Indirect support groups seek to absorb or annex sports development.
Service-specific policy paradigm	*Sport: Raising the Game* stressed national sporting heritage, the moral value of sport, and tradition. Increasing acceptance that international success requires investment and systematic preparation. But suspicion of 'state planning'. Heavy reliance on National Lottery for funding. Emergence of a 'bidding culture' among local authorities.	*A Sporting Future For All* and the *Government's Plan for Sport* both reinforce the twin focus of policy on high performance achievement and school/youth sports participation. Policy process is more strongly interventionist than in the previous period.
Dominant core policy paradigm	Dominance of neo-liberal economics reflected in privatisation and managerialism; but also partial return to 'one-nation' Conservatism on some aspects of social policy.	Dominance of neo-liberal economics reflected in privatisation, managerialism and non-intervention; contrasts with interventionism on the increasingly prominent cross-cutting social issues.

	Variables	Changes from the early 1990s to 1997	Changes from 1997 to the present
Deeply entrenched	Embedded structural values fundamental to the social formation	Mythology of British amateurism dispelled and replaced by an acknowledgement of the need for greater professionalism in the preparation of elite athletes. Concept of equity introduced into the sports discourse.	Less deference on the part of government towards amateurism and volunteerism. Concept of equity established within the sports discourse, though impact on policy inputs and outcomes is mixed.

probably safest to conclude that, while equity issues are firmly on the sports development agenda, equity itself in the distribution of resources and service impact is still some way in the future.

The second deep structural change, and one that often serves to reinforce the deep structural gender inequities that continue to exist in sport, is the consolidation of the commercialisation of sport. The abandonment of amateurism by rugby union and the huge sums paid by television broadcasters for major sports events and league competitions are simply the most recent examples in a history of commercial involvement in elite sport that stretches back at least to the early part of the twentieth century. More interesting is the extent to which commercialisation has become a key source of funding for sports development activity. Sponsorship from companies as diverse as Nike, Ecclesiastical Insurance and the Post Office has been used to support governing body and voluntary organisation youth sport development programmes; specialist sports colleges must raise £100,000 from local sponsorship before the government will provide matching funding; and schemes such as SportsMatch require clubs to seek commercial sponsorship for development activities. The growing commercial involvement in sports development can only strengthen the instrumental perception of sport and push further into the background the conception of sport as an intrinsically valuable and rewarding activity that deserves the priority of public expenditure. Coupled with commercialisation is the growing professionalisation of sport with many elite athletes funded to train full time through the World Class programme.

The third shift in values is the decline in deference towards voluntarism and amateurism in sports clubs and governing bodies. As outlined earlier in this study, when government did accept a role for public resources in sport those resources were initially directed through the voluntary sector. Only slowly did government begin to assert its priorities and overcome the deeply entrenched deference to governing bodies and clubs. The gradual move towards a contract-based relationship between the Sports Councils and the governing bodies during the 1990s was one firm indication of a changed attitude towards sports organisations. Parallel to this change was the equally slow, but equally significant, change in attitude of the courts to sports. From the landmark *McInnes* v. *Onslow-Fane* in 1978 when Justice Megarry argued that the courts should be slow to become involved in matters under the jurisdiction of sports governing bodies, there has been a steady weakening of that resolve as witnessed by the increasing number and range of disputes where the courts have been prepared to accept jurisdiction, including racism, offering contracts to youth team players and claims for compensation arising from injuries sustained during competition. The steady erosion of the privileged position of sports organisations has enabled local authorities and the Sports Councils to raise their expectations of the contribution that clubs and NGBs might make to public sports development policy in return for access to public funds, National Lottery income and other public resources. The move by the Sports Councils to more contractual relations with governing bodies and the attempts to incorporate governing bodies within partnerships are both illustrative of the depth of this attitudinal change. As Jones and Bird (2000) comment, partnerships need to be understood as a political strategy and not necessarily as mutually beneficial coalitions based on trust, shared risks and common aims as Hutchinson and Campbell (1998) suggest. Partnerships might well produce benefits for all those involved, but they are constituted from, and underpinned by, power relations and involve the displacement and recombination of inter-organisational relationships and the refinement and realignment of resource dependency relationships. Partnerships and the use of quasi-contracts are both examples of the 'rolling out' the state whereby the state extends its influence into areas of sport policy of previous relative autonomy.

Finally, over the last twenty years or so there has been a substantial change in the way that people connect with public services. As Goss has observed:

> For many people, public provision is no longer as important as it was …
> while most people still depend on public provision for health and education, fewer and fewer people depend on the public sector for housing, leisure and libraries. For a significant proportion of ordinary working people public provision has become marginal to their lives.
>
> (Goss 2001: 15–16)

With that marginality has come a greater scepticism about the role of the state, especially in areas such as sport, and a greater concern that public services should be able to demonstrate that they are delivering value for money. Although much of the supposed Thatcherite legacy has dissipated, there has been no return to the 'taken for granted' status of public services. While, for a significant number of citizens, public services remain a necessity, for an increasing proportion the utilisation of public services is a matter of choice.

One major consequence of this changing attitude towards public services, in general, and sport and leisure services, in particular, is that leisure services managers and sports development officers have to be able to demonstrate in easily recognised, if not quantifiable, terms that they are delivering a service which the consumers can recognise as an effective response to their needs, and which the generality of citizens or taxpayers can acknowledge as a politically desirable and efficient use of public resources. One clear implication is that public services, including sports development, must be better able to demonstrate their public value through persuasive and rigorous evaluation processes. Such concerns are at the heart of current experiments with benchmarking and Best Value, both of which are concerned to establish valid bases for service evaluation. However, attempts to evaluate service performance tend to rely heavily on quantitative rather than qualitative measures, and tend to focus on outputs rather than outcomes. Given that so much of sports development activity is directed towards the achievement of complex social outcomes, such as safer communities and social inclusion, it will be difficult indeed to identify indicators which provide valid evidence of the specific contribution that sports development is making to social outcomes.

Changes in the dominant core policy paradigm

If there were any expectations that the election of a Labour government in 1997 would mark an attempt to return to the pre-Thatcher welfare state, they were rapidly dispelled as Tony Blair made it clear that he intended that his government should reinvigorate the reform process rather than seek to unpick the reforms of the previous Conservative administrations. As Clarke *et al.* noted: 'The New Labour government ... proved to be just as enthusiastic about the reconstruction of welfare as a major political task' (2000: 1). Even accepting that much of the rhetoric surrounding the launch of 'New Labour' and 'The Third Way' was an attempt to distance the Labour Party from its past in the eyes of the electorate and also develop a distinctive identity in a less ideologically intense post-Cold War Britain, there was still a core of radicalism at the heart of the first Blair government. Whether that core represents continuity with the neo-liberal Conservative agenda or represents a new and distinctive trajectory for welfare policy is by no means easy to determine. On the one hand, there are those, such as Giddens (1998) and Driver and Martell (1998), who argue that the distinctive elements in New Labour are reflected in its pragmatism regarding service delivery, its priority of community over the individual, and its commitment to public services as the core aspects of society. On the other hand, there are those – Jones and Novak (1999), King and Wickham-Jones (1999) and Lavalette and Mooney (1999), for example – who identify firm evidence of continuity, both in terms of underlying ideology and in practical service decisions. Continuity is reflected not only in Labour's acceptance of Conservative government public expenditure plans for its first two years of office, but also in its rhetoric of traditional morality, its image of the active, self-reliant citizen and its enthusiasm for a mixed economy of welfare.

That there is such substantial disagreement over the precise character and antecedents of New Labour is hardly surprising and serves to warn against an over-simplification of the complex, often paradoxical and shifting character of current Labour policy towards welfare. However, with these caveats in mind, there still seems to be ample evidence that there is a commitment to reform the welfare system along lines closer to the radical agenda of the Thatcher years than the earlier period of welfare state consensus. Clarke *et al.* crisply summarise the continuity between New Labour and the Thatcher policy for welfare as reflecting a 'shared view of the primacy of economic competitiveness; of the subordination of public and social policy to promoting a competitive national economy; of the reduced or limited scope for government intervention or direction; of the significance of controlling public spending; and possibly, of the "incentivizing" effect of economic inequality' (2000: 13). It is against this background that more specific policies such as Best Value, social inclusion and modernisation need to be understood. The scope of these policies to deliver radical change is constrained by this more deeply rooted orientation to welfare and citizenship. Thus, for example, social inclusion is substantially defined as involvement in paid employment, with this priority incorporated into many of the contemporary sports-related programmes delivered by SDOs designed, in one way or another, to make young people in particular more employable.

At the local government level, the identification of a series of cross-cutting issues, including social inclusion, community safety, urban regeneration, life-long learning and healthy living, is one way in which the current welfare agenda is having an impact on the way sports development is undertaken. For example, the identification of 'disaffected youth' (itself a highly contested and vague term) as a cross-cutting issue draws together a range of problems involving some young people, including educational under-achievement, drug use, homelessness, abuse, family breakdown, and crime. The remit of the PAT 10 working group was, in part, to identify the potential contribution that sport could make to the alleviation of these problems and facilitate the reintegration of disaffected young people back into the social mainstream. The Positive Futures project, for example, is designed to satisfy objectives associated with both disaffected youth and community safety and is a partnership between Sport England, the Youth Justice Board and the UK Anti-Drugs Co-ordination Unit. Working through local authorities and other sports and non-sports organisations, the aim is to target young people 'at risk of disengagement' through a variety of programmes and projects, including the provision of sporting programmes as an alternative to a drug misuse culture, and the establishment of educational programmes linked to the development of sporting skills and healthy lifestyles. Sports-specific objectives are clearly subordinated to youth welfare objectives.

One of the themes to emerge from the government's debate on social inclusion, and related cross-cutting issues, is the importance given to the concepts of civil society and citizenship. It is in this area that there is some potential for social policy to take a different direction to that mapped out by the previous Conservative governments. As part of the process of reinvigorating democracy and creating opportunities for citizenship skills to be developed and used, there is an acknowledgement that if there was to be an effective rebuttal of Margaret Thatcher's famous claim that there was 'no such thing as society', some attention needed to be paid to supporting and rehabilitating the ingredients of civil society, most notably a democratic infrastructure at local level, citizens with the skills and confidence to use them and, perhaps even more importantly, a government which is open and responsive. The community development projects of the 1970s were often marginal to unreformed local authority bureaucracies which were loath to devolve power to communities and were, with one or two notable exceptions, unresponsive to local views. Effective local democracy requires the development of social capital, defined by Putnam as referring to the 'connections among individuals – social networks and the norms of reciprocity and trustworthiness that arise from them' (2000: 19), on the one hand, and a set of local institutions where social capital can be 'an actual, rather than potential, resource for democracy', on the other (Lowndes and Wilson 2001: 638). It remains to be seen whether the plethora of local partnerships will facilitate the deployment of social capital or simply manage it. In other words, good government requires the 'interaction between a civic-minded citizenry and civic-minded government actors' (Levi 1996: 50).

Even if local partnerships eventually disappoint, social capital may still be effectively deployed if there exists a network of institutions of civil society which are independent of the state and of the market and also sufficiently powerful to provide a counterbalance to both (Gellner 1995; Fine and Rai 1997). Diamond (1994) catalogues the significance of civil society to democracy arguing that it can provide a check on government power, aid the recruitment and training of leaders, and develop democratic skills associated with participation. Putnam, although writing about contemporary America, makes an eloquent case for the importance of sports participation in providing the social capital that binds society together. Charting the decline in sports participation and the increase in spectating, the decline in team sports especially among the young, and the rise of socially isolated and isolating sports and leisure activities, he concludes that sports trends both reflect and reinforce the diminution of social capital. 'In football, as in politics, watching a team play is not the same thing as playing on a team' (Putnam 2000: 114). As Allison (1998) has persuasively suggested, sports clubs are capable of fulfilling some of the functions identified by Diamond and are of particular significance primarily because of their sheer number, but also because of their occasional willingness to defend their autonomy, as illustrated by the rejection of Margaret Thatcher's proposed boycott of the 1980 Olympic Games by the major Olympic sports governing bodies. There is ample evidence of a recognition of the need to strengthen the capacity of clubs both within the four local authorities examined in chapter 5, and also within Sport England, which has a number of programmes aimed at supporting clubs and volunteers, including the Volunteer Investment Programme and the Running Sport training scheme for club officers.

A necessary complement to the support given to community organisations, including sports clubs, is the revival of the idea of citizenship. While it was ideologically convenient for the Conservative governments of Margaret Thatcher to prioritise economic individualism over citizenship, the latter now holds a place at the heart of the assumptions underpinning Best Value and is central to much of Labour's modernisation agenda. However, the concept of citizenship is ambiguous and has little practical significance unless it is accepted that the operationalisation of the attendant rights of the citizen require the recognition that citizenship rights are not bestowed externally but are built from within communities. It is in this regard that sport has a potentially important role to play. Much was made in the PAT 10 report of the extent to which sports development projects could support the reinvigoration of citizenship due to their capacity for 'valuing diversity, embedding local control, supporting local commitment [and] promoting equitable partnerships' (DCMS 1999: 8). More importantly, sports projects have the potential to move beyond Marshall's long-established conceptualisation of citizenship as comprising political, civil and social dimensions and accept that there is an important cultural element to full citizenship. Modern citizenship has two central aspects – rights and identity – with the latter becoming more significant in recent years. Both rights and identity have an important spatial dimension and are often spatially specific to the extent that the identity of Irish–British or black–British can most easily be fulfilled, and for some groups can only be fulfilled, within a particular local community. Cultural citizenship, which is an extension of, and not a substitute for, political citizenship involves the right to visibility rather than marginalisation, dignified representation rather than stigmatisation and the right to identity as opposed to cultural assimilation (Pakulski 1997).

Given the importance of citizenship to the Labour government and the area-based focus of many sports development projects, especially those established as part of the Active Sports programme and Sports Action Zones, there would seem to be a clear opportunity for local authority sports development officers to contribute to the development of citizenship skills and capacity building to produce what the PAT 16 report referred to as 'risk-takers, problem-solvers, people who make things happen – so there are people with the leadership skills, persistence and drive to design sensible programmes, invigorate partnerships and mobilise communities' (Social Exclusion Unit 2000c: 17). The concern to revitalise the concept of citizenship and boost the

institutions of civil society and the part that sport is expected to play differenti-
ates New Labour from the governments of Margaret Thatcher insofar as the
former acknowledges the importance of the fabric of civil society for the
achievement of many of its public policy goals. The institutions of civil society
and an active citizenry are, however, the means to goals which are broadly
similar to those of the new right, namely, the creation of more self-reliant,
wealth-generating and ambitious individuals and communities.

Changes in the service-specific paradigm for sports development

As mentioned earlier, the salience of sport in general and sports development in particular has been highly variable. Since 1990 sport has moved
from a position beyond the periphery of governmental vision to a location
much closer to the core agenda of government. The radical re-evaluation of
the utility of sport to government undertaken by John Major was not significantly altered by Tony Blair. Both governments produced policy statements
and both identified substantial sums of new and, for a time at least, additional money to support policy implementation. In their different ways the
administrations of both John Major and Tony Blair have contributed
substantially to shaping the current service paradigm for sports development. Perhaps the most important contribution from John Major was in
overcoming the long-established reticence on the part of government to
accept that international sporting success required a level of professionalism
and a resource base that was well beyond the capacity of the vast majority
of sports governing bodies. The allocation of substantial sums of quasi-
public finance in the form of National Lottery funding to the pursuit of
elite success marked a profound change in the paradigm for sports development. That the current Labour government endorsed so unreservedly the
previous government's policy is evidence that there has been a shift in the
sports development paradigm that is unlikely to alter over the medium term.

One consequence of the prioritisation of elite achievement is the stimulation of the trend towards a greater degree of compartmentalisation and
specialisation within sports development. In the early 1990s the sports development continuum provided not only an intellectual integration between
different sports development activities and policies, but also provided a practical framework within which organisations could relate their particular
projects and programmes to core policy aims and also make sense of the
activities of other policy actors. However, the level of policy integration of
the early 1990s was relatively short lived. The repackaging of existing Sport
England projects under the three Active programmes that followed the earlier
establishment of the World Class Performance programmes symbolised the
extent to which clusters of programmes were becoming associated with
increasingly discrete policy objectives (participation, high performance, etc.)
and were also being supported and delivered by increasingly specialist organisations. Throughout the 1990s there was a steady growth in the number of

specialist organisations with a relatively narrow remit in terms of both expertise and policy focus. The National Coaching Foundation was one of the first examples, followed by others such as the Youth Sport Trust and UK Sport. Table 7.3 summarises the emerging clustering of organisations, sources of funding and programmes around elements of the sports development continuum.

Table 7.3 Clustering of interests in sports development

Primary focus	Foundation	Participation	Performance	Excellence
Lead organisations	Youth Sport Trust and schools	Local authorities, clubs and schools	Sports clubs, National Governing Bodies of sport and Specialist Sports Colleges	National Governing Bodies of sport, and selected clubs; UK Sports Institute; British Olympic Association
Supporting organisations	School Sports Alliance and the Professional Development Board	Sport England	Sport England and Sports Coach UK (NCF)	BASES, National Sports Medicine Institute, UK Sport, Sport England, selected universities
Main programmes	National Curriculum for Physical Education, Active Schools, and TOPs	Active Communities	Active Sports	World Class Programmes
Primary source of funding	Local authorities, DfES, Sport England Sport Lottery Fund and the National Lottery New Opportunities Fund	Local authorities and Sport England Sport Lottery Fund	Voluntary sector (club subscription; fund-raising; club house trading), commercial investment, Sport England Sport Lottery Fund and DfES	Sport England Sport Lottery Fund, UK Sport Lottery Sport Fund, commercial sponsorship; broadcasting income
Increasingly marginalised organisations	Local authorities		Local authorities, schools and school county sports associations	

To an extent, such clustering is an inevitable consequence of the rapid growth in sports development activity over the last decade and the increasing maturity of the policy sector. However, while the greater degree of specialisation within sports development is welcome, it is important to consider what the consequences might be and how they will be managed. For example, the steady marginalisation of local government from involvement in most elements of the sports development continuum except participation has potentially major implications for sports development as a whole. Despite the extent to which the development of excellence is becoming more self-contained, illustrated by the establishment of specialist facilities and services at UKSI regional centres, it is easy to overlook the significant contribution that local authorities make to excellence (as well as participation and performance) through the provision and subsidy of specialist training and competition venues, including athletics stadiums, velodromes, ice rinks, and Olympic standard swimming and diving pools. Similarly, current compartmentalisation of sports development policy puts at risk the significant contribution that schools, outside the 150 or so specialist sports colleges, and the various schools sports associations make to talent identification and development. Much the same can be said with regard to the role of institutions of higher education and the British Universities Sports Association, which contribute substantially to sports development at the performance and excellence levels, but may well also be marginalised as talented student athletes are encouraged to attend universities that are strongly linked to a regional UKSI centre.

A much more significant danger of the growing segmentation of sports development policy is that organisations that are increasingly strongly linked through involvement in common programmes, or with particular categories of participant, evolve into protective coalitions seeking to preserve and expand their share or resources and policy influence, even if this is achieved at the expense of other sectors of the sports development network. At present it is possible to identify four potential advocacy coalitions within sports development with one of the strongest being that focused on high performance achievement in Olympic and major team sports. Three organisations, or groups of organisations, with strong overlapping interests (the BOA, UK Sport and the UKSI, and the relevant national governing bodies) provide a potentially powerful coalition to defend the substantial gains of recent years and further consolidate the central position of elite sports development. School/youth sport provides the focus for the second cluster of organisations which, while receiving strong support from governments in the last ten years, is not yet quite so coherent or cohesive as the elite coalition. The Youth Sport Trust, Sport England, the growing number of specialist sports colleges and the Department for Education and Skills have a strong interest in this sub-area and possess the potential to establish a formidable defensive and promotional advocacy coalition.

Much weaker, by comparison, are the clusters of interests concerned primarily with community sport/Sport For All and with the performance element of the sports development continuum. Sport For All relies very heavily on the leadership of local authorities yet, as has been demonstrated, local authority sports development units are being drawn ever more firmly into the orbit of policies concerned with the broader agenda of community regeneration. Similarly weak is the cluster of interests concerned with the provision of opportunities to play sport at the performance or routine competitive level. Sports governing bodies and their constituent clubs provide the primary organisational focus and the Active Sports partnerships the current policy initiative. However, as the partnerships are in their infancy, it would be premature to provide an assessment of their effectiveness. At present there is no serious shortage of resources to support activity in each of the four increasingly discrete areas of sports development work. However, as resources become more constrained – as they undoubtedly will – the coalitions associated with elite and school/youth sports development seem far better able to fulfil an effective defensive and advocacy function than those for performance and participation.

Interaction between structural interest groups

As mentioned in chapter 1, the interaction between structural interest groups provides an important dynamic for policy change and stability. In the previous section the growing demarcation between clusters of interest was noted as a significant factor in shaping the future of the policy area. The segmentation of interests cuts across, albeit unevenly, the various structural interests. Demand groups are still of marginal importance to the policy process, as indeed they have been throughout the history of sports development. The only limited exception is the presence of groups which represent the interests of elite athletes. Although professional sports have had players' unions of various kinds for some time, these have tended to have interests which were largely outside the scope of public policy for sports development. Only relatively recently have organisations such as the Professional Footballers Association become involved in broader sports development issues such as football in the community schemes and those linked to talent identification and development. In general, the exclusive focus of many of these bodies has been a narrow economism with there being few examples of engagement with broader sport policy debates. Outside professional/commercial sports the British Olympic Association's Athletes Commission has fulfilled a representative role, but it too has had little involvement beyond the narrowly defined interests of Olympic athletes. More recently, UK Competitors was formed with the aim of representing and promoting the interests of elite athletes in their relationships with organisations such as their governing body, sponsors and doping-control agencies. UK Competitors is still in its infancy and it remains to be seen how effective a lobby it will be, but it is one more addition to the range of organisations that represent the interests of the elite athlete 'demand groups' and highlights the dearth of demand groups to represent the interests of the young and the community sports participant, for example.

It is among provider groups that the clearest reflection of the segmentation of sports development can be found. Local authority SDOs are finding it increasingly difficult to sustain a perception of their work as being defined primarily by sports outcomes, and there appears to be a marked number who are taking a pragmatic decision to redefine their service outcomes in terms of cross-cutting issues and integrate their activities more tightly with those of larger directorates. The picture among sports clubs is more mixed with evidence from the case studies suggesting that, while the majority of clubs retain a broadly social/participation function, a significant number are being given/adopting a more central responsibility in the talent identification and development strategy of their national governing body. In hockey, for example, the switch from a loose series of largely knock-out competitions and informal or county-based leagues to a much more competitive and highly structured framework of national leagues was prompted by the clear motive of enabling elite players to experience top-class matches more regularly. The more intense specialisation among provider groups is reinforced by the emergence of additional organisations strongly focused on high performance sport, including the UK Sports Institute and its regional centres and the small group of universities that are playing an increasing prominent role in elite sports development. Between them this cluster of bodies has the potential to provide a cohesive lobby on behalf of elite sports development. There is a similar clustering of existing groups and the formation of new groups in the area of youth/school sport. The recent appointment of school sports co-ordinators and the establishment and heightened profile of specialist sports colleges has added weight to, but also sharpened and possibly skewed the focus of, existing physical education provider groups, such as the PEA UK.

A similar process of segmentation and clustering is also evident among direct support groups. Prompted by the Sports Councils, national governing bodies are linking their activities to the government's twin priorities of elite achievement and youth development. A strong resource dependency relationship has been created between the government and the major governing bodies, through the Sports Councils, given that the bulk of finance available to governing bodies is for facilities and services to underpin elite success. A similar cluster of organisations has emerged around school sport with the new School Sport Alliance likely to add weight to the already influential Youth Sport Trust.

It is possible to trace an increasingly tightly interlinked set of organisations associated with elite sport and school sport that cut across demand, provider and direct support groups, which have the potential to maintain existing policy direction and momentum. The recent publication of the Cunningham Report, which argued, inter alia, that elite sport needed a further £10 million each year over the next four years if the achievements of British competitors at the Sydney Olympic Games were to be defended successfully in 2004, reflected the growing confidence of elite sports interests. In the area of school sport, the strong support for specialist sports colleges in the government White Paper 'Schools: Achieving Success' is also evidence of the school sport lobby taking full advantage of a sympathetic government.

It seems that it is only at the level of indirect support groups that the interests of the general sports participant receives significant consideration, but only as an instrument of community development. The renewed interest in sport among land use planners, community workers, the police and local authority redevelopment directorates is largely limited to the contribution that it might make to non-sports objectives. Economic regeneration partnerships have substantial resources, access to which is firmly controlled and limited to those sports organisations and sports development units that can demonstrate a capacity and willingness to subsume their objectives within those of the partnership. The efforts to build sports-specific partnerships through the Active Sports programme is hampered by resourcing that can best be described as modest and which is also time-constrained. While these partnerships are likely to make a noticeable contribution to the range of opportunities for young people to make the transition from the participation level to the performance level, their scale of activity and the level of resource investment is dwarfed by that being channelled to schools and elite sport. Advocacy on behalf of participation and routine performance is appreciably weaker than that for other interests, and is likely to be squeezed once funding becomes more tightly constrained.

Changes in administrative arrangements

It is easy to over-estimate the significance of changes to the administrative arrangements for services. When faced with ineffective policy or inefficient service delivery, politicians turn to administrative reform as a highly visible solution when a more effective response might be to improve the leadership capacity of management, examine processes, modify cultures or provide greater clarity of goals. The administrative history of both central and local government is littered with bouts of structural reform and tinkering and the last few years have been no different. While it is easy to dismiss some administrative change as having little impact beyond the change of logo on the departmental letterhead, there have, in recent years, been some changes, especially at local government level, which have considerable potential to affect the structural context of sports development activity.

Structural change at local government level was prompted by a range of factors including: first, the increased political salience of issues, such as regeneration and community safety, that straddle the traditional single-profession/single-service department; second, the impact of the Local

Government Review and the creation of a number of new unitary authorities which were able to establish structures from scratch; and, third, pressure from central government to modernise. As a result, the authority with nine or ten service committees linked to professionally based, single-service departments is rapidly declining and being replaced, in many cases, by a small number of multi-service directorates. In a study in 1995, the Local Government Management Board found that the majority of local authorities which responded to its survey had changed their departmental structure, mainly to reduce the number of departments and restructure around multi-service departments with a stronger corporate core. The experience of Coventry, Kent and Herefordshire is thus far from being a series of isolated examples. One obvious consequence for sports development units is that they are now likely to sit within much larger, diverse and complex departments and thus have the opportunity to establish a profile across a broader range of services in their directorate or, less optimistically, run the risk of slipping beyond the field of vision of senior managers and policy-makers. Where the move to directorates is accompanied by the abandonment of the traditional committee system and its replacement by policy-making through cabinets, the risk of marginalisation is compounded as sports development will be one of many services seeking the attention of one cabinet member. Opportunities to lobby on behalf of sports development diminish as the number of traditional access points to the decision-making process through the ten or so committee members or through the larger membership of corporate management teams decline. If this problem is being experienced in some of the larger and well-established sports development units covered in this study, then the problems facing the more typical sports development units are potentially severe.

However, it is important to stress the opportunities that structural reform within local government has created. The period of intense reform in local government has been paralleled by radical change in many other public and voluntary organisations such that the architecture of service provision is substantially different from that of ten years ago. The health service has experienced numerous structural changes, creating many potential new partners at local level, including Primary Care Trusts and GP consortia; the police service has tended to devolve greater responsibility to divisional level; the voluntary welfare sector has seen a massive expansion in its contribution to care of the elderly and those with mental health problems; and the housing association sector has expanded, not only due to the transfer of local authority-owned housing, but also due to pressure from the Housing Corporation to broaden their community involvement beyond the simple provision of housing and collaborate in more widely defined community development projects. As Goss succinctly observes, 'New spaces for joint working are being created, and it is easier for organisations to come together at regional, locality and neighbourhood levels' (Goss 2001: 73).

A second change in the administrative arrangements of local government directly concerns the 'new spaces for joint working' identified by Goss and is one that has taken place much more quietly, but which has much greater potential to affect sports development – namely, the emergence of partnerships. Partnerships have become much more prominent for a number of reasons: first, the prominence of cross-cutting issues; second, frustration on the part of central government with the slow pace of structural change within local authorities to support the cross-cutting agenda; third, the steady shift in resources and responsibility for service delivery to the voluntary sector; fourth, the increasing requirement on local authorities and other public agencies to bid for funding and to meet the expectations of funding agencies for closer collaborative working; fifth, the continuing pressure on local authority budgets; and finally, the substantial pressure from the Department for the Environment, Transport and the Regions to use Local Strategic Partnerships as the primary vehicle for neighbourhood renewal.

Partnerships can take many forms and vary considerably in terms of formality, levels of resource commitment and lifespan. The key principle underlying the use of partnerships is that geographical boundaries and functional demarcation between organisations should no longer be a barrier to developing an effective response to social problems. Consequently, partnerships have linked local authorities across county boundaries as well as with a range of other public sector and voluntary bodies. Although partnerships are still in their infancy, there is already an emerging consensus that they offer tremendous potential, but there is also an acknowledgement that realising that potential is harder than first thought (Social Exclusion Unit 2000b; Richards *et al.* 1999). The evidence from the case studies confirms both the potential of partnerships and also the costs and frustrations involved. While the small-scale partnerships with a few well-established and sports-focused partners can produce remarkable results, as in Herefordshire, or offer the prospect of benefits, as with the Active Sports programmes, the larger multi-agency partnerships, such as that in Derbyshire, demand substantial initial resource investment and are inevitably slower to build momentum, although they promise to deliver substantial community benefits once they are fully functioning. According to Goss, the general view among researchers is that partnerships 'seem to be good at strategy, planning, document writing, research, data-gathering and so on, delivery is harder' (2001: 95). Processes within partnerships are inevitably slow due to the need for often extensive negotiation, the number of potential veto points and the absence of formal authority structures that are able to prompt compliance. Yet partnerships are often cumbersome vehicles for policy because each tends to have its own peculiar processes for accessing the particular government funding stream, as well as distinctive requirements for monitoring and reporting, often on an annual basis, resulting in high management costs and frustratingly slow decision-making. There is also the danger of partnership fatigue due to the rapid increase in the number of part-nerships which often involve the same over-extended staff. Partnership working can be a major drain on scarce senior staff resources within small sports development teams. Moreover, there is risk that partnerships overlap and end up competing with each other for resources and developing parallel expertise, as in the case of the Coalfields Alliance and the acknowledged sports development expertise in both Nottinghamshire and Derbyshire. Perhaps of greatest concern is that, despite the weight of government pressure to explore the potential of partnerships, 'crosscutting issues are driven to the margins by strong departmental interests and traditional silo mentalities, reinforced by professional alliances across central/local boundaries and by powerful incentives to concentrate on national service targets' (Goss 2001: 95).

Large-scale cross-boundary and multi-organisational partnerships are undoubtedly difficult to manage and will require continued powerful support from government if they are to overcome the deeply entrenched departmentalism within local authorities. Not surprisingly, the prospects are much brighter for smaller-scale partnerships between organisations with broadly similar objectives, as with Active Sports, and also as in many of the examples from the four local authorities. While the extent of contribution to cross-cutting issues varies, there is sufficient evidence of benefits to both the development of sport and to the development of communities to warrant their continued support and refinement.

One way in which government is attempting to increase the responsive-ness and flexibility of local service providers and also maintain the momentum behind the use of partnerships is by strengthening the regional level of administration. Over recent years there has been a steady expansion of the regional level of administration and government. The Government Offices for the Regions have had their remit gradually widened, regional development agencies are well established, and regional cultural consor-tiums have delivered their initial strategic plans. In addition, the Minister for Sport has made clear his support for a stronger role for Sport England at regional level and there have been discussions within the DCMS about expanding the role of the Regional Sports Boards to include some respon-sibility for the distribution of the National Lottery-funded 'Awards for All'.

In early 2000 the government published a report, *Reaching Out*, from its Performance and Innovation Unit (Regional Co-ordination Unit 2000), which made it clear that the regional level of government was to be the engine for driving the development of local partnerships/area-based initia-tives. The report addressed many of the factors noted by Goss which threatened to stymie the success of partnerships. In his foreword Tony Blair noted that the report confirmed that 'too many good projects are having to waste time negotiating their way through complex systems of unnecessary red tape, with different rules, time scales, and accounting arrangements', and went on to endorse the central recommendation of the report that there should be 'a stronger role for Government Offices in the regions in pulling together the different arms of central government; new arrangements in Whitehall; and new mechanisms to streamline the variety of different funding streams, initiatives and arrangements' (*ibid.*: 1).

Government Offices for the Regions were established in 1994 in order to co-ordinate the services provided by four departments (Environment, Transport, Employment and Trade and Industry) as the delivery arm of the four parent departments. Current recommendations are to give 'Government Offices a strongly enhanced role in supporting and evaluating local performance on strategic and cross-cutting issues' (*ibid.*: para. 3.16). The enhanced Government Offices will be 'the leading element of central government in the regions' (*ibid.*: para. 3.19) and have a responsibility to 'ensure that other Government Departments represented at regional and local level understand their relative role in relation to cross-cutting issues' (*ibid.*: para. 3.19). The reference to other central government departments would include the DCMS, which already has a small number of staff seconded to Government Offices. Moreover, the Government Offices are intended to have a much more proactive role in relation to local authorities and cross-cutting issues 'influencing the way bids are presented to Government by local players to ensure they accord with central Government priorities and relate to other local initiatives; [and] encouraging local and regional players to address cross-cutting issues' (*ibid.*: para. 3.20). To support the expanded role for Government Offices it is agreed that they should have greater flexibility over the use of public funds although the extent of change has yet to become apparent.

Reaching Out also reviewed the role of the Regional Development Agencies (RDAs), largely in response to a report from the House of Commons Select Committee on Environment, Transport and Regional Affairs in 1999 (House of Commons 1999) which noted, inter alia, confusion over the respective roles of the RDAs and the Government Offices, particularly with regard to social inclusion initiatives. Although the RDAs have a primary concern with economic regeneration and skills development, they have the potential to affect sharply sports development activity where it involves capital programmes or training and lifelong learning. The Regional Co-ordination Unit's review also offered the prospect of greater financial flexibility for RDAs, although it was cautious about any rapid expansion of their role until they were more firmly established. Also at an early stage in their development are the regional assemblies that parallel the work of the RDAs. Most regional assemblies work closely with their RDA and act as a sounding board and as a forum in which the wider community of the region can engage with the agency. While the assemblies have yet to establish fully their role, there are signs already that they will have an impact on the direction of RDA activity, and may be especially significant in promoting and defending sport and the other 'cultural service' due to the overlap of membership between the assembly and the Regional Cultural Consortiums recently established by the DCMS.

The Regional Cultural Consortiums were established to provide a unified voice for the cultural sector within the regions, especially with regard to other regional bodies, with one of their initial tasks being to formulate a regional cultural strategy. The establishment of the consortiums and the assemblies poses a considerable challenge to sports development in ensuring that their interests are not lost in the scramble for influence. While some SDOs looked upon the growing importance of regional bodies as a threat to their service because of the relative strength of competing lobbies, such as those for museums, libraries and the arts, others recognised that the developments at regional level provided a major opportunity to gain recognition and additional resources for sports development activity. For example, in many of the cultural audits undertaken as part of the process of developing the regional cultural strategies, sport and sports development featured prominently, not only in contributing to cross-cutting social issues, but also in contributing to the regional economy.

Sport is beginning to learn from the hard experience of the arts in the 1980s, which were dismissed by the Thatcher governments as solely elements of public consumption that made little contribution to the production of wealth. It took much of the decade before the arts lobby accumulated sufficient evidence to demonstrate that, far from being merely consumers of public subsidy, they made a major contribution to the service economy in terms of job creation and exports through tourism. Similar evidence is now being accumulated on behalf of sport. The research undertaken in preparation of the regional cultural strategy for the East Midlands, for example, emphasised the economic impact of sport. Not only did the Cultural Consortium stress to the RDA that one-quarter of all jobs in the region are in the cultural sector, but also that sports employment was both the largest employment sub-sector and also the fastest growing between 1991 and 1997, enjoying a growth of 92.5 per cent compared to a national figure of 52.9 per cent (Ecotec 2000: 19).

As suggested by the experience in the East Midlands, there is much evidence of the contribution that sport and sports development can make to the social and economic objectives of the various regional agencies and forums. However, in order to make the most of the evidence, there is a need for sports organisations at the regional level which can utilise the evidence effectively. The two bodies which might fulfil that role are the regional offices of Sport England and the Regional Sports Boards. While the former has the organisational capacity and the formal links with both the Regional Cultural Consortiums and the Regional Assemblies, Sport England's regional offices are constrained in their lobbying activity by their constitutional position and also by uncertainty caused by having three Sports Ministers in as many years and a change of Chief Executive in 2001. The Regional Sports Boards have the potential to fulfil a strong advocacy role at regional level as the Boards will be represented on the Regional Cultural Consortiums and may also be represented on the Regional Assemblies.

However, the Boards have generally yet to convince regarding their capacity to be successful advocates. In general they are under-resourced, often reliant on a part-time administrator and grant aid from Sport England, and, as a result, the DCMS delayed its decision to transfer responsibility for the award of small lottery grants to the Boards.

The emerging pattern of resource dependencies

Mention has already been made of the increasing self-sufficiency of particular aspects of sports development with bespoke programmes, specialist organisations and funding arrangements. However, the restructuring of sports development in each of the four sub-areas over recent years has largely been the result of the strategic use of National Lottery funds and, as such, has given the government, working through the Sports Councils, substantially enhanced leverage over the actions of a broad range of independent or semi-independent organisations. The significance of lottery funding is not so much that it is additional to existing resources for, as Table 7.4 shows, that is highly debatable, but rather that it is 'new' money in the sense that it is unencumbered by the accumulated historical commitments and consequent inertia that greatly limits the capacity of local authorities and schools, in particular, to refocus budgets over the short term. The dominance of a bidding culture in local government inhibits the establishment of local priorities, especially in non-statutory policy areas such as sport.

Table 7.4   Public expenditure on sport, England and Wales, 1992/3 to 2000/1 (current prices, £million)

Financial year	1992/3	1993/4	1994/5	1995/6	1996/7	1997/8	1998/9	1999/ 2000	2000/1
Sport England grant	50	54	53	54	52	50	49	52	52
Sports Council for Wales grant	5	6	7	6	7	6	7	7	7
Local authorities in England and Wales	957	988	986	994	1,014	993	1,013	1,020	1,022
National Lottery Sports Fund (England and Wales)	0	0	51	227	204	208	198	190	183
Total	1,012	1,048	1,097	1,281	1,277	1,257	1,267	1,269	1,264

Source: Po Wen Ku (2001)

A secondary trend in the pattern of resource dependencies – namely, the growth in specialist expertise – is one that might offer some counter-balance to the increasing centralisation of policy influence with the government due to its control of funding. In the last ten years or so a number of specialist bodies have emerged concerned directly or indirectly with sports development. The National Coaching Foundation (Sports Coach UK), the National Sports Medicine Institute, the Sport and Recreation Industry Training Organisation, a small number of university sports science departments, the UKSI and its regional centres, and the Youth Sport Trust are all highly focused and specialist bodies to which the government or the various Sports Councils must turn to for advice and service delivery in areas crucial to the success of policy objectives. However, while expertise undoubtedly provides leverage on policy, the capacity of these bodies to exploit their knowledge resources is limited by the fact that with few exceptions they too are locked into a financial dependency relationship with government.

Conclusion

It would be churlish to argue that sports development has not benefited hugely from the rise in the political salience of the service to both Conservative and Labour governments and from the availability of National Lottery funding. Much to the chagrin of those who would try and maintain the spurious separation of sport and politics, the last ten years amply demonstrate that a political profile (albeit a carefully managed one) is a prerequisite for attracting public resources to sports development. The emergence of sports development as a political issue has resulted in the injection of substantial sums of money into the policy area and has, as outlined above, led to both greater fragmentation and greater specialisation within sports development. Whether the emergent advocacy coalitions have a sufficient overlap of interests to enable them to lobby collectively on behalf of an inclusive conception of sports development remains to be seen. However, it is increasingly difficult to accept that the SDO delivering a primary school TOPs programme, the outreach worker organising street hockey in a deprived urban area, and the high performance coach of a national squad perceive themselves to be involved in a common endeavour. A perception of distinctive interests is the more likely outcome of the sharpening demarcation between different aspects of sports development and one that can only be intensified should the resource base for sports development decline, as it is likely to do given the tendency for the government to use lottery funding for a broader range of services and the decline in the sales of lottery tickets. Indeed, the fragility of the resource base must be a major concern to SDOs in both local authorities and governing bodies as far too many organisations perceive lottery funding to be a virtual 'free good' which requires little investment from their own core resources, so that if and when lottery funding declines there are few residual obligations that have to be met.

Earlier in this study it was suggested that the sports development continuum gave the service an intellectual coherence and offered the possibility of creating a service culture where quite disparate activities could be perceived as contributing to a broader, but common, endeavour. Although the continuum is still referred to, it has drifted into the background and is not part of the everyday language of sports development, having been displaced by the terminology of the various Active and World Class programmes. If the conceptual unity of sports development is weakening, so too is the integration at the level of day-to-day experience of SDOs where the emerging dichotomy between development of sport and community development is most apparent. There is an increasingly pronounced differentiation of activity between local authority SDOs, who are progressively being drawn into social policy partnerships, and governing body SDOs, whose focus is talent identification and youth development.

One important attempt to give a greater degree of coherence to sports development is the formation of the National Association for Sports Development (NASD), which does bring together SDOs from across the public and the voluntary sectors. Like so many organisations involved in sports development work, it is new and just finding its feet, but it does offer the prospect of an organisational focus for an inclusive definition of sports development that can emphasise the common interests of SDOs whether working in schools, with national governing bodies or for local authorities. The link between NASD and the Institute of Sport and Recreation Management provides a secure organisation context, while the strong expressions of support for career development and training for SDOs expressed by the government in *A Sporting Future For All* have ensured a sound start for the new body. However, it is indeed a formidable challenge to bind together SDOs who are involved in an increasing specialised range of activities, have a broad range of organisational locations and differing degrees of financial security.

Overall, the picture painted in this study is of a dynamic service operating in a turbulent, though relatively well-resourced, environment. On the positive side, SDOs have shown themselves to be highly adaptable and innovative and, with regard to those working in local authorities, in the vanguard of experiments in partnership working. On the negative side, there is little evidence of SDOs being influential in affecting the policy direction of their service; in this respect they are very much policy-takers rather than policy-makers and, as such, are constantly having to adapt to policy change that has its origins beyond their policy area. As with sport policy generally, sports development lacks the systemic embeddedness that exists in other service areas such as health and education, where the organisational and professional roots are multiple and go deep into the infrastructure of political parties, the government and the state. The challenge facing those involved in all aspects of sports development is to secure the status of the service politically, financially and organisationally – a daunting, but not impossible, challenge.

Notes

1 The origins of sports development: the 1960s to the mid-1970s

1   The fifth structural interest group is co-ordinating groups whose function is to rationalise programmes between sectors aimed at reducing inefficiencies. While this function can be identified in British public administration – for example, in the role of corporate planners at the local authority level – it is difficult to distinguish this group from the administrative group, and this function is therefore best seen as part of a broader administrative role.
2   See Kirk (1992) for a detailed history and analysis of the restructuring of the post-war PE curriculum.

2 The mid-1970s to the early 1990s: sports development comes of age

1   See Loney et al. (1991) for a broader review, and Dunleavy (1991) for a vigorous challenge to the right-wing analysis of bureaucratic self-interest.
2   This section draws on Wilding (1997).
3   Quango is an acronym for Quasi-Autonomous National Government Organisation.
4   The title 'Sports Council' will be used to refer to the British Sports Council; other sports councils or the regional offices of the British Sports Council will be referred to by their full titles.
5   Coghlan (1990: 220) reports that the employment arrangements added £450,000 to the cost of the programme over the three years through the necessity of paying value-added tax (VAT).

3 The early 1990s to 1997: welfare restructuring and Major's sporting glory

1   There will be a fuller discussion of contemporary sports development policy in the next chapter.
2   Category A sports were association football, athletics, cricket, cycling, gymnastics, hockey, judo, netball, rugby union and league, sailing and swimming. Category B sports (development of excellence) were canoeing, golf, rowing, squash, and triathlon. Category B (young people) were badminton, basketball, fitness/aerobics, orienteering, table tennis and tennis.

4 New Labour: the reinvigoration of sports development

1   http://www.sportengland.org/whatwedo/active_commune/zones.htm

5 Sports development in four local authorities

1 RECHAR, RESIDER and RETEX are European Regional Development Funds Community initiatives aimed at assisting areas or regions severely affected by the decline of the coal, steel or textile industries respectively by accelerating economic diversification and regeneration.

2 Hereafter referred to as the Derbyshire and Peak Park Strategy.

3 The figure is for the former local authority of Hereford and Worcester. The figure for Herefordshire alone would be lower as there are more higher-paid jobs in Worcestershire.

4 Active Sports is targeted at eight to sixteen year olds. To date, 45 Sports Partnerships have been established across the country with local authorities as the primary partners. The selected sports are: athletics, basketball, cricket, girls' football, netball, hockey, rugby union, rugby league, swimming and tennis.

6 Sports development and four national governing bodies of sport

1 Women's hockey was organised into counties and territories rather than counties and regions. Territories were larger areas than the regions which were adopted in the men's game.

7 Development of sport and/or development through sport?

1 Moore defines 'public value' as comprising two activities, first the production of 'things of value to particular clients and beneficiaries' and might include well-maintained pitches and indoor sports facilities and, second, meeting 'citizens' and their (representatives') desires for properly ordered and productive public institutions' (1998: 53). In other words public value is broadly equated with the generation of measurable improvements in service levels.

References

Advisory Sports Council (1965) *Terms of Reference of the Sports Council and its Committees*, London: Advisory Sports Council.

Albemarle Report (1960) *The Youth Service in England and Wales*, London: HMSO.

All England Women's Hockey Association/Hockey Association (AEWHA/HA) (1996) *Hockey: A Chance for All*, Milton Keynes: AEWHA/HA.

Allison, L. (1998) 'Sport and civil society', *Political Studies* 46(4): 709–26.

Amateur Rowing Association (ARA) (1998) *Oxford Adaptive Rowing (OAR): A Guide for Future Groups*, London: ARA.

—— (1999a) *Umpire Recruitment*, London: ARA.

—— (1999b) *Rowing Facilities Strategy 1999–2005*, London: ARA.

—— (2001) *Draft Forward Plan 2001–2005*, London: ARA.

Audit Commission (1989) *Sport For Whom?*, London: HMSO.

Bachrach, P.S. and Baratz, M.S. (1962) 'Two faces of power', *American Political Science Review* 56: 1947–52.

—— (1963) 'Decisions and non-decisions: an analytical framework', *American Political Science Review* 57: 641–51.

—— (1970) *Power and Poverty: Theory and Practice*, New York: Oxford University Press.

Baring, T. (1999) 'Head to head on question of additionality', *Lottery Monitor* 4(6) October: 6–7.

Benson, J.K. (1975) 'The interorganisational network as a political economy', *Administrative Science Quarterly* 20: 229–49.

—— (1979) *Interorganisational Networks and Policy Sectors: Notes Towards Comparative Analysis*, unpublished paper, University of Missouri.

—— (1982) 'A framework for policy analysis', in D.A. Whetton and D.L. Rogers (eds) *Interorganisational Co-ordination*, Iowa: Iowa University Press.

Birley, D. (1995) *Land of Sport and Glory: Sport and British Society 1887–1910*, Manchester: Manchester University Press.

Board of Education (1939) *Secondary Education* (Spens Report), London: HMSO.

—— (1944) *Teachers and Youth Leaders* (McNair Report), London: HMSO.

Brackenridge, C. (2001) *Spoilsports: Understanding and Preventing Sexual Exploitation in Sport*, London: Routledge.

Buchan, A. (1998) 'The strategic message that local authorities cannot ignore', *Lottery Monitor* 3(July): 6–7.

—— (2000) 'North beats south in local success', *Lottery Monitor* 4(8): 1–2.

Buchanan, J.M. (1978) *The Economics of Politics*, London: Institute of Economic Affairs.

Bunker, D. and Thorpe, R. (1982) 'A model for the teaching of games in secondary schools', *Bulletin of Physical Education* 18(1): 3–8.

Butcher, H. (1994) 'The concept of community practice', in L. Haywood (ed.) *Community Leisure and Recreation*, Oxford: Butterworth Heinemann.

Centre for Leisure Research (1993) *Sport and Leisure Management: Compulsory Competitive Tendering; National information survey report*, London: Sports Council.

City of Coventry (1995) *Coventry Sports Development Strategy: Leading Sport into the 21st Century*, Coventry: Leisure Services Department.

—— (2000a) *Best Value Performance Plan 2000/2001*, Coventry: City of Coventry Council.

—— (2000b) *Coventry Community Plan*, Coventry: City of Coventry Council.

—— (2000c) *Grant Aid Agreement: Coventry City Council in Partnership with Coventry Sports Foundation*, Coventry: City of Coventry Council.

—— (2001a) *Cultural Development Services Plan 2001/2002*, Coventry: Cultural Services Division.

—— (2001b) *Our Future in Our Hands: Wood End, Henley Green, Manor Farm and Deedmore 'New Deal For Communities' Partnership Delivery Plan*, Coventry: City of Coventry Regeneration Unit.

—— (n.d.) *A Charter for Sports Clubs in Coventry*, Coventry: Leisure Services Department.

Clarke, J. (1996) 'The problem of the state after the welfare state', *Social Policy Review* 8: 24–37.

Clarke, J., Gewirtz, S. and McLaughlin, E. (2000) *New Managerialism, New Welfare?*, London: Sage.

Coalter, F., Long, J. and Duffield, B. (eds) (1986) *Rationale for Public Sector Investment in Leisure*, London: Sports Council and Economic and Social Research Council.

Coghlan, J.F. with I. Webb (1990) *Sport and British Politics since 1960*, Brighton: Falmer.

Collins, M. (1993a) *Research on Sports Development*, mimeo, Loughborough: University of Loughborough.

—— (1993b) *Sports Development Revisited: Threats and Opportunities in the '90s*, mimeo, Loughborough: University of Loughborough.

—— (1995) *Sports Development Locally and Regionally*, Reading: Institute of Leisure and Amenity Management.

Conservative Political Centre (1958) 'The future of the welfare state', in I. Macleod (ed.) *The Political Divide*, London: Conservative Political Centre.

Deakin, N. (1994) *The Politics of Welfare*, Hemel Hempstead: Harvester Wheatsheaf.

Deakin, N. and Edwards, J. (1993) *The Enterprise Culture and Inner Cities*, London: Routledge.

Department of Culture, Media and Sport (DCMS) (1998a) Press Release 110/98, London: DCMS.

—— (1998b) *The DCMS Comprehensive Spending Review: A New Approach to Investment in Culture*, London: DCMS.

—— (1999) *Policy Action Team 10 (Arts and Sport): A Report to the Social Exclusion Unit*, London: DCMS.

——(2000a) *A Sporting Future For All*, London: DCMS.

—— (2000b) *A Sporting Future For All: Action Plan, Report to the DCMS and DfEE*, London: DCMS.

—— (2001) *A Sporting Future For All: The Government's Plan for Sport*, London: DCMS.

Department for Education and Employment (DfEE) (1998a) *Specialist Schools: Education Partnerships for the 21st Century*, London: DfEE.

—— (1998b) *Sports Colleges: A Guide for Schools*, London: DfEE.

Department of Education and Science (DES) (1991) *Sport and Active Recreation*, London: DES.

Department of the Environment (DoE) (1975) *Sport and Recreation*, White Paper Cmnd. 6200, London: HMSO.

Department of National Heritage (DNH) (1994) *Sport for the Twenty-first Century*, London: HMSO.

—— (1995) *Sport: Raising the Game*, London: DNH.

Derbyshire and Peak Park Sport and Recreation Forum (1998) *Derbyshire and Peak Park Sport and Recreation Strategy*, Matlock: Derbyshire and Peak Park Sport and Recreation Forum.

Diamond, L. (1994) 'Toward democratic consolidation', *Journal of Democracy* 5(3): 4–17.

Draper, R. (2000) 'The club strategy', internal paper submitted to LTA Council, 25 May 2000.

Driver, S. and Martell, L. (1998) *New Labour: Politics After Thatcherism*, Cambridge: Polity Press.

Dunleavy, P. (1991) *Democracy, Bureaucracy and Public Choice*, Hemel Hempstead: Harvester Wheatsheaf.

Dunning, E. and Sheard, K.(1979) *Barbarians, Gentlemen and Players: A Sociological Study of the Development of Rugby Football*, Oxford: Martin Robertson.

Ecotec Research and Consulting Limited (2000) *Regional Cultural Strategy for the East Midlands: Source Document*, Birmingham: Ecotec.

English Hockey Association (EHA) (2000) *Identifying and Developing Potential International Hockey Players: Talent Development Strategy*, Milton Keynes: EHA.

English Hockey Association/Sport England (1999) *The Active Sports Development Framework for Hockey*, Milton Keynes: EHA.

English Sports Council (ESC) (1997) *England: The Sporting Nation: A Strategy*, London: ESC.

—— (1998a) *English Sports Council: More People, More Places, More Medals*, London: ESC.

—— (1998b) *Young People and Sport*, Information Sheet 15, London: ESC.

Evans, G. and Smeding, S. (1996) *Survey of Leisure Services Budgets and Capital Intentions 1996/97*, London: Centre for Leisure and Tourism Studies, University of North London.

Evans, H.J. (1974) *Service to Sport: The Story of the CCPR 1935–1972*, London: Pelham.

Evans, J. (1988) *Magic Moment or Radical Critique: The Rise and Rise of the New PE*, paper presented to conference on Leisure, Labour and Lifestyles, July, Sussex University.

Evans, J. and Clarke, G. (1988) 'Changing the face of physical education', in J. Evans (ed.) *Teachers, Teaching and Control in Physical Education*, Lewes: Falmer.

Field, F. (1996) *Stakeholder Welfare*, London: Institute of Economic Affairs.

Fine, R. and Rai, S. (1997) 'Understanding civil society: a preface', in R. Fine and S. Rai (eds) *Civil Society: Democratic Perspectives*, London: Cass.

Gellner, E. (1995) 'The importance of being modular', in J.A. Hall (ed) *Civil Society: Theory, History, Comparison*, Cambridge: Polity Press.

Giddens, A. (1998) *The Third Way: The Renewal of Social Democracy*, Cambridge: Polity Press.

Goodin, R. and Klingemann, H. (1996) 'Political science: the discipline', in R. Goodin and H. Klingemann (eds) *A New Handbook of Political Science*, Oxford: Oxford University Press.

Gore, T., Dabinett, G. and Breeze, J. (1999) *Coalfields and the Lottery: Phase 1*, Sheffield: Sheffield Hallam University.

Goss, S. (2001) *Making Local Governance Work: Networks, Relationships and the Management of Change*, Basingstoke: Palgrave.

Granovetter, M. (1985) 'Economic action and social structure: the problem of embeddedness', *American Journal of Sociology* 91: 481–510.

Herefordshire Council (1998) *Service Delivery Plan 1999–2000*, Hereford: Herefordshire Council.

—— (2001) *Leisure Services Business Plan April 2001–March 2002*, Hereford: Herefordshire Council.

Herefordshire Council and Herefordshire and Worcestershire Chamber of Commerce (2000) *Herefordshire Economic Assessment 2000–2002*, Hereford: Herefordshire Council and Herefordshire and Worcestershire Chamber of Commerce.

Herefordshire Council and Herefordshire and Worcestershire Chamber of Commerce, Training and Enterprise (1998) *The County of Herefordshire Economic Assessment 1998*, Hereford: Herefordshire Council and Herefordshire and Worcestershire Chamber of Commerce, Training and Enterprise.

Herefordshire Cultural Consortium (2001) *Herefordshire Cultural Strategy: Summary*, Hereford: Herefordshire Cultural Consortium.

Herefordshire Partnership (2001) *The Herefordshire Plan*, Hereford: Herefordshire Council.

Herefordshire Sports Council (HSC) (n.d.) *Membership Application*, Hereford: HSC.

Heron, E. and Dwyer, P. (1999) 'Doing the right thing: Labour's attempt to forge a new welfare deal between the individual and the state', *Social Policy and Administration* 33(1): 91–104.

Higgins, J., Deakin, N., Edwards, J. and Wicks, M. (1984) *Government and Urban Poverty*, Oxford: Blackwell.

Hill, M. (1993) *The Welfare State in Britain: a Political History Since 1945*, Aldershot: Elgar.

Hockey Association (1989) *Official Handbook*, London: Hockey Association.

Hodgkins, T. (2000) *Gravesham Disability Sportslink Project: 5 Year Report*, West Malling: Kent Sports Development Unit.

Holt, R. (1989) *Sport and the British: A Modern History*, Oxford: Oxford University Press.

Houlihan, B. (2001) 'Citizenship, civil society and the sport and recreation professions', *Managing Leisure: An International Journal* 6(1): 1–12.

Houlihan, B. and King, N. (1999) 'A survey of sports development officers in English local government', unpublished paper, Loughborough University.

House of Commons (1999) *Tenth Report of the Environment, Transport and Rural Affairs Select Committee, Rural Development Agencies*, London: HMSO.

House of Lords (1973) *First Report from the Select Committee of the House of Lords on Sport and Leisure* (chairman: Lord Cobham), London: HMSO.

Hutchinson, J. and Campbell, M. (1998) *Working in Partnerships: Lessons from the Literature*, DfEE Research Report 63, London: Department for Education and Employment.

Hutton, W. (1996) *The State We're In*, London: Vintage.

Jessop, B. (1992) 'Fordism and post-Fordism', in A.J. Scott and M. Stormper (eds) *Pathways to Industrialization and Regional Development*, London: Routledge.

—— (1994) 'The transition to post-Fordism and the Schumpeterian Workfare State', in R. Burrows and B. Loader (eds) *Towards a Post-Fordist Welfare State?*, London: Routledge.

—— (1999) 'The changing governance of welfare: recent trends in primary functions, scale, and modes of coordination', *Social Policy and Administration* 33(4): 348–59.

Jones, C. and Novak, T. (1999) *Poverty, Welfare and the Disciplinary State*, London: Routledge.

Jones, K. and Bird, K. (2000) ' "Partnerships" as strategy: public–private relations in education action zones', *British Educational Research Journal* 26(4): 491–506.

Kent County Council (1999) *Kent Economic Report: Informing Kent's Future*, West Malling: Kent County Council.

—— (2000) *Opportunities for Kent: The Vision*, West Malling: Kent County Council.

Kent Sports Development Unit (2001a) *Business Plan 1.4.2001–31.3.2002*, West Malling: Kent SDU.

—— (2001b) *Annual Report 1.4.2000 to 31.3.2001*, West Malling: Kent SDU.

—— (n.d.) *Mission Statement and Principles*, West Malling: Kent SDU.

King, D. and Wickham-Jones, M. (1999) 'Bridging the Atlantic: the Democratic (Party) origins of Welfare to Work', in M. Powell (ed.) *New Labour, New Welfare State?*, Cambridge, Polity Press.

Kirk, D. (1992) *Defining Physical Education: The Social Construction of a School Subject in Postwar Britain*, London: Falmer.

Klein, R. and Millar, J. (1995) 'Do-it-yourself social policy: searching for a new paradigm', *Social Policy and Administration* 29: 303–16.

Labour Party (1996) *Labour's Sporting Nation*, London: Labour Party.

Lavalette, M. and Mooney, G. (1999) 'New Labour, new moralism: the welfare politics and ideology of New Labour under Blair', *International Socialism* 85: 27–49.

Lawn Tennis Association (LTA) (1995) *The Development of Tennis in Great Britain 1996–2001*, London: LTA.

—— (1999) *British Tennis and You: A Strategy for the New Millennium*, London: LTA.

—— (2000) *National Tennis Performance Plan 2000*, London: LTA.

—— (2001a) *An Outline Submission to the National Lottery Panel of Sport England*, London: LTA.

—— (2001b) *Club Vision Year One Interim Report*, London: LTA.

—— (2001c) *British Tennis*, Issue 57, London: LTA.

Lentell, B. (1993) 'Sports development: goodbye to community recreation?', in C. Brackenridge (ed.) *Body Matters: Leisure Images and Lifestyles*, Eastbourne: Leisure Studies Association.

Levi, M. (1996) 'Social and unsocial capital: a review essay of Robert Putnam's *Making Democracy Work*', *Politics and Society* 24(1): 45–55.

Lindblom, C.E. (1977) *Politics and Markets*, New York: Basic Books.

Loader, B. and Burrows, R. (1994) 'Towards a post-Fordist welfare state? The restructuring of Britain, social policy and the future of welfare', in R. Burrows and B. Loader (eds) *Towards a Post-Fordist Welfare State?*, London: Routledge.

Loney, M., Bocock, R., Clarke, J., Cochrane, A., Graham, P. and Wilson, M. (1991) *The State or the Market*, London: Sage.

Lowndes, V. and Wilson, D. (2001) 'Social capital and local governance: exploring the institutional design variable', *Political Studies* 49(4): 629–47.

Lukes, S. (1974) *Power: A Radical View*, London: Macmillan.

Marshall, T.H. (1963) *Sociology at the Crossroads*, London: Heinemann.

—— (1981) *The Right to Welfare*, London: Heinemann.

Maslow, A.H. (1943) 'A theory of human motivation', *Psychological Review* 50(4): 370–96.

McDonald, I. (1995) 'Sport For All – "RIP": a political critique of the relationship between national sport policy and local authority sports development in London', in S. Fleming, M. Talbot and A. Tomlinson (eds) *Policy and Politics in Sport, PE and Leisure*, Brighton: Leisure Studies Association.

McIntosh, P. (1987) *Sport in Society*, London: West London Press.

McIntosh, P. and Charlton, V. (1985) *The Impact of Sport For All Policy 1966–1984 and a Way Forward*, London: Sports Council.

Milson, F. (1974) *An Introduction to Community Work*, London: Routledge & Kegan Paul.

Minford, P. (1984) 'State expenditure: a study in waste', *Economic Affairs* April–June: 22–36.

Moore, M.H. (1998) *Creating Public Value: Strategic Management in Government*, Cambridge, Mass.: Harvard University Press.

Musgrove, F. (1975) 'Education and physical education in the 1980s', in A. Hargreaves (ed.) *Teaching Physical Education Today and Tomorrow*, conference report, Madeley: Madeley College of Education.

Muter, A. (1998) 'The bidding culture is here to stay', *Lottery Monitor*, September.

Niskanen, W.A. (1973) *Bureaucracy, Servant or Master?*, London: Institute of Economic Affairs.

North Derbyshire and North Nottinghamshire Coalfields Alliance (2000) *Positioned for Prosperity: An Economic Development Strategy, 2000–2005*, Mansfield: North Derbyshire and North Nottinghamshire Coalfields Alliance.

Pakulski, J. (1997) 'Cultural citizenship', *Citizenship Studies* 1: 73–86.

Parliamentary Debates (1994) *Official Reports Session 1993–94*, Vol. 244, col. 8, 23 May 1994.

—— (1997) *Official Reports Session 1997–98*, Vol. 296, col. 1058–1062.

Pickup, D. (1996) *Not Another Messiah: An Account of the Sports Council 1988–1993*, Bishop Auckland: Pentland Press.

PMP Consultancy (1999) *A National Facility Strategy for Hockey*, Guildford: PMP Consultancy.

Po Wen Ku (2001) *The Development of the UK Sport Policy since 1992*, unpublished paper, Loughborough: Loughborough University.

Powell, M. and Hewitt, M. (1998) 'The end of the welfare state', *Social Policy and Administration* 32(1): 1–13.

Putnam, R. (2000) *Bowling Alone: The Collapse and Revival of American Community*, New York: Simon & Schuster.

Quest (2000) *Quest for Sports Development: Policy and Strategy Questionnaire – Herefordshire return*, mimeo.

Regatta (2000) 'Awesome Oarsome', Issue no. 132, London: ARA.

Regional Co-ordination Unit (2000) *Reaching Out*, London: Regional Co-ordination Unit.

Rhodes, R.A.W. (1994) 'The hollowing out of the state: the changing nature of the public service in Britain', *Political Quarterly* 65: 138–51.

—— (1997) *Understanding Governance: Policy Networks, Governance, Reflexivity and Accountability*, Buckingham: Open University Press.

Richards, S., Barnes, M., Coulson, C., Gaster, L., Leach, B. and Sullivan, H. (1999) *Cross-cutting Issues in Public Policy and Public Service*, London: DETR.

Rigg, M. (1986) *Action Sport: An Evaluation*, London: Sports Council.

Rowe, N. (2001) 'Sport and social inclusion: the research evidence', paper presented at Loughborough University Sports Research seminar series.

Rowe, N. and Champion, R. (2000) *Young People and Sport National Survey 1999*, London: Sport England.

Rugby Football Union (RFU) (1988) 'Internal Report to RFU Development Sub-Committee'.

—— (1995a) 'Internal Report to RFU YDO Steering Group'.

—— (1995b) *New Image Rugby: Introducing the Game to People with Different Abilities*, London: RFU.

—— (1996) *Report of Working Party on Youth Rugby* (Horner Report).

—— (1999a) 'The Evolving Roles of YDO Team Leader and YDO', internal paper prepared by Director of Development for the Chief Executive.

—— (1999b) *Equal Opportunities Policy*, London: RFU.

—— (2000) 'Annual Financial Statements Season 1999–2000'.

—— (2001) *'Putting England First' Strategic Plan 2001–2007/8*, London: RFU.

Rugby Football Union for Women (RFUW) (1995) *Development Plan 1995–1999*, London: RFUW.

—— (1996) *Partnership for Progress: An RFUW Policy for Development of Junior Rugby for Girls*, London: RFU.

—— (2000) *Development Plan 2000–2004: To Create a Level Playing Field*, London: RFU.

Rugby Football Union/Rugby Football Union for Women (RFU/RFUW) (1999) *Child/Young Player Protection Policy*, London: RFU.

Sabatier, P. (ed.) (1999) *Theories of the Policy Process*, Boulder, CO: Westview Press.

Saunders, P. (1975) 'They make the rules: political routines and the generation of political bias', *Policy and Politics* 4(1): 31–58.

Schattschneider, E.E. (1960) *The Semisovereign People*, New York: Holt, Rinehart & Winston.

Scottish Sports Council (1988) *Laying the Foundations: Report on School-Aged Sport in Scotland*, Edinburgh: Scottish Sports Council.

Social Exclusion Unit (SEU) (2000a) *Report of Policy Action Team 16: Learning Lessons*, London: SEU.

—— (2000b) *Report of Policy Action Team 17: Joining It Up Locally: The Evidence Base*, London: SEU.

—— (2000c) *National Strategy for Neighbourhood Renewal - report of PAT16: Learning Lessons*, London: The Stationery Office.

Sport England (1999a) *Investing For Our Future: Sport England Lottery Fund Strategy 1999–2009*, London: Sport England.

—— (1999b) *Active Sports Guide*, London: Sport England.

—— (2000a) *The Use and Management of Sports Halls and Swimming Pools in England*, London: Sport England.

—— (2000b) *Making English Sport Inclusive: Equity Guidelines for Governing Bodies*, London: Sport England.

—— (2000c) *Child Protection in Sport Task Force Action Plan*, unpublished paper, London: Sport England.

—— (2001) *Active Communities: Active Communities Projects*, London: Sport England.

Sports Council (1973) *Annual Report*, London: Sports Council.

—— (1976) *Annual Report*, London: Sports Council.

—— (1977) *Annual Report*, London: Sports Council.

—— (1978) *Annual Report*, London: Sports Council.

—— (1979) *Annual Report*, London: Sports Council.

—— (1980) *Annual Report*, London: Sports Council.

—— (1981) *Annual Report*, London: Sports Council.

—— (1982) *Sport in the Community: The Next Ten Years*, London: Sports Council.

—— (1983) *Annual Report*, London: Sports Council.

—— (1988) *Sport in the Community: Into the '90s*, London: Sports Council

—— (1991a) *Annual Report*, London: Sports Council.

—— (1991b) *Sport in the Nineties: New Horizons*, London: Sports Council.

—— (1991c) *National Demonstration Projects: Major Issues and Lessons for Sports Development*, London: Sports Council.

—— (1993a) *Black and Ethnic Minorities and Sport: Policy and Objectives*, London: Sports Council.

—— (1993b) *Women and Sport: Policy and Frameworks for Action*, London: Sports Council.

—— (1993c) *People with Disabilities and Sport: Policy and Current/Planned Action*, London: Sports Council.

    (1993d) *Young People and Sport: Frameworks for Action*, London: Sports Council.

—— (1994a) *Developing Sport Through CCT*, London: Sports Council.

—— (1994b) *The Brighton Declaration on Women and Sport*, London: Sports Council.

Sports Council (North West) (1991) *Sportsnews Fact File Two: Sports Development*, Manchester: Sports Council.

Stead, D. (1987) 'Six areas for action', in D. Stead and G. Swain (eds) *Youth Work and Sport*, London/Leicester: National Youth Bureau, National Council for Voluntary Youth Services and the Sports Council.

Stepney, P., Lynch, R. and Jordan, B. (1999) 'Poverty, exclusion and New Labour', *Critical Social Policy* 58: 109–27.

Swain, G. (1987) 'Sport, Youth Service and young people', in D. Stead and G. Swain (eds) *Youth Work and Sport*, London/Leicester: National Youth Bureau, National Council for Voluntary Youth Services and the Sports Council.

Talbot, M. (1995) 'Physical education and the National Curriculum: some political issues', *Leisure Studies Association Newsletter* 41: 20–30.

Taylor, P. (1993) *The Financing of Excellence in Sport*, London: Sports Council.

Timmins, N. (1995) *The Five Giants: A Biography of the Welfare State*, London: Fontana.

UK Sport (1999) *The UK Vision for Coaching*, London: UK Sport.

UK Sports Council/International Working Group on Women and Sport (1998) *Women and Sport: From Brighton to Windhoek: Facing the Challenge*, London: UK Sports Council.

University of Birmingham, Physical Education Department (1956) *Britain in the World of Sport*, London: Physical Education Association.

White, A. (1996) *Building a Sporting Future: Corporate Work with Governing Bodies in England*, paper presented to meeting with National Governing Bodies, May 1996.

—— (1997) 'Towards gender equity in sport: an update on Sports Council policy development', in A. Tomlinson (ed.) *Gender, Sport and Leisure: Continuities and Challenges*, Aachen: Meyer & Meyer.

White, A., Mayglothling, R. and Carr, C. (1989) *The Dedicated Few: The Social World of Women Coaches in Britain in the 1980s*, Chichester: West Sussex Institute of Higher Education.

Whitehead, N.J. and Hendry, L.B. (1976) *Teaching Physical Education in England: Description and Analysis*, London: Lepus Books.

Wilding, P. (1997) 'The welfare state and the Conservatives', *Political Studies* 45(4): 716–26.

Williams, F. (1994) 'Social relations, welfare and the post-Fordism debate', in R. Burrows and B. Loader (eds) *Towards a Post-Fordist Welfare State?* London: Routledge.

Wolfenden Report (1960) *Sport in the Community: The Wolfenden Committee on Sport 1960* (chairman: Sir John Wolfenden), London: CCPR.

Youth Sport Trust (1996) *Sports Colleges: You Can Be Part of Our Sporting Future*, London: YST.

Index